What Happens When the World's Racial Cultures Clash?

Sterlin D. Williams

Stew Books Publishing— Southaven, MS
ISBN: 978-1-7335893-1-4
Library of Congress Control Number: 2021923451
Title: *What Happens When the World's Racial Cultures Clash?*
Author: Sterlin D. Williams
Digital distribution | 2022
Paperback | 2022

Dedication

To the memory of my parents, Eunice and Dorothy M. Williams, siblings, Evester L. Darrough and Charles L. Williams, father-in-law, Dr. Joseph W. Samuels, sister-in-law, Jonette M. Carter, brother-in-law, Frank A. Samuels, and Dr. Steven M. Neuse, former Master of Public Administration (MPA) Director of the University of Arkansas, who challenged me to think critically and analytically in problem-solving.

An insightful and contextual look at race and its global impact historically and in modern times

Understanding the Far-Reaching Global Impact of the World Racial Order

Sterlin Williams

DISTINGUISHED FAVORITE

www.NYCBigBookAward.com
#BigBookAward

About the Author

Sterlin Dwayne Williams is a native of Pine Bluff, Arkansas. He had a successful career with the Federal Motor Carrier Safety Administration (United States Department of Transportation) and retired after thirty-two years of federal service. During his career, he served as the Division Administrator for twenty-six years for the states of Louisiana and Mississippi. He was responsible for the statewide implementation of federal interstate motor carrier safety/economic/hazardous materials programs where he collaborated with numerous partners and stakeholders. While with the agency, Sterlin served as the first chairperson of the National Diversity Committee. Because of his leadership, he received the agency's Diversity Champion Award and the Secretary of Transportation's Equal Employment Opportunity (EEO) and Affirmative Action Award in directing and implementing the agency's Diversity Initiative.

Sterlin attended Dollarway High School and received his Bachelor of Science degree in Business Administration and a Master's degree in Public Administration at the University of Arkansas in Fayetteville, Arkansas. As a steadfast supporter of social justice issues for voicing the needs and concerns of marginalized cultures,

Sterlin was a recipient of the University of Arkansas' Black Alumni Society (BAS) 2021 Myron "Mike" Macechco Diversity Advocacy Award. His interest includes art, traveling, golf, sports, and reading. He is a member of the Alpha Phi Alpha fraternity, Inc. Writing provides an opportunity to combine those interests by using his knowledge to help promote the causes that make the world better.

This book, entitled *What Happens When the World's Racial Cultures Clash?*, is Sterlin's second book. It is a sequel to his first book, *Understanding the Far-Reaching Global Impact of the World Racial Order.* His first book focused on an understanding of the world's racial caste system. The second book explores the interaction dynamics between cultures and racial groups. It examines the role they play in the continued development of our global society. This provocative book offers a thoughtful analysis yet the riveting and haunting impact of past unresolved global-racial-cultural clashes and the present cultural discourse in which many cultures still experience deeply demeaning racism. The second book places a much greater emphasis on our shared cultural history but an unshared vision. The book provides an opportunity for societal discussions on complex topics of culture evolvement and development to stimulate further learning, analysis, and cultural advancement. It examines the world, celebrate it, and even try to make it better. Both books give an insightful and critical analytical look at culture, race, and its global impact historically and in modern times to help heal and create lasting change. The first book earned the 2020 International African American Historical and Genealogy Society (AAHGS) Book Award in the multicultural category and a 2021 New York City Big Book Award distinguished favorite in the racism category.

Table of Contents

Acknowledgements

As an Elder, in the tradition of my African ancestors, the author wants to distribute the knowledge that he has learned in his lifetime and share it with future generations. He especially wants to give thanks to his ancestors in whose path that we follow paved the way for us. We now set an example for those who follow us.

This book could not have been completed without the contributions of many trusted friends and associates who touched and shaped my life at some point. The contents of this book are not just about the author's opinions about the subject matters but theirs as well along with many other people from all walks of life. There is a heartfelt appreciation to all. However, there are a few who must be especially noted.

Special thanks to my wife, Priscilla Samuels Williams; my daughter, Alexis Shennell Williams; sisters Dr. Bettye J. Williams and Dr. Brenda F. Graham; Shirley M. Williams and my mother-in-law, Martha L. Samuels for their comments, feedback, candid critiques, and appraisal of the manuscript that made it a reality.

To my siblings and their spouses, Evester L. Darrough (deceased) and James Darrough Sr (deceased), Dr. Bettye J, Williams, Shirley M. Williams, Dr. Brenda F. Graham, Dr. Margarette A. Williams and Lewis J. Williams, Charles L. Williams (deceased), N. Lucille Gilkey, Ted W. Williams, Robin N. Baylock, and Sonnya N. Adams and Dwight Adams Sr. for your inspiration over the years. To all my nephews, nieces, great-nephews, great-nieces, aunts, cousins, and friends for always supporting me.

Sincere thanks to Welton Boyce, Jerrold Brantley, Richard Bullard, Diane Butler, Cynthia Williams-Campbell, Harold Carter, Randolo B. Cuttino, Charles Dove, Augusta Farver, Barry Garland, Keith Gibson Sr., Eugene Graham, Michael Kevin Gray, Lonnie R. Green Jr., Jackie Thomas Grissom, William Hall, Kirke "Rocky" Herman, Audrey C. Howard, Monica Carey-Lanos, Taft Kelley,

Veron Kirkendoll Sr., William Matlock, Ronald Nichols, Tyrone Robinson, Gordon R. Seawood, Oliver L. Sims III, Shelia Shannon Spiller, Billy Sprinkle, Curtis Thomas, Ricky Tobias, Barry Turner, Jerrauld Turner, Marlon Weems, Victor A. Wilson, Willie Wilson Jr., Michael Woolfolk, and my 1976 Pine Bluff Dollarway High School classmates for their unbiased valued comments throughout the years in our debates of this subject matter and many others whose opinions heavily contributed in the unstinting support of my aspiration to make this book possible.

Preface

Writing objectively and analytically about a contentious and highly divisive sociopolitical subject can be difficult. Depending upon one's socioeconomic background, perspective, and culture, each side in the debate selectively takes issue with details while abandoning the big picture and the core problem that most demands critique. The desire to back one's culture is universally understandable. Generally, some people get defensive when their benevolent and magnanimous held beliefs are challenged and questioned. Especially if there is a belief the information used to bolster them is thought to be inaccurate or unreliable. The author tried to stick to the ideas and facts and remain objective in his critical analysis.

The present global cultural dilemma in our distorted and dysfunctional world is a product of a collective effort and social structures that provide opportunities to some cultures and racial groups, and obstacles to countless others. When global societies are full of chaotic culture members grappling with recurrent conflicts and clashes based on racial and cultural differences, they can never achieve sustainability and may eventually lead to their demises. Humankind sets and accepts lower and lower social standard practices and calls the Truth a lie and a lie the reality. Some cultures have cemented historical untruths into their cultural reality and made them logical to their members. Over generations, a new reality is formed and maintained. They make it out to be whatever they want it to be. The world has a lost sense of social cohesion due to widening inequality gaps between the racial cultures. We live in a very flawed and complex atmosphere of cultural mistrust and volatility – a world of constant war, poverty, starvation, hostility, and the unquenchable thirst for power to rule over humanity.

One must apply the intellect to a thing and discern its reality. The development of civilizations on Earth is a complex matter. The human history of this planet has always been centered against a backdrop of reckless optimism and a state of despair. It is the sociopolitical and cultural scene of our shared global space. It cannot be handled with the omission of authentic history. For humanity to progress, we must be willing to understand its literal history, especially when it contradicts our programmed beliefs. We should respect the achievements of all cultures to educate ourselves proficiently about them and not glaze over unpleasant facts. These issues cannot be oversimplified or over specified in the way some cultures are trying to do. When things are untrue and not based on the discovery of Truth, we should try to put them right. The cultural fault lines of the past will continue to haunt our future without an honest and truthful conversation on our shared global history. We all want the world to be in a better cultural sphere but change only happens when humans search the depths of their souls. The searching of one's soul involves debunking learned generational culture behaviors. It is hoped that when a mass of opposition against the Truth grows enough, cultures might stand up and put an end to the delusion and the circle of insanity.

We live in a global society that has no agreed-upon consensus about what is the unvarnished Truth. There is only one Truth, but different opinions and versions have sprung from it. Cultures create their reality. Some cultures have departed the plane of reality and lost sight of reliable Truths. There are competing narratives, talking points, and ideologies peddled in the marketplace of ideas. As culture members, we choose our version of the Truth that fits our sense of cultural identity. Everyone wants to know the Truth until they realize that it runs counter to their cultural beliefs. Instead of fully embracing the Truth, we recoil in a state of denial. We tend to place greater trust in sources that conform to our learned cultural generational values. In our cynical world where there is no unconcealed Truth, we seek out our version of Truth using our valued judgments. We trust those voices that reflect our values and shared ideas to decide on who to believe. Once we settle on a version of the Truth, despite some of their stretched credulity and cowardly conception, we become emotionally invested with this affiliation. Switching allegiance to a different version of the Truth can be challenging and confusing. We protect ourselves from competing Truth versions and sometimes accept bias as reflecting some greater Truth. Very few people can stay completely unaffiliated with some version of peddled Truths. If people become so emotionally attached to their culture to the point that the Truth becomes a secondary consideration, their cultural reality is a liability to humanity.

Some people do not want to hear the unvarnished Truth. And then they want to deflect and cast blame elsewhere. With no understanding nor a will to have social awareness, they will never grow. In this global society, some people will only embrace changes when directly impacted by their beneficial outcomes. It can be painful to know the Truth when presented with curated versions of reality through various information sources. Our global history is so dramatic that there should not be a need to add or subtract from it. There are some glaring omissions, lies and startling Truths that have thickened the stew of cultural mistrust that never fail to shatter and awaken. It was the collective weight of all that history that has kept some global cultures in denial. That has kept them believing they could beat these latest challenges in the same way they had done in all the others. The present widely-touted global historical misinformation about all cultures needs to be made right. Some cultures live for the present and think they can escape history. This short-term thinking and near-time future mentality do not bode well with a preferred collective global long-term frame of reference.

Throughout the history of humankind, first as tribes and now as nations, human rights have existed in some form. World national societies by force provide partial protection of these rights. Essentially, those rights and privileges are bestowed by nations on their citizens but can be taken away on a whim. The world has never lived up to its lofty goals. The standards it sets in words are very high. When the words were written, it was hoped that the global societies would live up to them in the future. Because of the national discordance, there is no universal agreement of rights. Some global governance institutions have developed widely acceptable human rights declarations, but they are very abstract and offer no enforcement. Does this dilemma lead to two theories of thoughts involving human rights inherent from birth or emanating from positive law?

The dominant mainstream cultures cannot deny other global culture members the fundamental rights of a human being. All humans, regardless of their cultural affiliations, were born with natural and human rights. During the past five centuries, numerous social constructions have deprived many people of color of those fundamental human rights despite their enshrinement in world Constitutions. Historically inequalities and disparities in our cultures across our global communities operate along a constitutional fault line that we must somehow cross. There is this mythology surrounding the interactions that have given some cultures the power to ruin the lives of other culture members completely based solely on what part of the world they came from, the religion or spirituality they practice, or the color of their skin. That power cannot be squared with the global Constitution or basic human fairness. No matter what the Constitutions say, the global societies are not even close to establishing herd immunity to racism, human rights abuses, cultural xenophobia, and misogyny. If the world is to survive this cultural-racial reckoning, and others to come, it must be dedicated to perfecting its founding ideals, documents, and subsequent amendments to the Constitutions. There must be more than blind allegiance to the founding culture members who wrote them. The newer generations must commit to the Truth in ways previous generations refused to.

Unfortunately, global cultural behavior may be more acceptable than one might think. It is the broad and unintended exposure that may be the problem that brought bad press and negativity to the mainstream culture brand.

Unfortunately, in this global society, some people must contend with living and existing in societies controlled by dominant cultures that have shaped their entire existential reality that sometimes has resulted in a diminishment and devaluation of their lives. This inescapable cultural phenomenon and harrowing reality have required them to deal with a multitude of social issues throughout their lives that have infringed upon their universal natural and human rights to life. Presently, there are no rights fully guaranteed for all humans living on planet Earth. As societies progress and we mature as a human species and begin to see the value of each human being, this narrative will hopefully change. We can become the noblest cultural versions of ourselves.

There have been a few notable books written about culture clashes in our global society. However, history, language, culture, tradition, and, most importantly, religion were the primary emphases of those books. Those books viewed civilizations as a hypothesis which people's cultural and religious identities will be the primary source of conflict in the post-cold war world. The proposition was derived not from nationalities and ideologies but from cultural and religion-based differences. [i] This book will not debate the merits and contents of those books.

The human condition has always had a feeling of connection to something greater than oneself. The world has been mired in religious-cultural differences for most of the past two millennia. The roles that religion and many other cultural elements play are interrelated in our global society. Religion is one of the many elements of a society and one of its strongest foundations. There are other cultural aspects of a society that may be indistinguishable from the religious doctrine.

Religion and spirituality should be about a personal pursuit, relationship, and communication with someone's God, Goddess, deity, or idol without interferences with other members and cultures of the human species. One's religion and spirituality ideology should not be used within the context and experience of the culture, and not as a tool for conversion. The spiritual needs and religious ideologies of some people should be separate from others of the human species. Everyone has the right to express their religious or spiritual belief systems and believe whatever doctrine or concept they choose. But cultures should have no authority to dictate how other cultures should express their opinions. However, some modern cultures have engaged in religious ideologies and doctrines which have led to horrific atrocities and wars. In their effort to fundamentally impose their political and religious will by conquest or conversion, consolidate economic power, and control the natural resources around the globe. Some religious culture leaders took an increased role in political affairs through political and judicial activism, further complicating societal governance. Cultures must learn to respect other cultures' religious or spiritual beliefs and refrain from imposing religious ideologies and beliefs that do not suit them. Cultures should focus on things that unite them regardless of their religious or spiritual differences.

From the author's perspective and the purpose of this book, humankind divides also cleaved the global landscape into another crisis. One of the challenges we have seen not only in the Americas and the Caribbean, but in Africa, Europe, Asia, Australia, and other world's regions, is the increasing conflict based on cultural and racial inequality and injustices. There has been a worldwide movement that started in 2020. These activities fight racial injustices and raise global awareness and consciousness. There has been a broad movement, which is different from past more localized or regional human and civil rights movements, in which all cultures and racial groups have participated. This iconic global movement has led other nations to see their racism within their societies. This book will address the extreme polarization that still exists in our global society involving our cultural, racial, and physical profile differences.

This book provides some insights and catalyzes all members of humanity to increase their understanding and awareness of the dynamics and interactions that our global societal cultures and race play in our lives. Hopefully, the global racial awakening that we are presently experiencing will be the impetus to finally allow members of humanity to live and exist in harmony. The roles of culture, race, ethnicity, ethnocentrism, xenocentrism, and nationality are analyzed. All six concepts play a major role in the development of the identities of all members of humanity. Their interaction is important to our reality and is a large part of what forms it. People are usually not aware of how important these concepts are in every aspect of their lives. [ii] Although all these factors and others play major roles in the development of world's societies, culture and race will be the primary focus.

The purpose of this book is to help all members of humanity understand the roles that culture and race play in our global society. The book reviews the impact of societal intercultural racial intermixing and multi-culturalism. It examines the formation and developments of major world's cultures, subcultures, and societies. The book also evaluates the concepts of counterculture, subculture, and cancel culture. Finally, the book discusses ways to achieve a multi-cultural global society.

Introduction

As human beings, we exist as social human species on planet Earth. We are cultural creatures, formed extensively by the social structures within which we live. Our human species have survived for millenniums mainly because of the creation of learned shared social cultures transmitted from one generation to the next. Some of the other Earth's species inhabitants became extinct because of natural catastrophes and disasters, lack of genetic diversity, inability to cope with nature, among other factors. The human species have survived because cultures can communicate and understand one another in more complex, sophisticated ways than other species. Human beings are the only known species to have successfully migrated, populated, adapted to, and altered a wide variety of land and water regions around the globe. The human species may be the most adaptive because of this flexibility.

Human beings appear to have the intelligence and mental ability to cope with nature and endure it, but do we have the political will and the moral courage to get along with our fellow human beings? However, our intelligence has grave tragic consequences to some of the social constructions that we create. We must ensure that the goals of our social constructions align with the humanity of all world cultures and the standards used to judge an action are equitable. As such, we should shift our goals from creating purely misdirected, ill-conceived, misguided, disguised, obscured, and unguided concepts to beneficial humanistic social constructions. It appears that some members of humanity still have an intentional vested interest in eliminating their members through wars and genocide because of cultural and religious differences or perhaps greed and racism based on physical profiles, and the competition for environmental resources. In essence, our human species prey on other world cultures. In our constantly changing, ongoing invasive parasitism, symbiosis, amensalism, mutualism, and commensalism relationships, we have become the cultural misfits in the custody battle over the world, and the human predation species to our mere existence.

Since the beginning of humankind, thousands of cultures and subcultures have existed in our global society. Even before the establishment of civilizations, cruel, oppressive tribal atrocities between cultures existed on planet Earth. Each unique sovereignty culture entity had its own distinct cultural, spiritual, and technological development. Unfortunately, over centuries, that number has steadily dwindled. Human inhumanity against each other has often led to the destruction of entire cultures. Some were prominent in establishing some of the earlier and ancient civilizations in the world. Some of these societies have survived over time but are less recognizable and prominent since their peak performance periods. Other societies have completely vanished from existence. Many of these societies were dismantled because of cultural and racial differences. The world is faced with opposing cultural forces that separate powerful cultures from more vulnerable ones. Cultural clashes are an integral part of society because they have emanated into the global community. This inescapable cultural phenomenon has always been part of the human experience. Its present levels of acceptance in an ever-evolving multicultural global society landscape are critically analyzed and debated. It may be the global cultural adaptable way of humanity, but it is not the way life started. It is not natural but by design and subliminal imagery made out to be commonplace when it is not.

When one or more of these cultures are integrated and intermixed into one environment, most of the time they cause disruption and often challenge their previous contemporary traditions. This integration of different cultures, if not harnessed, can result in a culture clash between the members. The people feel threatened by what the other believes - their values and practices. This threat can be based on a person's race, ethnicity, nationality, culture, religion, sexual orientation, age, gender, and others. This continuing threat becomes even more problematic when it occurs in societies in which an abundance of raw materials and natural resources are present. This vulnerability can happen in homogenous societies as well, albeit to a lesser extent. In many instances, a more dominant predatory conquering culture is the reason for their demises.

Science has its biases, and some people have attempted to debunk the theory that humanity comes from Africa. With intolerant sentiments and tendencies influencing the way people view the evolution of all humankind, some believe that humans did not come from Africa, even though many scientific types of research justify this query. There is a consensus among scientists that all human beings originated and descended from Africa. Some of whom migrated and settled in Europe, Asia, the Americas, Australia, and other places around the world. This opinion has been demonstrated archaeologically and anthropologically as well as with the genetic record. Lighter skin is the mutation that came about as people began to migrate farther north of the equator to cooler climates and adapted to local environments. Human beings are the same species. Our differences are minor and superficial. There are no superior or inferior people or cultures. Before early human beings practiced vagility and migrated to other territories around the world, mountains, deserts, forests, and oceans isolated human beings from each other for thousands of years. Members of the ancient civilizations circumnavigated to most inhabitant places around the world. As the human species migrated to various parts of the world, tribes were formed, and values were created as ways to signify one's association or belonging to said group. Our global history involves global migration and cultural invasion. This reality has led to a mass exodus of many cultures from their native homeland worldwide. New cultures and populations have replaced others. This scenario has become an integral part of those societies that reflects different cultures from the original ones on the same global lands in past centuries and millenniums.

However, since the beginning of antiquity and human emergence, the human species have never been disconnected from each other but interwoven into a complex culture web of interconnectedness and commonality. The trunk of Africa formed the winding roots and tangled branches through the movement of human population global expansion that eventually covered the whole continent and spilled out into Madagascar and the Arabia Peninsula. The indigenous aboriginal people whose genetic fingerprints and footprints are in every continent, country, hamlet, and island on the planet. Although some human species lived in isolation from each other, we have always continually mixed in back and forth between various cultures of people. The historical roots of the symbolic tree of life, the oldest and strongest living species on earth, are still developing today through numerous cultures. Ancient genetic and discovery links in arts, science, religion, spirituality, education, technologies, philosophy, linguistic were formed. Humankind has been tasked with unifying work that pruned all these twigs of knowledge into a single coherent tree – one that will continue to bear humanistic fruit for future generations. This connection makes us one humanity, although the genetic analyses point to a continued reevaluation of our tales, mythologies, and conspiracies of the past. Cultures are but one thread that is woven into the web of humanity. What one culture does to this web affects all cultures. All world cultures are inextricably interlinked, locked, mixed, linked, bound, tied, interwoven, intertwined, and connected. All cultures are pieces of other cultures wrapped in multiple cultural contexts.

Since the advent of the Transatlantic Slave Trade in the fifteenth century and worldwide Colonialism, most world's citizens now live in a global society. Most world cultures now are appropriated from an existing foreign culture or evolved into what it is today from a mingling of different racial groups and cultures. As a result of these major world events, a few dominant cultures began to practice cultural racism. They saw this integration of cultures as an opportunity to fundamentally impose their culture and political will on the rest of the world. The dominant cultures accepted the cultural conflicts and clashes as inherent in their culture's human nature and built their institutions and systems to support it.

These two primary events were primarily responsible for steering the world in a direction that started a compulsion of one racial group over another in a global society that is becoming more pluralistic. These events were responsible for creating a deranged ideology of racial superiority and inferiority. It cannot pass through the gates of a multicultural global future. The present cultural global dilemma is the product of a collective effort and social structures that provide opportunities to some cultures, and obstacles to countless others. These global events completely threw the world cultural life off balance. Since their inceptions, all global cultures grew up and around them, but we must grow above them. We must stop living in the shadows of these events but into the light. The world is presently experiencing the aftermath of those events, and they have caused a primary reverberation of racial relationships on a global scale. One-half of a millennium later, the full scope of these atrocities is still hard to fathom.

As a global society, we need to evolve from a complex, difficult, bitter, and racist cultural past and transform it into a reinvented multicultural future. We need to fully embrace our cultural difference with an open mind and end our present collective internal global fear that tested the measure of our global humanity. We need to focus on our similarities and acknowledge the human commonalities and values that we all share while respecting our cultural differences. We need to acknowledge and study our global history to stop the damage and prevent the continuation of disparate treatment. All cultures need to come to terms with their past. Each society needs to find its intercultural balance. All cultures, except those located in a few global remote, isolated, and inaccessible locations, interact with other cultures, and all cultures have subcultures within them. Therefore, all cultures except the ethnic enclaves can be considered multicultural to some extent.

Five centuries ago, rather than invest in human capital, inclusiveness, education, technological advances, and economic development, we chose to conquer, divide, control, and destroy other world's cultures. "Now we live in a world beset by cruelty and destruction"[iii] under the disguise of laws, untruths, and religions to justify our hypocrisy. As our cultures "disintegrate and their spirits numb, they lose their moral compass and creative vision".[iv] But greed and narcissism is the winner in our species' present values of choice of self-destructing or evolving. Now, we must prove to the world that we are finally ready to embrace bold new cultural interventions and initiatives to deal with our stained cultural internal strife and historical legacy. This cultural behavior is who we are and has been for centuries and millenniums. This stain is the creation that will forever taint our tarnished legacy and global reputation.

During one's journey through life on planet Earth, the average human being regardless of cultural affiliation should be grateful for the way his life turned out and likewise feel an obligation to other members of humanity along the way. It should not take an awful lot to return the good feelings humanity brought to each other and to make others feel good about themselves and their lives. We can transcend our present global society and traditional boundaries and look to end conflicts and clashes. We can become culturally ubiquitous, create the conditions for epiphany, achieve multicultural solidarity coalition of religiously, racially, culturally diverse populations, deepen our understanding and skills of human engagement, enhance our education, and become a world cultural treasure that embodies the best traits of all the global cultures.

Historians have recognized over seventy major empires, civilizations, or societies in humankind global history. Unfortunately, some had mandates to fundamental force their political will on other cultures and fulfill their scorched earth doctrine of the victor over the vanquished. Some primary empires include Ancient Egyptians, Ancient Greece, Ancient Rome, Persians, Qing, Turks, Arabs, Mughals, Abbasid Caliphate, Yuan, Japan, Chinese, Brazil, Kushan, Byzantine, the Mongolians, Phoenicians, Crusaders, Spanish Conquistadors, Portuguese, Germany, British, Russian, French, Ottomans, and others. The European empires consisted of tribal territories of the barren landmass in large global areas such as the Americas and the Caribbean, Australia, and New Zealand, Africa, India, and others. The Mongol Empire, the largest contiguous land empire in world history, stretched across one-fifth of the globe. At its height, encompassed the major of territories from Southeast Asia to central Europe. However, it covered a lesser global land base than the British and European empires. The Mongolians were barbarians, marauders, pillagers, and thugs who would raze and murder every man, woman, child, and livestock in every town and village they encountered. The Mongols lived in the age (thirteenth & fourteenth centuries) where sadly killings, murders, and genocide were the normalcy in human relationships. [v] The European powers were enabled by advanced technology in weaponry, maritime, seafaring travels, and industry. Technological advances in the eighteenth and nineteenth centuries allowed a small number of European nations to control a wide area of global land. Throughout humankind's history, these cruel world mandates were carried out by numerous predatory empires. The European empires are just the latest in world history from the fifteenth to the twentieth centuries to yield great destruction and violent hatred on a large segment of global humanity. Unfortunately, human beings have never reliably seen the humanity in all members of their kind. Humankind has never completely acquired the transcendental connection of other cultures, particularly foreigners from other tribes or nations. Science and technology differed throughout the eras, so it is hard to compare different empires, civilizations, or societies.

The story of the Transatlantic Slave Trade and worldwide Colonization, and its aftermath is world history. By the 1700s, these archaic institutions were the main global trading business and economic engine. The continent of Africa, with its strategic global location, and natural resources, and proximity, was the envy of Europe. Great Britain, which was the world's dominant Colonial power, was involved with these institutions. France, which was Great Britain's main rival on the imperial stage, was involved with them. Other European powers including Portugal, Spain, Belgium, Denmark, the Netherland, Germany, the United States, and a few other European nations such as Sweden, Courtland, Norway, Russia, Scotland, and others played a minor role were involved with these institutions. "Colonialism is an expansionist military and economic policy that seeks dominance over other peoples. At its peak in 1914, Europeans controlled 84% of the globe".[vi] This colonization would not end until the 20th century.

The Transatlantic Slave Trade was initiated and orchestrated by the European powers, beginning with Portugal, and followed by Great Britain, France, the Netherlands, Spain, Denmark, the United States, and others. The European powers were the main vectors and played a foundational role in the slave trade by buying and selling enslaved Africans from the fifteenth to the nineteenth centuries, and their Colonial presence throughout the world well into the twentieth century. They built their empire of African bodies and indigenous people. They played a foundation role in setting up anti-African and anti-indigeneity racism and demonization globally. The Europeans Americans were and still are now the primary beneficiaries of the trade in human beings from Africa five centuries later with the establishment of a well-coordinated heinous and brutal system.

Some African kingdoms, tribal rulers, families, or merchants, "mostly for financial or short-term political gains",[vii] were complicit or collaborated with the European powers in the Transatlantic Slave Trade. Some culture members from the continents of Europe and Africa capitalized on a mutual understanding of the slave trade. In many African cultures, slavery was an accepted domestic practice. In

Africa, the slave usually had rights, protection under the law, and social mobility that was more akin to indentured servitude. Africans captured by other Africans could marry into their African capture's families, but this was not the case with the European involvement of the Transatlantic Slave Trade.

The European powers expanded the slave trade into a brutal enterprise. The Africans did not have the massive apparatus such as slave castles, guns, ships, or ports to transport millions of Africans across the Atlantic to three continents. This chattel form of slavery based on physical profiles and skin tones was legal construction by the societies as a permanent form of existence for the enslaved. Chattel slavery was supported by European governments, monarchs, and religious leaders during that era. Their entire former way of life was outlawed. They had to endure the loss of their ancestral cultures, languages, names, identities, generations and centuries of customs, rituals, and traditions, family structure, forbidden from reading and writing, not allowed to worship their religious or spiritual concepts, celebrate their festivals, and numerous other human rights abuses. Chattel slaves were individuals treated as property, to be bought and sold. The Europeans involvement in the slave trade was predicated on the belief that Africans were inherently genetically inferior to the Europeans.

However, the continued discriminatory practices and disparate treatment at the symbolic conclusion of the atrocities cannot be blamed or attributed to other cultures. These atrocities were followed by institutionalized/systemic racism and other human rights abuses that continue to perpetuate trauma on their descendants today. In more subtle and covert ways, decision-making about hiring practices and employment searches, awarding of contracts, voting rights - gerrymandering/suppression, police brutality, unequal criminal justice system, redlining and gentrification, healthcare disparities, mass incarceration, unequal forms of compensation, boardrooms decisions, what history is being taught in schools, and many others. This brand of slavery, worldwide colonialism and its aftermath consisted of a perpetual condition that was virtually unique in the history of humanity. It ranks among some of the worst atrocities involving the traumatization and dehumanization of human beings in recorded humankind history. Their ideology breeds underdevelopment to the Africans. Colonialism, and slavery as institutions were born out of greed and necessity, which later condemned the Africans and indigenous populations to their present piteous state. The oppressors left an evidentiary documentary trail. There are hundreds of years of evidence as to why such a perspective would be maintained. This opinion is not a figment of one's imagination.

There are varying degrees of culpability and shared responsibility by some members of several cultural groups for this monstrous atrocity. All major global atrocities (Arab-Muslim Slave Trade, Transatlantic Slave Trade, Apartheid, and the Holocaust) had some collaborators who were members of the distressed subordinate cultures. Historically, there has always been some voluntary members participation of other lesser cultures in the human arena of power struggle. The human dominant cultural predators would not have been as successful if they did not have accomplices. But on the other hand, cultures blaming everybody except themselves, particularly the principal contributors, for their roles in the atrocities and the aftermath is a bad look. Some cultures are trapped in a mentality that cannot see the full picture of their role in the global atrocities. Out of shame for their cultural behavior, they will convince themselves that others are the culprits and simply not admit their mistakes. In a bond built on greed, exploitation, and manipulation, they were complicit with the dominant cultures in committing these heinous atrocities. The responsible cultures need to take responsibility and accountability for their actions and the present condition that still exists.

In the past, there has been an outright refusal by certain countries directly involved in the Transatlantic Slave Trade and worldwide Colonialism to even apologize for these atrocities. An apology is an admission of guilt. They believe it would create legal implications that would force them to pay reparations. Instead, they release statements of regret about what happened. A few West African countries have apologized for their role in the Transatlantic Slave Trade. The dismantlement of the system of oppression built from the atrocities that is still maintained and benefited by their descendants would be preferable. These two atrocities are among the most dishonorable and abhorrent chapters in the history of humanity. [viii]

Chattel slavery, in the form that existed in the Americas and the Caribbean, rarely existed on the continent of Africa as a principal form of production. This new form of racialized chattel slavery deemed enslaved Africans and their offspring slaves for life. [ix]The Transatlantic Slave Trade fueled the industrialization that gave Europe and the United States their economic, cultural, military, political, and social advantages during the past five centuries. [x] Before the colonial era, many countries and kingdoms participated in extensive trading networks and trans-oceanic travels. Some pundits believe it was the international trades that exposed Africa to destruction and looting from other cultures. [xi]

These two archaic institutions are a world's shame. The world must confront them. The world must eventually come to terms with them. The world must bear some responsibility and accountability for them. Those responsible for these appalling abuses and subversionary behaviors should be ashamed of themselves for participating in atrocities that have been disgraceful to humanity. Most people with any conscience should have known that their forays into the world's global land to seize omnipotent control over its natural resources and all the inhabitants would not end well in the long run. The long-term damage will forever tarnish and threaten the distinctive legacies of these cultures and become an imminent peril to humanity.

These global institutions involving the commercial trading of human beings and the colonization of global lands must be viewed and debated in a global context because of their far-reaching impacts and consequences. Without a global perspective, it is difficult to understand the current economic, social, and political situations in many undeveloped and impoverished countries, especially with people of color and their connections to these institutions. They have severely damaged their ability to prosper in the global community in its present form. The relationships between the cultures are not conducive to global success that should be based on harmony, dignity, cooperation, inclusiveness, and mutual respect instead of winning at all costs. There is no reason to think that the world's racial cultures can co-exist in this global space going forward with the roles and the power each one has or does not have. There are a lot of variables that go into it and it can be extremely complicated. It will be interesting to see where things go from here over the next decades and centuries. But fixing the present cultural differences that developed between the cultural groups over the past two millenniums, and especially the five centuries is easier said than done. Their depths and tentacles are varied and deeply interwoven in a modern global society. The remnants, relics, vestiges, and residual effects of their existence still have their fingerprints and footprints all over the world one half of a millennium later.

Yet, in the twenty-first century, the world's leadership is still in cultural denial of how race and culture have played a major role in many past and present soaring racial inequalities and injustices that have existed since the fifteenth century. Ironically, racism and race relations have never been a major topic when the dominant cultures meet in most of the global governance institutions to discuss the world's agenda. These issues are rarely mentioned among the biggest or relevant global challenges or problems. Many social ills are acknowledged but may arguably be the symptoms of racism and race relations. As a global society, we may not be getting to the root of the problem. The dominant world societies make these decisions and determine what is discussed on the world's stage, particularly in the global institutions, involving the world's major powers.

The countries in Africa and very few nations with a majority population of color, except South Africa, a former British colony, are offered seats at the table at some of the global governance institutions like the G7 and G20 that address significant international issues. Likewise, no African leaders were invited to Berlin, Germany when thirteen European countries and the United States met at the Berlin Conference of 1884-1885. In this Scramble for Africa meetings, they haphazardly carved up the continent of Africa like a pie without even telling the people who lived there that it was happening.

This unfathomable, cultural arrogance or indifference and lack of introspection by the European powers at the Berlin Conference to not even acknowledge and recognize the humanity of hundreds of cultures on the second largest continent in the world, is of monumental epic proportions. In utter disregard and not a single iota of conscience or concern for the cultures or the families of the continent, the map was redrawn, and land claimed.[xii] What followed was the systematic scramble and undoing of Africa and a total disregard of its future implications. Those brutal unilateral actions in Berlin by the European powers and the United States were despicable and unacceptable.

In addition, the Doctrines of Christian Discovery (DoCD) originate with 15th century Papal Bulls that were issued by the Vatican and implemented by Monarchies, that specifically sanctioned and promoted the domination, conquest, enslavement, Colonization, and exploitation of non-Christian global territories and people. The Doctrine of Christian Discovery (DoCD) is a series of Papal Bulls written between 1452 and1493 by the Roman Catholic Church that authorized the takeover of global land not ruled by Christians. Other Europeans powers adopted the global DoCD concept. It had disturbing and devasting consequences worldwide for the indigenous populations and people of color. Their far-reaching global impacts continue today.[xiii] As a result of these atrocities, there have been zero consequences and no repercussions. At the end of European global Colonial conquests, all but ten countries were not colonized by the Colonial powers.

Race and culture were and still are the "albatross" around the neck of the world and have been for centuries. The story of the Transatlantic Slave Trade had its origin fifty years before Christopher Columbus set out for his first voyage to the Americas in 1492. Since 1441, the first European mass slave expedition of 12 captured Africans, [xiv] and in 1444, Portuguese traders brought the first large number of 235 kidnapped Africans to Europe.[xv] Africans were brought to present-day Georgetown, South Carolina on September 29, 1526, by Lucas Vasquez de Ayllon. The first African slaves arrived in the present day in the United States as part of the San Miguel de Gualdape colony (most likely located in the Winyah Bay area of present-day South Carolina). The ill-fated colony was almost immediately disrupted by a fight over leadership, during which the enslaved people revolted and fled the colony. De'Ayllon and many of the colonists died shortly afterward of an epidemic, and the colony was abandoned, leaving the escaped slaves behind on North American soil. In 1565, the colony of Saint Augustine in Florida became the first permanent European settlement in North America, and included and unknown number of African slaves. [xvi] Ignoring the racial component in our global society which was created by numerous social constructions during the past one half a millennium will not make it go away. They have been woven into the fabrics of our global society. This inaction will just prolong the inevitable ongoing cultural racial clashes between members of the global societies.

Some people who happen to be born with the skin tones and physical profiles of the dominant cultures have benefitted from being members. They do not see the urgency of this matter. Some have not been directly or personally affected by systemic or cultural racism, so indifferences and apathy set in. Some culture members are unaffected by its consequences or repercussions. The actions of some people are based on personal rewards and outcomes. Unfortunately, some of them will not become allies unless they are personally impacted. Generally, they are not aligned with the subordinate culture members. These group differences have made some of them oblivious, ignorant, and benumbed insensitivity to the racial issues and plight that people of darker skin tone experience.

But billions of their fellow global members of humanity are adversely affected by global institutions and systems that have treated them differently simply because of their skin tones, physical profiles, and lineages. The strain against cultural forces is persistent to them but invisible to others. It makes it more difficult when ignored. They are the hidden faces of subordinate groups around the world who are excluded from the table involving their interests. The table does not belong to any culture group. Every culture group should be at the table as guests. Most of the time, they are hardly ever heard about or seen unless in a negative light. Usually, they are the descendants of the first inhabitants in those territories bearing perpetual scars and enduring loss of pain. They possess a core of strength that survives the worst that life can bring with a hope that even their longest nightmares end. They are a cultural outsider in a global community they have been a part of since its early formation. For numerous reasons, the world's mainstream cultures have eluded them. Yet, their culture and land are the foundation the mainstream society was built on. It is much older than their newly created borders during the past few centuries. They are seen within the context of this global society as a modifier based on their physical profile. To begrudge another culture because of their physical profile is absurd. It is based on fear, fear of the other, fear of what is not like you. As a global society, cultures must somehow rise above this irrational, paranoid, racial-cultural xenophobia, and all its guises. It dehumanizes a whole community of people that were not otherwise invisible. Cultural racism was the answer to the overwhelming monstrosity of people of color globally. However, their indomitable spirits live on and will continue to inspire their descendants to achieve lasting peace, stability, and prosperity. Their significant past must not be relegated to the landfill of history.

The only success that culture must live up to is their cultural standards if aligned with beneficial humanistic social constructions for its members. Defining success for one culture may differ from another culture. This cultural paradigm does not mean one culture is better than another culture, but their outlook and way of life may differ. One of the primary missions of a culture is to advance the collective aspirations of the people. Society must first be able to meet the needs and demands of its members and be able to solve their problems. Each succeeding generation is expected to lay claim to leadership by formulating an ideological outlook and clear vision of where they want to see the continued evolution of the culture. If the culture members can thrive and prosper within their shared cultural core values and priorities, the culture and society met their social obligation.

One of the things that all cultures must recognize in their continued evolvement is the possible trauma they may impose on other cultures. These atrocities heralded the dawn of a human era of political trauma and turbulence. Their actions are a flagrant abuse of their position of humanity cultural trust. Historically, cultures have unintentionally or purposely inflicted intentionally triggered trauma and caused a lot of generational pain to other cultures. These actions are unacceptable in our global community, and the action matters far more than any intention. We must acknowledge the trauma it evokes regardless of intentions. "Some racial groups are experiencing communal trauma that is acerbated live through social and new media platforms. This active traumatic stress has led to harmful coping devices that further added to communal stress, particularly during a global pandemic. The stigma of dealing with trauma has generally improved in society. Some culture members have sought help as awareness efforts have increased."[xvii]

These impacted cultures have endured traumatizing wounds that may never fully heal. The torment that these culture members endured at the hands of other cultures has left generational scars on their souls. Many had to relive their historical stories over generations and centuries. The impacted cultures bear some responsibility for dealing with trauma even if other cultures caused it. How the aggrieved cultures deal with the pain from the trauma is their choice. Taking a proactive stance despite the dire circumstances should be the preferred option. Ideally, the afflicted cultures should make a good faith effort to reclaim, redefine, recreate, reshape the narratives, and improve their previous cultural practices.

A poor culture refuses to acknowledge its role in the trauma of other cultures, a good culture apologizes for the damage and pain they cause to cultures, but a great culture makes amends. Cultures cannot grow and evolve if they cannot face and acknowledge their historical past realities. The progress comes from healing the trauma that was caused by some of their cultural members. In offering an apology for these harms, the culture recognizes that awareness and apology only resonate when accompanied by action; by not bringing understanding of the past into the present but in acting to ensure reconciliation, reconstruction, and restoration.

Some culture members even evoke traumatic responses by their failure to come to terms with these issues. Some cultural members will not even acknowledge that they exist. By responding passively only perpetuate the core issues at stake. To recognize the cultural behavior in its mistreatment of other cultures is the beginning of the healing process and is transcendent to the ancestor realm. If a culture's trauma transmits from generation to generation, so can the healing process. If cultures practice transcendent compassion, cultures will need time and nurturing so that the recovery process serves their evolution into their highest cultural traits. All cultures are a work in progress.

The world is a conglomerate of different cultures and people with different physical profiles and skin tones. Anywhere there are people, there will be problems and issues between them. "To have problems in life is an inherent part of the human condition. But it takes self-examination, humility, grace and empathy to take the time and space to truly understand that some racial groups and cultures of humans truly have it much better than others." [xviii] This phenomenon does not mean that life for some members of the dominant mainstream cultures has not been hard. It just means that their cultures and skin tones and physical profiles are not making it harder. The world should not be a homogeneous place to fit in anyone's specific fixed cultural mold. The human species can come together to work on common interests and good but respect our cultural and racial differences. Since the beginning of humankind, there has always been a dynamic interdependency and interactions between cultures and racial groups. Why must there be a clash instead of coexistence?

Our cultural and skin tone differences should not mean there should be an inevitable and inescapable conflict of one culture to dominate another culture. Just more respect and tolerance of other cultures and their differences in a humanistic way will go a long way to resolve our hostilities and conflicts. Showing humility for our fellow people goes a long way in restoring respect for others and learning more about other cultures, which is an essential ingredient in world harmony. We must never lose sight that there are people from all cultures and backgrounds with the potential to avoid an escalating conflict through the ability to be empathetic. They have the moral courage and political will to espouse the highest form of humanity. All of us can be a beacon of guiding light, a safe harbor, a journey of hope, and a solid foundation to bring people and cultures together. We can develop a cultural evolution driven by the most successful memes among all the world's cultures and put this locust plague period behind us.

There is only one race, and it is humanity. No single culture can achieve enduring fame at the expense of other cultures. No human species of the global society should be the divisive figments of another culture's imagination. The reroute to humanity for cultures of color should not be barricaded by complex set of laws, mired with the condescension, insults of rejection, and irresistible disdain by some mainstream culture members. This divisive global tribalist mentality is the source of our failure to operate as a collective multicultural global society. Planet Earth belongs to all cultures of the world, including the original African forebears, their descendants, and the diaspora. Cultures represent the collective wisdom of our forebearers. In the twenty-first century, we are yet again at the crossroads of some very trying global racial cultural issues. Malign forces in our world community should not turn every disagreement and debate into a clash of cultures. The present culture clashes between the world's racial cultures do not have to be the continued epitome of irresolution and become a cultural boneyard.

Chapter I
The Impact of Intercultural Racial Intermixing

During the past one half a millennium, each generation has inherited an intercultural racial global society and an unequal broken world order from our ancestors in previous generations. Some incremental strides and gains have been made during the past decades and centuries through transformational world events to address these injustices and inequalities. But we still must make some profound changes in our global society as we continue to evolve as a human species. We must seek to become stewards of cultures with many diverging viewpoints held together by one common belief of restoring unparalleled decency to humanity. We must become better stewards of planet Earth and custodians of valued cultures.

This often unexploited and unharnessed cultural frontier that we are presently facing is a platform that presents yet another opportunity and challenge by which we can finally come together as one united global society and one humanity. At the present rate, it appears the present methods by which we live in our global society, and our cultural behavior will not be sustainable in the long run. As a global society, we must critically examine some of the social constructions that we have created and their impact on all world's citizens and other planet inhabitants.

The world is amid a global racial awakening. An insistence that subordinates culture members be afforded the same basic universal natural and human rights presumed by every global citizen tore at the world's conscience. We are presently facing yet another critical juncture in the United States and our global society that is burdened with history and laden with new challenges. Monumental positive changes in race relationships could be on the horizon in America and around the world. There have been several previous major transformational events in world history that have provided incremental changes. But only with time will we know if this event

1

will truly change and finally turn the corner in global racial relationships and reconciliation. There is a call for all cultures to do more to meet the challenges that we face today. Meaningful actions are required without delay to address the growing inequality, injustice, division, and clashes between the world's racial cultures.

For the first time in humankind's history, major protests, rallies, and marches for police reforms and an end to systemic racism and racial injustices that happened in midst of a global pandemic around the world. Cultural and political change are chipping away at the world as many global members are fashioning a multicultural society. We are uniquely positioned to do better and usher in an epoch of cultural goodwill. They were billed as the largest civil rights protests in humankind's history. Protests and demonstrations for enacting economic and inequality changes are ongoing in many countries and have been for centuries. These protests can be a powerful tool for enacting changes, but they are no guarantee that the changes will occur or be permanent. The present global wide support does not necessarily result in real-world changes. People and institutions need to be willing to do the work over a prolonged period to promote and exact lasting, meaningful, and permanent changes. Our present culture global dilemma developed over centuries. Transforming societies will involve some quick fixes and long-term solutions. It is important that all stakeholders have access with those in power, be on the same page, stay the course, and be held accountable for their actions.

The protestors are up against deeply embedded and entrenched institutions, systems, and networks that have been around for centuries. However, overcoming cultural ingrained attitudes is another matter. Past resistance was strong and sometimes met with brutal, harsh, intimidating, and violent outcomes. This iconic global movement's warm embrace may signal a broader change in attitudes toward race and cultural relationships. The United States is the current epicenter of this systemic global racial protest that was triggered in May 2020, as a result the slaying of the Mr. George Floyd at the hands of the police in Minneapolis, Minnesota. This action shocked the conscience of the nation and the world. Many countries around the world have joined the United States in this effort. The global protests have created a transformative mood that is less patient, much larger, and more determined to enact changes than freedom movements of the past. It is also an opportunity for other affected groups whose rights were trampled on to address grievances in their residing countries.

Now, we have a golden opportunity to evolve and transform our global society. We must take advantage of this moment in history. We are at a unique point where we can grow as far more inclusive societies and nations. We can become more aware of the struggles and challenges that some members of the subordinate cultures go through. We need to stand in unison with all the cultures and move forward in race relationships. We need to examine why some dominant cultures continue to predominately base the identity of their members on their skin tones and physical profiles instead of the other numerous cultural elements. Generally, subordinate culture members are not placed in positions to reach their potentials. The world should be putting them in positions to succeed, as opposed to placing barriers and roadblocks. If given the ability to step up and lead, they would strengthen overall humanity.

We live in a global society that contains thousands of distinct cultures, subcultures, and racial groups. However, only a few dominant mainstream cultures define the major cultural patterns for the entire world. The dominant cultures are firmly entrenched in virtually all the world's social institutions and systems. Western culture is presently the most dominant culture in the world. Most cultures in the world are under the umbrella of the Western culture. It had a vested interest to rule over the world for the past five centuries. However, the Eastern culture, particularly China and India, have made great strides in exerting their cultures and worldview during the last few decades. The Eastern culture has now become a major rival of the Western culture through a renewal of its cultural identity during the past few decades. China was one of the ten global countries that was not entirely colonized by the former European powers.

These dominant mainstream cultures set the world's agenda and determine what is discussed and implemented on the world's stage that impacts minor cultures. Despite the cultural distinctiveness and group solidarity of some subordinate cultures, the dominant cultures still exert strong influences from health care, education, economics, science-religion, politics to other sectors of their societies. Historically, there has also been a refusal of dominant cultures to

3

share power with other racial groups. The major cultures generally are also in denial of how race has played a major role in many past and present inequalities and injustices that exist around the world.

Throughout the history of humankind, the dominant cultures have generally decided whose culture is the best by their ability to fundamentally force their culture and political will on other cultures. However, the forcible takeover and haphazard assimilation of other cultures into their society do not mean that the dominant culture has the best culture but perhaps the most advantaged. It may be the best culture for the members of the dominant culture but not necessarily for the subordinate members who have been the subjects of forced assimilation, subjugation, a cargo of misery, mass carnage, an imperiled existence in an ambiguous state of liberty, and a tortured cultural saga that has been meted out for centuries.

Most of the subordinate cultures finally gained their symbolic independence from colonization after World War II. Although the "Colonial" and "slave" statuses have officially been removed, a new framework continues through renamed identities such as mass incarceration and Neocolonialism. It is not always about the previous statuses of their past turbulent relationships but their present and ongoing subservient relationship of domination with the previous Colonial powers. The former European Colonial powers are still in complete control of the businesses from most of the formerly Colonized nations. Most of the former Colonized impoverished countries in Africa, the Middle East, Southeast Asia, Latin America, and the Caribbean have strong indirect Western culture or Eastern cultures' control over their economies, regardless of who heads the window-dressing political governing of the people. The European culture is still very much evident and dominant in countries of predominantly African descent worldwide. The local economies are heavily dependent on foreign economies. No African majority country fully controls its policies, economy, defense, or finances.

There is a strong historical argument to be made that the Transatlantic Slave Trade and worldwide Colonialism during the past five centuries, helped shape the entire existence of the modern cultures that exist today. These two world events played a major role in the capital accumulation assumed by the European powers through their global imperialism ideology and worldwide mandate. This world's conquest led to the post-industrial information

4

movement which was significant in fostering globalization via international trade and commerce. It resulted in an unequal and broken world social order which severely and adversely impacted the Colonial territories and resulted in the inequalities and injustices of the impoverished and undeveloped nations across the globe, particularly in Africa, the Middle East, Southeast Asia, Latin America, and the Caribbean. It has impacted generations of descendants of African descent with massive poverty, malformed economies, and the destruction or loss of entire ancestry cultures. Many people are caught in a bleak cycle of toil and poverty whose lives are dominated by their bitter struggle for existence.

When a culture does not have a historical framework of reference on its past, it is hard to map a plan to govern themselves internally in a manner that respects their members and society. Even if some of the formerly colonized cultures wanted to fully reclaim their ancestral cultures, it would be hard to do so. They have been cut off from their cultures for generations and centuries. They can make a good faith effort to restore some aspects of their original cultures but their concepts of what they were formerly may be distorted by a worldview of the dominant culture, propaganda, and brainwashing over the years. In essence, they can try to reclaim them but generally, they will be in the present worldview mold and images of the dominant culture. It would be tough to fully recapture the uniqueness and authentic elements of their original cultures. To completely restore one's culture, their land, resources, inventions, technologies, religion and spirituality, style and arts, language, music, and scientific knowledge must be restored as well. That is a very difficult task to undertake, particularly when the cultures have been assimilated into a dominant culture for generations and centuries. But it is better late than never to reconstruct the most viable ancestry elements. Culture members need to know where they came from to best determine their destiny and charter a path to rediscover and reclaim some aspects of their lost cultural heritage and history. Cultures are not defined by their successes but by how they bounce back from their failures and adversities.

Without a cultural ancestry identity, a subordinate culture can become anything the dominant culture wants it. This scenario is what happens when subordinate culture members no longer understand their original culture. The culture loses it cultural identity because of generations of not practicing the concept regularly. In many cases, the dominant culture fundamentally imposes its culture and political will on the subordinate culture and understands their former culture better than some present members of the subordinate subculture. They took oral communication from the cultural elders and remixed and twisted them to suit their agendas. This knowledge has allowed some unsuspecting members to do things contrary to their best interests without being aware of it. Some members of society who are uncertain of where they fit and belong in their mainstream culture are in pain and anguish. The subordinate culture members may feel alienated by the very culture that they should have been rooted. To practice the standards of one's ancestral traditional culture, one must first understand them, but without knowledge of one's traditional ancestral history, modern dominant mainstream standards will prevail. Aboriginals and indigenous populations should not feel like orphans, expatriates, exiles, and castaways in their ancestral homelands and foreign territories of their domicile. Like inhabitants of a besieged territory, the people are often caught in the middle, ignored as their humanity is being debated by the dominant cultures.

History has shown that most great civilizations/empires/societies eventually lost their long-standing status because of complacency, corrupt leadership, inability to deal with multiculturalism, lack of technological advances, and lack of national identity, [xix] and being too inclusive with other cultures, among other reasons. Those subordinate cultures tried to be friendly and helpful to other cultures, but all the time, those predatory cultures were lurking and plotting against them to take over their natural resources and cultural best practices. All the foreign cultures saw and cared about were the natural resources in their ancestral land. They did not really care about the humanity of the natives. This chicanery concept has been used for centuries by some cultures to secretly create problems and issues for another group of people. Then the culture plays the role of the guardian angel or liberator of the group under the pretense of saving the culture from itself, thus subjecting the group to generations and centuries of pain and suffering.

During the international trading network between the cultures, the invading cultures were assessing goods and services of real value while bartering their usual goods and services under the guise of

6

partnership and friendship. Later, they forcibly and cunningly acquired the property and services they desired and controlled anyone who objected. The deep sinister spirits of a fake universe of inclusion had long been operating on the fringes of some cultures found their way to mainstream statuses. It was the increased intermixing of their government, educational institutions, spiritual system, economic production and technology, and military that eventually caused their downfall.

The dominant culture sometimes steals from subordinate cultures that they conquered, colonized, and enslaved and does not give them proper credit for their contributions. This preclusion is cultural theft. When this omission happens, they not only steal from the person(s) who contributed but also from the cultures of the subordinate racial groups. The looting of artworks and architectural treasures by predatory cultures is an insidious cultural force at work. Many of the stolen artifacts are in foreign museums and vaults in Europe and the United States. In addition, the dominant culture has purposely ignored the history and culture of subordinate cultures and nations. The removal of all evidence and knowledge of the local culture deprives the youths of their history and achievements. The rightful owners of the artifacts have a vested interest to provide an accurate account of their history. This situation is equally deceptive as it is unjust. This dishonesty has thwarted the traditional generational cultural transfer process between global culture members. This cultural theft will not allow future generations the ability to deal with racial and cultural issues more openly and honestly than what occurred in previous generations. The newer generations cannot fully understand the world they inherited to hopefully build a better global society for future generations. To move forward, you must understand what the past was like. Learning about one's history will lessen their cultural fragility and keep culture members from digressing as a group. It brings them into the global cultural hood fold. Culture members need to connect the dots to let them know how things were. Every effort must be made to preserve their sense of reality from the false distortion of history. In the age of enlightenment, all that was hidden is now coming to light.

Centuries later, descendants of the originating cultures are copying descendants of the copier cultures who imitated them instead of tapping in with first frequency. The predatory cultures generally copied some of the useful concepts of the subordinate culture but not its practices, and then reinvented them into their cultural practices. Those cultures would later become dominant, learned from some past dominant cultures, and were determined not to make the same mistake in being too inclusive with other cultures. The dominant cultures promoted full exclusivity from other cultures. In many cases, the adopted stolen concepts were so intricately changed that they were not even recognizable from other cultures of origin. The predatory cultures used helpful concepts and beliefs of other cultures then created a misinterpreted version of them in another form that was even unknown to the distressed cultures. This same old camouflage of distortion has been used for generations. There is nothing that cultures do now that is original and superior to their ancestor's accomplishments. The interconnectedness of humanity represents the collective human progress, accomplishments, and lessons learned from past millenniums. Ideas of today are developed, built off, and expounded upon from past eras. The variation of the framework keeps getting dressed in a different facade to maintain its effectiveness. As a result, the balance of power among the various cultures shifted because of religious, cultural, political, economic, and social changes.

This lack of inclusiveness among the world's cultures wherein the dominant cultures refuse to share power with other cultures and integrate with them in harmony may be the main reason why cultures today are so polarized. In addition, the inability of dominant cultures to see the perspectives of other cultures and the lack of understanding of the interconnectedness of human beings have been very problematic. These past and present conflicts and tensions between racial and cultural groups are an indirect result of the ever presence-dangers of this polarized mentality that exists in our global society. The dominant culture has purposely ignored the history of other cultures and their societies. There has been a worldwide removal of ancestral cultural reminders that had lineages that could be traced back millenniums. During worldwide Colonialism and the Transatlantic Slave Trade, most of the landmarks and geographical locations across the globe now bear names given by the European settlers. Additionally, new geographic regions were established based on cultural differences, language, and phenotype. For example, the regions of Asia and its subcontinents were established by the British. The Middle East is based on its location from Great Britain and Kemet, the ancient name of Egypt and its remarkable African civilization, was taken from Africa. This omission is harmful to the pride and history of ancestral cultures, and a major part of the issues that we are experiencing today. Our global society is facing a turning point that will determine whether its cultures grow more inclusive or exclusionary.

When cultures believe in things about other cultures that they do not understand, all cultures suffer. We are, too often, misguided by our misunderstandings. This cultural lack of awareness and inclusiveness is not the way to go. Until we own up to this lack of inclusiveness and misunderstanding about other cultures because of greed, paranoia, willful ignorance or tactical stupidity, the fear of the unknown, and suspiciousness; the unequal broken world order will continue. As calls for culture inclusivity grow, these change agents work to showcase a broader spectrum of multiple perspectives, backgrounds, and experiences on problem-solving on any issue. Cultures must purge this lack of cultural inclusiveness and the fear of empowering other cultures from our global society's existence, or we will never regain the humanity we lost from our ancestral cultures.

Unfortunately, most of the African cultures, the origin of humankind and the cradle of civilization, collapsed centuries and millenniums ago because of the intervention of more aggressive predatory cultures who destroyed and undeveloped their ancestral culture and history. Those cultures tried to move Africa from its rightful and respectful commentary of history. The mass migration and cultural invasion of Kermit/Egypt is a biased version of the truth now taught by mainstream cultures to disconnect the original culture from Africa. However, Africa's history and the memory of its history disciplines of study have not been completely erased, reprogrammed, and replaced by predatory cultures. All knowledge in the world belongs to all cultures in the world, and not any self-obsessed, narcissistic culture trying to take full credit for it as the originator. Hopefully, at some point soon, this global society will recognize that our past is a historical connective account of all the cultures' stories. One of the certainties of life is that nothing remains the same forever. The self-inflicted historical amnesia of the dominant predatory culture will not prevail in the long run.

Africa is the root of all civilizations on planet Earth. The Colonialism of Africa, the Arab-Muslim Slave Trade, and the Transatlantic Slave Trade played a major role in distorting the global perception and history of the continent. A strong compelling argument based on the long deep-rooted past and present history of inhumane treatment and atrocities can be made that a culture of great enmity shapes a subconscious fear and distrust of the original fellow human beings from Africa and its diaspora. Acrimony builds walls around nations, cultures, and races, forming limiting, restrictive, and conditional cultural identities. When a superiority mindset culture identifies itself over and against other cultures, it narrows the possibility of who we can become as a global society.

There is always a risk of alienation among two or more factions owing to overexposure to each other's beliefs and value systems. When these competing cultures are fixated on the same territories and when different concepts are making up these cultures, the major conflict is inevitable unless there is agreed-upon cooperation among the cultures. Unfortunately, in most cases, an agreement, or its adherence thereof, between the cultures was not the norm. Historically, this conflict has led to hostilities between the factions which unfortunately have escalated to violence, wars, and atrocities. The clash of cultures is what primarily accounts for the racial divides that still exist. Race is used as a tool to inflame passions. Race looms as a wildcard, with a cultural divide further shaping the contours of the global society.

Human beings now live in a global society that emphasizes a worldview perspective. There are thousands of distinct cultures and subcultures within the various nations. Because of globalization, the world is now more interconnected more than ever before. The various social media networks and media sharing sites have allowed instant free-flowing of information and ideas to the masses that was greatly influenced by the elites and political entities. However, this interconnection between cultures does not guarantee that globalization will turn the world into one giant, homogeneous world culture, even with an ever-accelerating cultural homogenization around the world. It may lead to a sense of togetherness via the sense of shared cultural experience. It also has the potential to break down cultural barriers and increase harmony among ever more heterogeneous people. [xx]

Physical barriers such as mountain ranges, deserts, forests, and oceans no longer hinder people's movement, and there is a resultant spread of cultural ideas from dominant cultures to the rest of the world. These physical barriers had isolated human beings from each other for thousands of years. The internet and advertising through the many forms of mass media have allowed people worldwide to see what is popular in the dominant cultures. As a result, some of these new cultural ideas and products can be found in even some of the most remote places on Earth. In whatever ways cultural diffusion occurs now or in the future, it has happened many times throughout history and will continue to do so as new areas grow in power and pass on their cultural traits to the world. The ease of travel and modern technology will only aid in speeding up the process of modern cultural diffusion as social change sweeps across the world.

Is race a component or element of a culture or is culture an element or component of race? Each race has its own culture. Race can also have multiple cultures and subcultures. On the other hand, race is a meaningless outdated concept. It is a system of classifying people according to their skin color and physical profiles. Biologists, geneticists, and anthropologists, and others long ago reached a common understanding that race is not a "scientific" concept rooted in discernable biological differences. However, race remains an extremely important and hotly contested social issue. [xxi]

In our existing global society, despite culture being an umbrella for so many things, race has been placed above it. Unfortunately, recent world events from the fifteenth century have made race an extremely important and problematic global issue. What made this period so unique is the clash between worldviews and ideologies involving race. Many human beings around the world are still unfortunately judged by their race every day in their societies. [xxii] All foreign ideologies and beliefs that are introduced to cultures should not always be accepted as face value and need to be fully vetted. An ideology that injects toxicity of racial division into the global society must be challenged, particularly when it leads to atrocities, instability, violence, and wars.

The human condition has always had a feeling of connection to something and a propensity to feel a need to belong to something. It can be a culture, tribe, people, caste, nation, society, club, fraternity or sorority, team, church, school, and many others. Some people want to be around a like-minded group of people that look or think like them. There is a tendency for many people to want to label and identity themselves with some entity or group that they recognize. This association is a very basic instinct that is not inherently morally wrong. However, human beings should also have the intelligence to rise above the sum of their instincts and understand the humanity of others. Cultures should realize that the belongingness to a culture or group because of many commonalities may make them more comfortable but not better than other cultures.

Unfortunately, because of Colonialism, the Arab-Muslim Slave Trade, and the Transatlantic Slave Trade, many people of African descent in the Americas and the Caribbean, Europe, and other places around the world who form the Africa diaspora have an identity crisis. In some educational cultural history curriculums, there are three questions on identity that are always asked. They are: who am I?; where in the world am I?; and how in the world did I get here? Some culture members are not able to answer the three questions. Because of the inability of some members to answer the three questions, they exist in an evolving perpetual pattern with no end in sight, particularly when the dominant culture does not accept them as full members of its culture. Additionally, they do not know the ancestral history of their ancestors from five millenniums ago, the chronology events of what happened during that period, the predatory cultures who were responsible, and why it occurred. "If you understand the beginning well, the end will not trouble you." [xxiii]

The mainstream cultures have the financial means or resources to connects all the dots to display their cultural origins in museums, Smithsonian, libraries, or universities. Knowledge of one's history gives a strong sense of belonging and an identity that provides the basis for group unity, which further provides the basis for economic and political power to become self-sufficient and control one's destiny. [xxiv] Recently, the use of genealogical DNA ancestry tests has helped individuals learn their cultural identity. However, because of the loss of physical records and lack of African DNA samples, panels and algorithms presented distinct challenges although the numbers are increasing yearly.

Culture

Culture is a way of life for a group of people. Culture refers to the external environment which influences people. It is a social heritage that is learned and shared by the group. Culture provides a basis for common understanding, and cooperation among people in a society. It dictates that we and others like us who learn and share the same social heritage and will have the same initial outlook on life. It allows cultural members to think, feel, and act at least initially, in a certain manner. [xxv] Crime and criminal activities are not part of people's culture and their way of life. [xxvi]

Culture is learned through shared experience by a group of people that takes years to form. It undergoes gradual changes over time. Culture is transmitted across generations in the form of symbols and stories. Some beliefs, traditions, languages, or rituals are eliminated or changed. Culture cannot remain isolated. Every culture is influenced by cultures in the surrounding regions and countries through trade and commerce, migration, or travel of people. [xxvii] Every cultural process leads to culture, and by the relationship between cultures, a society is born.

Culture is an umbrella for many things. Major elements of culture include language, beliefs, customs and traditions, rituals, behaviors, faith/religion, attitudes, values, arts, music and literature, education, family, food and cuisine, clothing, tools, social organizations, governments, shared ideas, law and politics, economy, housing, institution, technology, symbols, norms, and many other things. The cultural elements are the parts that make up the culture of people, country, ethnicity, or region. They give shape, cohesion, and identities to societies, and allow clear identification and differentiation from other cultures, and are transmitted from generation to generation. [xxviii]

A subculture is also a group of people who share the value of the mainstream culture, but at the same time, they have their own set of identities. Subcultures do not go against the dominant culture, but they have their way of distinguishing themselves from the primary culture. Examples include youth, university, music, organization, and others. These sub-cultural groups may have their style, vocabulary, set of rules, and others; however, they reflect but do not oppose the mainstream culture. Members of subcultures may exchange their ideas which might not be understood by non-members of the group. But their ideas do not undermine the core values of the mainstream culture. [xxix]

The problem is most global societies are not balanced proportionately when it comes to cultures. Some societies may have a predominantly culture and a myriad of other cultures that are in the minority. When there is a melting pot of cultures with one dominant culture, culture conflicts and clashes will be inevitable if the integration of cultures is not handled delicately. During assimilation of the various cultures, some cultures may lose a sense of belongingness and loss of some cultural identities. Some cultures may be positioned between their own culture, the predominant culture, and other minority cultures.

This myriad of cultures can lead to multicultural tensions. When different cultures have multiple perspectives, there is bound to elicit one reaction to an issue while another culture will have another reaction to the same issue. The culture members would have to choose between one or the other issue. In a multicultural society, this scenario among cultural members initially struggling with their identity is the norm.

A culture can remain static or change with time, particularly as it develops. Also, the change can occur because of prolonged exposure to a different culture. Exposure to these different cultures can result in either positive or negative changes. "The integration of different cultures in one environment leads to disruption of traditions. Contacts between different cultures are also viewed as cultural clashes for they are bound to result in undesirable consequences or even destruction of one or all the cultures. Therefore, culture clash is a conflict that occurs when people with different cultural values come together." [xxx]

When two or more cultures intermix in a society, either because of conquest or in a more conciliatory voluntary manner, all the cultures will not maintain the consistency of their cultural history. Typically, one culture will assume a more dominant posture and the other culture(s) will experience a cultural evolution in which a merger and union with the other culture(s) take place. The subordinate cultural members will undergo a transformational period and give birth to a new cultural entity. They will experience a culture shock in their new society when they are immersed in a culture with customs so different from their own. Although the dominant culture may maintain its cultural history, the diversity of cultures and their merger with each other, is the beginning of a new society for all the members.

The time frame for the stability of the new culture may vary by the level of development, political system, region, or type of economy. The new society may undergo periods of great achievements, cultural activities, vitality, setbacks, and revolts. Finally, the culture may at some point reach its maturity with the merger of the new elements of the other culture(s). On the other hand, some cultures may collapse and suffer an ending date if the infusion of the new culture(s) failed to successfully integrate and assimilate the new culture(s) into its society. In that respect, cultural evolution is not much different than biological evolution in that both may take a long time. Oftentimes, with changes going unnoticed in real-time and jumpstarted by transformational events and revolutions.

The diffusion of interracial and intercultural racial groups in many societies has caused some cultural clashes in their internal and social identifications. For example, a person of both African and Latino genetic mix may encounter an identity culture crisis not only from the two groups but also from the broader euro-centric representative culture of the society. In certain areas, the separation of cultures still exists in certain areas of society. An internal form of racism may be expressed in separate spaces that force people who move between the two cultures to limit themselves to a single culture when operating in social circles. The person may experience stereotypes and conceptions of one or more of his cultures in some social circles because of ignorance or miseducation. [xxxi] This type of cultural clash highlights the complexities of cultural identity in an integrated, intercultural, intermixed society.

When a culture diffuses with the new culture(s), the primary focus in the past has been about the differences between the cultural makeup and all the elements' characteristics that make them different. Rarely do the culture members focus on the numerous elements that make them very similar. This mindset needs to change. Once we do that, we will find out that diverse people are human with flaws and have a lot more in common than we ever realize. The acknowledgement can change the narrative if we also focus on the positive instead of the negatives all the time.

Some, but not all interracial societies, are also intercultural. Some of the societal members may have different cultural backgrounds. Likewise, not all intercultural societies are interracial. A societal cultural background is not explicitly tied to its race or ethnicity. Rather, it may be shaped by the nation and community they grew up in, their religion and politics, and their proximity to and relationship with the family. What is more, member's cultural backgrounds often influence their attitudes about gender roles, family relationships, expected and appropriate relationship behavior, and others. [xxxii] The coexistence of multiple cultures within member's communities and societies can be complex and challenging.

As global society members, we should stop pitting cultures against each other. As humankind has evolved from a traditional culture to modern culture during the past few centuries, human beings have tried to mold their environment. "Because of this conflict, it can be said that the more subordinate a culture, the greater passivity it displays. The culture mainstream reveals itself through its domination of the material condition in which it is born and develops, showing itself as dominant and triumphal as an artist opposite the material with which he works." [xxxiii] "In his Lyrical and Critical Essays, Albert Camus writes, "Men express themselves in harmony with their land. And superiority, as far as culture is concerned, falsehoods in this harmony and nothing else. There are no higher or lower cultures. Some cultures are more, or less true.": the goal should be to emulate the truest, noblest aspects of every culture and try to learn about each culture's people. [xxxiv]

This pitting of one's culture against other cultures has created cultural racism in most societies. "Culture racism occurs when the dominant culture exerts the power to define cultural values for the society. Cultural racism involves not only a preference for the culture, heritage, and values of one's group but also the imposition of this culture on subordinate culture groups. The consequences of cultural racism are that subordinate groups are encouraged and sometimes forced to turn their back on their own culture and to become assimilated into the dominant culture." [xxxv] Culture is a learned behavior that is not biologically inherited.

When culture members venture outside the cultural zone of their culture by accident, curiosity, or adventure, transcendent experiences can happen. Perhaps they may lead to new perspectives and enlightenment from other cultures. These transformational events may dispel previous myths, conspiracies, and lifetime behavior patterns about other cultures. They may seek additional transcendental experiences that debunk previous untruths of how their culture suppressed them. This self-discovery may allow for members to seek new thresholds to breach and discover new cultural realities. If more culture members become willing to overcome the cultural fears of their brethren with different cultures, physical profiles, and skin tones, it could bring on a domino effect and evolve into a new culture.

Race

There are no "races" with the human species. Race only exists in peoples' minds. Race is a concept that is often abused as well as misunderstood, particularly given how it has been historically corrupted generally by humankind. In general, race is arbitrary, unscientific, and harmful and a term that should not be used. There is no biological justification of race and racial classification of the human species. There is a common set of genes for all the morphological and skin color shades across the globe and different populations. However, given the way the term "race" has been used for centuries, it will be difficult to convince the public to discontinue its use. In a race-obsessed, narcissistic global society since the fifteenth century, it has been used out of convenience. We have latched onto "race" for political reasons.

Race has mostly been defined by our physical profiles. It has been placed in a continuum from one extreme to the other for all physical traits without displaying any clear-cut "racial" boundaries. This arbitrariness of categories is harmless if there are no draw or "sociological" conclusions from biological categories. No race is no better than another, but they are different. "In some cases what are perceived as racial differences are primarily cultural differences between people whose genetically based physical characteristics are not markedly distinguishable." [xxxvi]

Race has been used to subjugate people. It is biological and racial characteristics cannot be hidden. Race is socially and fundamentally imposed and hierarchical. There is an inequality built into the

17

system. You have no control over your race; it is how you are perceived by others. Race may be outdated, but racism is alive and unfortunately not decreasing even in the twenty-first century even after several global major transformational events in recent decades. Race is a social construction invented by the European powers in the fifteenth century to control other people by categorizing them and trying to prove all humans are not the same members of humanity.

Racism is a corrupted misunderstanding of other cultures and being culturally uneducated in the makeup of their characteristic elements, norms, and factors. In general, people were never taught the essence of another culture. The real issue with society is not hated towards each other for not being each other but just fear of the unknown. Our global society is too uneducated with the concept of clashing cultures. Everyone seems to not understand why racism is still such a huge issue within our society. Some members of our global society are treating race as a cultural category but not as a biological reality.

Racism is a very dark, deep concept. We just happen to live in a society that is so uneducated with cultural clashes. Everyone feels a need to argue that they are misunderstood. The only rational excuse may be that they are too full of their own culture and a false sense of infallibility. This failure to understand or accept the reality of other cultures can lead to crime, atrocities, violence, and war. Throughout the history of humankind, this failure to understand and appreciate other cultures has led to thousands of atrocities and the destruction and elimination of the world's cultures. Racism corrupts the soul of the cultures that practice it.

Instead of educating ourselves about other cultures, we decide to build physical and mental walls, barriers and create new laws and public policies to make others feel unwanted and keep them at arm's length. That approach is a recipe for disaster. It has never worked and will not work in the future. Our society is just too uneducated with the concept of culture clashing. This lack of knowledge of each other's culture has regarded many members in some societies as racists and bigots. Learning more about other cultures can break down these cultural and physical walls and prevent future generations from building new walls. [xxxvii] Addressing the inequalities and injustices by members of the subordinate cultures does not mean that life for some dominant culture members has not been hard. It just means that race is not one of the social constructions making it harder.

When unharnessed in a cultural frontier, race leads to racism and has led to thousands of inexcusably heinous atrocities. Racial ideology runs deep in our culture and global history and is the lenses through which we interpret these injustices and inequalities in our global society. Racism divides the world's cultures, and societies, and fractures the idea of a global common hood. Race is the principal force that will underdetermine the future of our mere existence if we refuse to get a handle on it.

Most scientists, geneticists, anthropologists, and biologists and many others have long ago discarded the concept of race and determined that it is not a scientific concept. It was always difficult to describe the characteristics that made up a race, and who was in what race. Now, because actual genetic studies have shown that there are more genetic similarities among different populations than there are genetic differences. However, the idea of race in Western thought is very old and very entrenched, and many people do not understand or believe in the modern science of human genetics. Race has been part of their "world." Most people have not been taught that races do not exist biologically. They do not have a good education or an education in modern human biology. Cultural history is not a part of the normal educational curriculum. [xxxviii]

However, race will continue to be a very controversial issue until future generations have the political will and the moral courage to decide that its usefulness is no longer applicable in a multi-cultural global society. Noted scholar, activist, and Black nationalist, W.E.B. DuBois, said that the problem of the 20th century is "the problem of the color line". [xxxix] Unfortunately, his words still ring true today. One of the primary issues of the twenty-first century and beyond remains that of race and lack of inclusiveness with other cultures around the world.

Ethnicity

Ethnicity refers to a state of belonging to a specific nation or national origin, race, people, or culture. It is being part of a group whose members have a great deal in common with each other. It has both biological and cultural aspects. The members may share cultural norms, values, identities, and patterns of behaviors. Its members tend to share similar interests, tastes, problems, backgrounds, and experiences.[xl] In some areas, ethnicity has replaced cultural identity because the culture was too broad of a term.

Race and ethnicity can overlap. For example, a Japanese American would probably consider herself a member of the Japanese or Asian race, but, if she does not engage in any practices or customs of her ancestors, she might not with the ethnicity, instead of considering herself an American. Some people may also share the same ethnicity. Two people might identify their ethnicity as American, yet one is a Black person and the other White. A person born of Asian descent growing up in Britain might identify racially as Asian and ethnically as British.

When Italian, Irish, and Eastern European immigrants began arriving in the United States, they were not considered part of the White race. This widely accepted view led to restrictions of immigration policies and on the entrance of "non-White" immigrants. Around the start of the 20th century, people from various regions were considered members of sub-categories of the White race, such as "Alpine" and "Mediterranean" races. These categories passed out of existence, and people from these groups began to be accepted into the wider White race, though some retained distinction as to ethnic groups.

Ethnicity is cultural. It can be displayed or hidden. It can be adopted, ignored, or broadened. Unfortunately, race and ethnicity have been used historically to subjugate people rather than uplift them. [xli] Race can be confused with ethnic or cultural identity. Although someone might look like another race, that assumption alone is based on restricting one's identity to physical profiles.

Hispanic and Latino are often grouped and used interchangeably when it comes to cultural identity. These two groups hold distinctions that are regional and linguistic. Someone who identifies as Hispanic may descend from Spanish-speaking countries such as Mexico, the Dominican Republic, and Puerto Rico. On the other hand, people who identify as Latino may come from Latin American countries such as Brazil. The official language of Brazil is Portuguese, so someone from there may identify as Latino/Latina but not necessarily as Hispanic. Likewise, people might consider themselves both Latino and Hispanic, depending upon their descendants.[xlii]

The term *Hispanic* evolves from people living in Hispania – the Iberian Peninsula in modern Spain – during the Roman Empire. Although Hispanics might share the same language or religion, they still might come from different cultural backgrounds which may equate to their ancestor's country origin or an ethnic group within their residing country. The term came into use by the United States government from 1968 – 1974 and first appeared on the United States census in 1980. The term *Latino* refers to geography and has a Spanish origin. Both terms, often considered an ethnicity, are often refer to race in practice that may not fit within definitions of political systems in the policy. In the United States, the term *Latino* first appeared on the United States Census option in 1980. Over the years, the United States Census, which allows self-reporting of one's identity has offered different options of racial categories. People of all races have identified as Hispanics or Latinos. [xliii]

Indigenous peoples are another large subgroup in which their identities are sometimes misunderstood. Some culture members might consider themselves first people, aboriginal or natives in the area. This group can be broken down into several subgroups and tribes all over the world. These groups are each classified by their languages and unique tribal traditions and religions.

For example, those native to the Americas might classify themselves as Cherokee, Iroquois, Navajo, Sioux, or Cheyenne, among many others. Other examples around the world include the Sami indigenous to Nordic countries, the Kurds indigenous to the Middle East, the Aborigines in Australia and New Zealand, and the Tamil indigenous to Sri Lanka. [xliv] All terms and concepts involving race and ethnicity are considered social constructions.

Ethnocentrism

To be ethnocentric is to judge and evaluate another culture solely by the values, and standards of one's own culture. In other words, one's worldview is based on the beliefs, assumptions, expectations, and values shaped by your culture's elements. Then you judge others according to that singular 'ethnocentric' worldview rather than being open to considering or accepting other worldviews. Ethnocentrism involves a belief in all positive aspects of one's culture and or ethnic group to the exclusion of all others. "Ethnocentrism can either be overt or subtle and although it is regarded as a natural reaction, it has a negative connotation.

It was "ethnocentrism" that created the world as we know it today. Settlers who started venturing out to the Western states during the expansion era of America did so under the assumption that they had a Manifest Destiny to follow. It was God's will that the "civilized" cultures of the East begin to migrate West to begin taming the final frontier. The work was completed under the idea that missionary work was occurring, bringing new opportunities to the tribal cultures already living there.

Culture, which leads to ethnocentrism led to worldwide Colonialism. "Colonialism can be defined as cultural domination with enforced social change. Colonialism refers to the social system in which the political conquest by one society of another society leads to cultural domination with enforced social change." [xlv] In almost every instance of worldwide Colonialism, the colonizer had very little or no understanding of the culture in the colonized society. These interactions create problems and unrest between cultures.

Every Colonization attempt for the past five hundred years has been an effort to develop new resources in foreign locations because of the belief that one's home country is better than the colony itself. It is a rule that is similar is to "finders' keepers" because of the role that ethnocentrism plays in our approach." The concept continued with the worldwide Colonialism of all but ten nations on planet Earth. [xlvi]

Below is an incomplete but useful list of examples that helps define the term, Ethnocentrism.

American Exceptionalism

The term American exceptionalism was first used in 1831 by French political scientist Alexis de Tocqueville. Today, it can be used to describe the United States in three distinct ways:

- The United States is very unlike over countries found in the developed Western world. This view has most likely been around since the time of the American Revolution, in the 1700s. The idea of a uniquely

American identity that was separate from its European counterparts was first born during this time.

- The idea is that the United States has a desire to shape the world to be more "American". This identity exists in the form of things like Manifest Destiny.
- The idea is that, because of their customs and belief systems, the United States holds superiority over every other nation in the world. This belief is close to the idea of ethnocentrism.

Religiocentrism

Religiocentrism operates from the viewpoint that one's religion is more true, important, or valid than the religion of others.

Sinocentrism

Sinocentrism refers to the belief that China is the center of the world. It has held complicated economic and cultural implications overtimes, often eliciting reactions from neighboring countries throughout history.

Consumer Ethnocentrism

comes into play when people create groups of people, determined by the consumption of goods.

Chronocentrism

Chronocentrism refers to the attitude that certain periods throughout history were superior to others.

Afrocentrism

Afrocentrism is a worldwide through the lens of people living in, or with a close connection to, the continent of Africa. Unlike other types of ethnocentrism, many argue that Afrocentrism is not a negative concept, as many African voices and stories have been silenced over recent centuries. " [xlvii] The indigenous term *Kemetic* has historically been the most useful term in it refers to a nation (Egypt) and a continent (Arica) similarly to the term *America* refers to the United States and North America and South America.

Xenocentrism

The term "xenocentrism is a culturally-based tendency to value other cultures more highly than one's own, which can materialize in a variety of different ways. Xenocentrism serves as an antithesis to ethnocentrism, wherein a person believes his culture and its goods and services are superior to that of all other cultures and people. Xenocentrism relies instead on a fascination with others' culture and a contempt for one's own, often spurred by gross injustice of government, antiquated ideologies, or oppressive religious majorities.

In some extreme cases of xenocentrism, the impact on the local culture of its people favoring others' cultures can be devastating, sometimes even neutralizing one's cultural practices almost entirely in favor of a more desirable counterpart. Another downside of xenocentrism is that cultural appropriation, rather than appreciation, often results from this love of others' cultural and expressive practices. An extreme example of idolizing other cultures includes the Japanese anime genre idolizing American beauty in its art, wherein it emphasizes such features as large eyes, angular jaws, and light skin. As a result, Johnson and Johnson say it will stop producing skin-whitening creams that it sells in Asia, the Middle East, and India.

Xenocentrism is considered a type of deviant behavior because it sways from the norms of society. Unexpectedly, that an individual would value the goods, services, styles, ideas, and other cultural elements of another society. However, in some limited circumstances, it has been noted that xenocentrism can help to shed light on cultural deficiencies, whether it be ideas or products, and offers the opportunity to fix that which may be legitimate inferior to another country or culture. It is also noted that self-perception and self-esteem can contribute to xenocentrism. In certain circumstances, some individuals may attempt to elevate their perception among others by eschewing domestic products for foreign ones." [xlviii]

The two major world events since the fifteenth century led to "the process of globalization has made it possible for cultures to learn

24

about the other cultures that exist around the world. These events allowed cultures to get in touch with the global markets that allowed access to the various products, styles, and lifestyles of outside cultures. The knowledge of other foreign cultures is what gives rise to xenocentrism.

Much of the credit for the rise of xenocentrism can be given to the globalization that has taken place that enables cultures to gain access to material as well as non-material cultures of other countries.

Xenocentrism leads to cultural diffusion, which is the spread of culture. It may also lead to hostility towards one's own culture, as one may find that the other culture is superior to his own and tend to lean more towards that culture. This interaction plays a great role in how and which culture we choose to adopt, and with which culture we relate more or adopt its mannerisms more." [xlix]

Nationality

Nationality is the identity of a large group of people having a legal connection and personal allegiance to a specific place. It is an individual's nation of origin. It is the feature of a person's individuality, resulting from his membership in a nation. Nationality can be acquired by birth or naturalization. It bestows the state, authority over the person and confers the person, protection of the state. The rights and powers of the state and its nationals may vary from state to state. [1]

The historical origin of nationalities by birthright in world history has a racial connotation to it. There are nearly two hundred countries in the world. However, only about thirty of these countries grant citizenship at birth. Most world countries do not grant citizenship just because someone was born in the country. Almost all the countries located in the Americas (North American and South America), including the United States, recognize birthright citizenship.

The countries in the Americas that allow birthright citizenships are tied to the European powers' conquest and settlement of their citizens. They invaded the Americas and the Caribbean, stole the land, and validated their descendant's ownership of the stolen land by claiming it as the right of their birthplace. This concept of birthplace by citizenship was a Colonial strategy by the European's power to permanent and legally secure the stolen global lands.

Birthright citizenship is a holdover from Colonial times when European countries granted lenient naturalization laws to conquer new land. The practice is used exclusively in the Western Hemisphere, but a few countries in the Eastern Hemisphere offer citizenship by birth on a conditional basis. [li] Furthermore, despite nationality acquired via birthright, naturalization, and inheritance, immigrants and many people who live in disadvantaged, marginalized, and disenfranchised communities in many formerly colonized nations do not enjoy the full benefits of their citizenships that dominant culture members enjoy.

Concluding Thoughts

During the past five centuries of shared cultural history but an unshared vision, the world has been in a global social construction culture game with rules stacked in favor of the dominant cultural group. When the cultural game is flawed, what is the norm is usually the issue. Humanity is more than a game. It is a cultural phenomenon.

In understanding the game and its levers of power, cultures must realize how much everything around it matters too – from the languages to the expectations, the routines/activities, the environment, interactions, and more. [lii] For some mainstream culture members, ensuring cultural gains over other cultures is another rigged game in which public policies benefit them. Unfortunately, some members from other cultural groups found themselves amid a partisan cultural onslaught sweeping the globe with no geographic or moral boundaries in which no tactic, no matter how cruel, offensive, and unfair, was out of bounds. This game is about the dominant cultures ruling every sector of the global community, including its history.

As much as any other game, the history of humanity tells the history of our global cultural-race relations. History provides some clarity of atrocities that is absent in real time. But it cannot record the pain and anguish of those afflicted by the terrible human rights abuses that drove the decision-makers. You cannot appreciate the cultural complexities without knowing how the long road has been and continues to be, towards human rights. The gameplan of the dominant culture shaped the entire existential reality of some subordinate culture members, and sometimes the cruelty of their actions placed them in hopeless and dire lifetime situations. Some culture members cannot reach their life's ambitions, potentials, niches, opportunities, dreams, hopes, and aspirations by following the dominant culture mainstream rules. Some members were stripped of their humanity, unable to contribute positively to society, and some even perish amid burgeoning prosperity and unlimited opportunities. This global hegemony has diminished the overall well-being of humanity.

The human species have evolved with a capacity of intelligence and culture to interact with our environment. But many times, those abilities are sometimes suppressed or advantaged by the culture or racial group that they are affiliated with. With so many rampant injustices and inequalities across the globe, the luster of the few success stories fades. This cultural divide has led to a resultant saturation of wasted talents of depth they never used that need to be redeemed. During the modern and post-modern information eras, global societies made great strides in scientific research, technological innovations, and inventions. Although human beings are capable of immense intellectual achievement, there is an overall lack of culture rational scrutiny, easily distraction, and self-introspection to truly learn from one another. However, if all cultures were able to fully participate, the world's performance outcomes in technological advancements could have been even greater. When the global society suppresses some of its cultures, all the cultures will eventually suffer in the long run.

But some cultures have no sense of history and marinate in their own cultures to see the benefit of being inclusive with other cultures. Some members have used their culture membership as the ultimate social lubricant to protect their narrow inherited personal interests and gain an advantage over other cultures. Some cultures have become the culprits of the world's most successful pyramid scam of deception when they recruit their kids generationally. As a global society, we need to decide where do we go from here in our shared culture future? Most of us know our problems and solutions but, few of us are doing anything about it. It is time for a break and for us to reassess where we want to go.

The world's perception of the unvarnished Truth by the dominant culture is dictated by its avoidance and a false indoctrination narrative. It is one thing for cultures to not remember their historical past so they will not repeat the same mistakes, but it is another ball game when they have been miseducated about the Truth. A re-education of previously taught miseducation is the first step that will liberate the minds of the culture members. It is never too late to find our way out of this cultural wilderness and face reality. There will always be interactions and interdependency between cultures. All we need to do is have fairer and equitable game rules for all global cultures. All cultures must reevaluate their interpretation, perception, and preconceived notion of reality in their relationship to other cultures. The dominant culture wields more economic, political, and social power. It possesses most of the wealth and privileges in the global society is presently in a better position to inject some needed reality into this global situation. Some descendants of the dominant culture have inherited and lavished with a bountiful supply of global resources and privileges that other cultures lack for numerous reasons. Some cultures are in a position of economic strength because of unpaid debts from other cultures incurred from their ancestors. Therefore, more returns should result from these cultures in return. They should use the power they acquired to protect the integrity of other traumatized cultures. With great power, inherited or inherited, comes enormous responsibility and accountability.

The global subordinate cultures need to be unleashed from five centuries of physical, cultural, and mental chains. Their ancestral culture already had a body of established world's work and some wondrous accomplishments well before the present dominant culture was even formed. They do not have anything to prove to other cultures and do not need their validation. Their contributions to the global society have remained largely unknown, unrecognized, ignored, neglected, or underappreciated to the mainstream cultures. Historically, dominant predatory cultures have always stolen and copied cultural concepts from other cultures. The subordinate cultures have always shown strength and tremendous resiliency throughout their history. Yet the current dilemma represents another obstacle that must be subdued by improved fortitudinous and reduced vulnerability to other Earthling human predatory cultures. Nothing that has followed can tarnished their honor or diminish their accomplishments and human achievements. Their legacy is secure, but the struggles continue. These subordinate culture members should not have to be the subjects of another culture's specific fixed culture's specific fixed mold that place them at odds with themselves and in violation of their innermost self and the sacred inviolable principle of humanity.

Those cultural members earned their freedom, liberty, and independence cards when their ancestors formed the origin of humankind and the cradle of civilization. Their ancestors paid their cultural world's dues decades and centuries ago with their blood, sweat, and years of tears from their hearts. Incredibly, they paid society for damage and harm that they did not even commit, and the lifetime curse needs to be lifted. The members are casualties of global-wide culture clashes; therefore, they are not eligible for pardons or paroles. The dominant culture's ideology and defense of using their social constructions as a basis for determining beliefs of other cultures is a supposition steeped in their presumptions of innate guilt. After five centuries, this disgraceful falsity of the charge against them has never been confirmed. And it is important that they finally be given their unconditional release. Many unknown sacrifices were made for their freedom and the continued quest to maintain them. Many wounds and hidden scars from these numerous sacrifices have never been revealed. Some of the modern descendants from dominant cultures should not continue to determine their future fate. Who designated these cultures as the world authority on history other than themselves, which is a self-serving abomination of hypocrisy? There is sufficient evidence for conviction far beyond a reasonable doubt but very few indictments.

Cultures should reframe from defining and typecasting other cultures. Some people are often more in sync with the conscience of their culture than their conscience will allow them to acknowledge. These dominant cultures never examine the outcome of their actions in the eyes of other cultures but rather in the eyes of themselves only and the benefit that would be reaped from this action. These traumatic events place a roadblock in the progression of the distressed cultures and an opening for further exploitation and dependency. Allow others to live within their culture too. Forcibly imposing one's own ideological culture on other cultures is almost bound to lead to conflict and tensions if not managed delicately. Some cultures' outlooks and ways of life differ from others.

Dominant mainstream cultures should not expect other cultures to be molded into their cultural image. A square peg cannot be shaped into a round hole any more than each human being has a unique fingerprint and footprint because of their genes and the environment. Subordinate culture members should be allowed to find their global cultural niche and be freed from their racial and ethnic culture prisons. During the past five centuries, many opportunities have been closed and stifled by other predatory cultures. In past millenniums, those cultures displayed much creativity and unabashed intellectual boldness and dominance in every sector of earlier global societies. The harness needs to be taken off the subordinate culture members. They need to be allowed the opportunity to unleash their creative power and technological prowess in the same manner that their ancestors did to make the world a better place to live for all cultures.

Since past global transformational events, we have already witnessed the spirit of human embodiment. It revived each time they were given the opportunity. Each time that transformational events occur, subordinate groups made incremental gains, but some members of the dominant culture stifled their progress and retreated to their old cultural behaviors and the status quo. These events produced high expectations, but their cultural reality produced poor results that are unrealized. Historically, a backlash usually follows progress which continues our long legacy of global racism. When there is a progressive action to change the status quo, the reaction forces fight back with everything in their power to reverse the clock. Likewise, whenever there is a revolutionary act, a counter-reaction is a certainty. This repetition of centuries-long bitter and divisive transformational turmoil creates a wave of cultural and racial anxiety fueled the dominant culture's obstructionism. They have repeatedly signaled distressed calls to other cultures in numerous attempts to weigh anchor to deal with their inherited plight, but with no better success than the previous times. Repeatedly, the lesser cultures have been deceived and denied by the dominant culture's continued radical resistance. This unequal treatment of subordinate cultures has kept them in a continuous holding pattern, trapped in a time loop, doomed to relive the most tragic, traumatic parts of their history as they motored through a global society so deformed by race and culture.

No matter what region of the world people of African descent and Indigenous populations live or the political system of their society, they are unable to escape the historical legacy of subjugation, horrors, oppression, suppression, and degradation. These patterns of inhumanity raise their ugly head in every sector of society, and no one is insulated from them. The world is running out of chances by continuing to allow arcane methods of denying progress to all culture members. Unfortunately, this treatment will continue to exist indefinitely until the members demand a diversion or finally reach a cultural pact. Subordinate cultures cannot regain their hard-earned freedom by signed fraudulent treaties and laws which historically have been broken at the whim of those cultures who put them into place. Freedom is won by the acquisition of equality in economic, social, and political power in a society. These cultures have not reacquired these levels of power in the global society to protect the integrity of their best interest.

All culture members should be allowed to learn their true past cultural history that will provide them a sense of belongingness and identity. Without having a base identity to connect them to their vast cultural wealth, over time, the group becomes further fragmented with little hope and group unity. This disconnection happens to some marginalized and disenfranchised cultures over the past generations and centuries. Their existential reality as human species has been threatened and endangered. Over generations, they have adopted a web of insidious laws, ideologies, and value systems of the mainstream dominant culture unconsciously but not all the benefits, privileges, and rights. Learning about their real cultural history will allow subordinate culture members the ability to see how they fit into the world environment as equal partners and stakeholders. In some societies, the use of laws has historically been applied as a key component to cement racism. They have been fully entrenched and embedded into society's fabric. There is an ongoing effort to dismantle racism in those societies. However, opposition to teaching about them has been met with strong resistance. On one hand, they claim that the teaching curriculum is false, then turn around and pass new laws against teaching them, further exacerbating unresolved historical issues. A culture which is proud of its history will not pass new laws to ban people from learning about it. However, due to a lack of inclusiveness, historically, the dominant mainstream cultures have been reluctant to provide other cultures with the education and true knowledge needed that will help set them free.

Although the modern society was not shaped or designed for subordinate culture members, they will need to learn how to overcome the obstacles and barriers to be what they need to be in this world. The social constructions developed in the wide range of long-established social systems and institutions from education, health care, criminal justice, law, labor, economics, science, politics, religion, and spirituality were created against their well-being. Usually, when something is promoted, it is in the special interest of the mainstream culture, and usually, a trap for subordinate cultures predicated on baseless falsehoods. As a result, subordinate culture members must think outside the box and become critical thinkers. Blindly following the cultural patterns of previous generations who were traumatized by other cultures for centuries should not become the precedent. Their situations were very different and more challenging due to searing racial injustices and inequalities. Sometimes their mere existence was in a survival mode. Therefore, they did things against their best interest because they did not know any better. Subordinate groups now have a greater knowledge of what happened centuries and millenniums ago. Therefore, everything taught to them should not be taken at face value. The newer generations have access to greater information because of the internet and other opportunities of their history and current plight. This repeatedly generational vicious cycle by cultures need to be broken. Learning about their culture's historical past will help the members develop social awareness. It will allow more cultural members to develop a positive sense of identity and self-worth which benefits the overall global society.

No culture that has lost its connections to its ancestry culture can survive. Over generations, the culture will adopt the cultural practicing behaviors of the dominant culture and use them internally against their own members. Two millenniums of oppression intensified in the last five hundred years with the advent of the Transatlantic Slave Trade and worldwide Colonialism. The atrocities have been a terrible accelerant on what was already a cultural epidemic. These events, including the Arab-Muslim Slave Trade from the seventh to the twentieth centuries, have been problematic to people of African descent in allowing them to control their cultural socialization practices. However, for a culture to become liberated again, the members must understand their history and freedoms before these archaic institutions.

It is understandable that some subordinate cultures want to present the reality to their inheritors that the society they live in can be unjust. When some culture members grow up in an environment where they are treated differently based on their physical profile, it is wise to prepare them for the demands they will face. They should have the ability to reach their potential but may face resistance and obstacles in the world because of that profile. On the other hand, culture must know their worth and never tolerate injustices and any type of mistreatment. They should never allow other cultures to benefit from their achievements by setting boundaries. Many culture members have fought against injustices from a position of strength made significant changes to them. Those culture members should never believe that who they are as culture members is the cause of the injustices. Those cultures are a part of social constructions that were caused and designed by dominant cultures. This dilemma does not mean they have no responsibility for improving their lives but only those things within their control. They cannot change the outcomes because an outcome is out of their control. However, they can change the decisions made along the way to address the injustices. Cultures should not allow what they cannot do to interfere with things they can do. Cultures cannot change their past or the way other cultures act toward them. However, they can change their attitudes to deal with the plight of their unearned circumstances. In other cultures, hatred expressed as racism is not their responsibility. It is the responsibility of those who impose those injustices against other cultures.

There will be no culture winners in this high-stake global cultural racial game. We were taught by the present mainstream culture that "to the victor belong the spoils" [liii] of the defeated cultures. However, if that cultural mindset were the norm, previous great societies would have practiced it on a worldwide basis. This global conquest approach had never occurred in the previous history of the world. If ever there is one game that does not have a clear distinction between winners and losers, it is an integrated culture in this global society. Every culture and subculture have their values and exist in different ways. Is it important that everything in our global society always is thought of in competition in terms of wins or losses, the best or the worst, and the good or bad? Perhaps these subjective criteria may be useful in comparing individuals but not cultures. The formation of cultures should not always be about focusing on winning at the expense of other cultures. All cultures share the same humanity. Advantaged global cultures should create paths for other cultures to help them succeed. The focus should not always be about conquering cultures or racial groups. Although winning looks good, building lasting legacies on a level cultural playing field will endure. Global cultures should build a welcoming, inclusive diverse legacy. No single culture should determine whose culture is the best.

Each time world's cultures were formed, either voluntarily or forcibly, they became part of a new culture. The cultures have the option to cooperate or clash. There is no clear path in how the merger of new members will evolve with the other cultures. In the end, all that matters is how the diffusion of new cultures integrates and assimilates into one culture. A newly formed culture is one game that all members must all play, not for winning or losing, but for finally emerging as one strong, mature, stable, and multicultural society.

This dark period in world history involving racial culture clashes needs to come to an end. This turbulent relationship between cultures has gone on for two millenniums; much too long in this global society. Regardless of the great accomplishments that were achieved during this Modern era, history will not be kind to the way the world has treated its fellow human species of color. It is too heavy of a price to pay in terms of the inhumanity that billions of people have had to endure. Centuries of worldwide colonialism, slavery and the dismantling of cultures driven by religious interpretations and concepts to spread a civilized culture was just an excuse to hide thievery and greed. The accomplishments of this era could have been achieved without the horrendous treatments that were inflicted upon billions of people simply because of cultural and racial differences. Unfortunately, these accomplishments are not evenly displayed in undeveloped and impoverished sovereignties on the continent of Africa, the Middle East, Southeast Asia, Latin America, the Caribbean, and other places around the world.

The time has come to leave the sins, evilness, and wickedness of the present unequal and broken world order and place them into the annals of history and the end of an epoch. At some point, chartering a new global cultural course needs to evolve from an era of gradualism and deliberate pragmatism to a new dispensation of culture power-sharing. It is just a matter of time before the long arm of humanity will finally accelerate its demise. We need to turn our attention and energy to the challenges and opportunities of a reinvented multicultural future. Allowing ourselves to be held captives in the shadowy corners of those three archaic institutions during the past two thousand years serve no culture except some members of the present narcissistic, self-obsessed dominant culture. They think other cultures are their possession and they own them. The vestigial powers of the depraved cultural elements of the dominant culture have been sustained for decades, and centuries are on global life support. The world is presently on CPR – or Culture + Power + Race - to resuscitate itself. It is now better to spend our energy making a difference in seeing global societies following through on promises of serious reckoning with systemic cultural racism. To tackle those challenges, we must stop holding back history. We must look to a multicultural future and a brand-new start.

There has always been dissension, conflicts, and clashes among global cultures but never on a global-wide-basis. Many cultures in world history have done horrible and unspeakable things against other cultures, but they were localized or regional. "By opening up sea routes to Africa, Asia, the Americas, Australia, and other territories, the European powers rose globally to become internationally active trading and colonial powers that turned Africans as commodities for Europeans" [liv] and exploited the indigenous populations. This European global hegemony was formed from an alliance in the European region on Earth in the fifteenth century in an ambitious attempt to construct an international world order.

For a particular culture to have a superiority mindset, a doctrine of imperialism, and a Manifest Destiny to rule over the entire world and make it their sole province, to have complete dominion over it, all the cultures, the global natural resources, other Earth's inhabitants, and species, and to create a global human caste system is astonishing. The despicable characteristic elements of such a culture that could justify such a global dominance and horrific cultural global behavior from some of its members, need to be critically analyzed and completely dismantled. The dominant culture's mythological spirit of resistance has justified making the reality their atrocities and sacred myths and conspiracies that chain all cultures. This cultural mindset resulted in the introduction of atrocities as the norm that ushered in a kind of pacification into the ordinary that became and considered respectable domestic and foreign policies. No dominant culture by their nature of power should make other cultures' virtues a deficiency and their depraved conduct admirable.

A global racial and cultural awakening is on the horizon for the unforeseeable future. After the past five centuries, the clashes of the world's racial cultures can no longer sustain themselves. It is very disheartening that a single dominant predatory culture, consisting of a small number of European countries, allowed to achieve hegemony over most of the globe. The variables culminated in the exploitation and genocide of the indigenous people in many of the world's territories, the enslavement of Africans in the Americas and the Caribbean, and the institution of worldwide Colonialism.

It is very difficult for an outside culture to fully understand the sociopolitical, geopolitical, socioeconomic, and socioemotional factors of a dominant culture to explain why the characteristic elements, cultural disorder norms, and factors involved in the makeup of it would compel some of its members to conquer, enslave and colonize all the other cultures around the world. What internal organizing forces are at play, that would help explain this deranged cultural behavior? What manner of culture would allow this type of global behavior among some of its members? "The rich and rigorous cognitive science of identity, status, and risk unites the discussion of our current cultural crisis. It should be an essential component of any analysis that attempts to explain how we arrived at this global cultural divide and an invaluable tool for bridging it." [lv] Many of us have tried to make sense of these human atrocities. There is no simple explanation for the reasons some cultures set in the direction of the lives of other cultures. Heinous atrocities committed by culture are extremely dangerous and much more volatile than personal hatred. We must find out the anatomy and the underlying principles of this global cultural divide before understanding it. We must make some attempt to put this cultural phenomenon into some understandable form.

Perhaps the **"science of risk perception" and "culture of denial"** research studies discussed in the second chapter may provide clues. There has been a collaboration to develop a theoretical analysis and framework to help understand this racial-culture-divide. It is such a complex issue with continuing moving parts. Many strategies and tactics have been applied only to see additional frameworks developed to oppose those efforts. Multiple tools in the toolbox are needed to help reduce the oppression imposed on some segments of humanity. Presently our understanding of this cultural dilemma and dynamics is more of a theory than a certainty. All the culture members - past and present - certainly have not complicit in the cultural behaviors and actions were undertaken by some of its members. This shared cultural association should not subsume into guilt by association. But the overall behaviors of culture are characteristics of the individuals within it. Some individuals from different cultures choose their lifestyles and associations. It is not incumbent upon the rest of us to bear the burden of these types of decision unless we want to maintain the status quo as evidenced by the fact that it continues to happen. Otherwise, it is not a reflection nor the responsibility of all of us unless unearned social benefits exist at the expense of other cultures, and we are complicit in the acts. All cultures have members with extreme ambivalent conflict in them, but individuals should not be judged collectively.

The insistence to define and control history ensures the ability to manipulate facts to strengthen their agendas. It is a tremendous source of power. Some people tend to believe the purported generational narratives or at least rationalize their existence was because of innate quality that was inculcated upon them. How else could someone justify seeing centuries of unearned human suffering, global atrocities, rampant inequalities, and injustices and still want to maintain the status quo?

Some dominant culture members have a deep-seated, complex, unhealthy obsession with race. This delusion is fueled by a distorted racial ideology and captured by absolute despotic inhumane hatred toward some cultures. The world has a big, deep, gaping racial scar that slices across our cultures and divides us. This scar messes with all our minds. All cultures need to take a deep breath, exhale, and reclaim their uncluttered mind space. Some dominant culture members cannot even begin to understand and relate to the experiences of some subordinate culture members who are on a different side of the same complex culture coin. That racial culture coin obsession with new social codes, artificial criteria differentiation, rigid social codes and labels, and the vicious self-perpetuating cycle is continually flipped in some global societies.

Unfortunately, it is difficult to deprogram some culture members when they have become spiritually and mentally affected by some reprehensible elements of their culture. Some cultures have trained their members to unconsciously think in a certain way about people of other backgrounds, beliefs, or physical profiles. This subliminally generational linear transmission into the subconscious minds of some culture members engrains certain myths and conspiracies that make them more compliant to their cultural mores. Cultural peer pressure creates beliefs that some culture members follow blindly and prevent them from developing critical thinking skills to see the world from other perspectives. This constant gaslighting and cultural indoctrination have brought some culture members to the point where they cannot mentally process truth from fiction. They developed an emotional bond to their cultural mores that makes them oblivious to the plight of other cultures. This familiarity keeps them in lockstep with other cultural members and precludes them from learning something new.

Sometimes, some culture members will act in servitude of their cultures and contrary to their own social-economic, survival, and interest. Their socialization and livelihood demand it. The predispositions to their cultural beliefs distort their perception of reality and manipulate its members to work against their best interests. It seems that their strong tribal cultural instincts will not let some members override anything that goes against the grain of their wants and group cultural needs. They inherited some cultural elements that have been transmitted from past generations, centuries, and millenniums that are almost difficult to overcome. It is virtually impossible to change the mentality of a cultural force of some members. They have been conditioned to hate and compounded by generational and environmentally taught racism. Those cultural traits adversely affect members of other cultures whose lives have been dramatically impacted when they assume power and authority over them.

The cultural mindset of some members of the dominant culture will need to permanent change. Global societies are becoming increasingly multiracial, multicultural, multiethnic, and interfaith. The newer generations are challenging the dominant cultures to reshape their societies to become genuine alliances of a broad multiracial, multigenerational, and multicultural coalition. As other cultures demand some semblance of parity and equality, the dominant culture will no longer be seemed like the default, presumed, and baseline culture for all other cultures. The subordinate cultures will continue to question the fundamental values, institutions, and systems through increased heightened political rhetoric, activities, and awareness. There will be pushback from the dominant culture because change, particularly by demand, disrupts the core values, beliefs, and norms which took generations and centuries to create. Regrettably, these types of generational traditions and customs die hard in our global society.

This pushback by the dominant culture is spurred not only by a possible loss of power and its unwillingness to share power but the belief that it will be excluded from future power, just as it excluded the other cultures. In their efforts to hold on to power, they fight back through whatever means necessary, which only acerbates the cultural divide problems ever further. This notion of subordinate cultures that once they assume some parity and semblance of power will treat other cultures the way they were treated in the past is largely unfounded. Perhaps, it is fueled by a possible fear of the unknown, paranoia, willful ignorance, or tactical stupidity, greed, and suspiciousness by the dominant culture. Some think back to how this same intolerance was used against other cultures in their historical past. They believe that history may become cyclical, further entrenching their disinclination to join a cause spoiled by their culture. This stinging duality complicates some of them from reaching across cultural aisles. Through the advancement of human progress and the reclaiming of ancestral cultures, the full human and natural rights of subordinate culture members can only be restored by sensible, humane, committed, and due diligence by human beings who truly value freedom.

We must know the connection between our shared global cultural history. It will allow us to create a place to examine our cultural past and support and celebrate the work of our ancestors in building a stronger global cultural future. We must reframe the historical narrative which has always centered on the dominant culture's perspectives and paradoxes that leave out lots of history. This fact-based narrative will identify, elevate, recreate, and support previously untold stories, places, achievements, voices, and activisms. [lvi] This important work in educating other cultures is not about defining what their cultures should be, rather it is about informing them of what other cultures have earned and contributed to the progression of the world.

We must honor the global land space as a place for all cultures to connect and ponder as caring members of humanity. All cultures should enter this space with reverence, humility, and openness. It will be a space where different opinions and perspectives could be heard.

Sometimes our cultural perspective and where we fit within society determine how we show up in those global spaces. Despite the good intention of some cultural members, some may not be particularly well versed of other cultures. We must seek to contribute to the vigor and vitality of the global land space rather than drain it. This universal interconnection will no longer allow those cultures to content themselves with their humanity contested as geographical spaces might be. This cultural connection must be rippled with honesty, which is a depth of understanding that will hopefully finally rest its head in a soft-landing place.

Global cultures need a deeper-reason moment of reflection. Some people are caught up in their own cultures and imaginary races; therefore, cannot see the merits of other cultures. This reflection may set us on a course to preserve and respect certain iconic features of past glorious cultures which have laid the foundation of our modern global society. There is nothing wrong with a culture trying to continue some aspects of its culture. Only if it contributes positively to the continued rebuilding and redevelopment of our global society. Being proud of yourself or your culture should not imply any degree of supremacy. We can seek to come to terms with the past one half a millennium reign of cultural terror while simultaneously recognizing the admirable contribution credits that they have brought to humanity. However, trying to comprehend and understand our present cultural dilemma does not necessitate empathy, especially when the atrocities committed are inexcusably heinous. A reflection of past global transformational events is not a denial of any accomplishments but the acknowledgment of their inadequacies. This reflection will also allow cultures who know very little about other cultures and transform a whole barrier-breaking practice of centering cultures in the long road toward racial reconciliation.

We need to continue to build from those cultural bases which provide strategies for counteracting some cultures that have done some horrendous and unspeakable racial acts against other cultures. Some world's subordinate cultures that are now misunderstood and unvalued were highly revered during their past peak performance periods. Other dominant predatory cultures learned from them, adopted some of their traditional cultural concepts, and then committed horrific atrocities that in some cases, led to their destruction and demise. Those cultures understood the unique cultural connection and linked among all humanity better than their successors and must always have an honored place.

Those subordinate cultures may have been ahead of their times or isolated from other world's cultures because of lack of technological advances. Fortunately, the work that some enlightened cultures are doing now is eternal because their impact will last into the unforeseen future. This cultural mentorship is spurred by cultures intentionality about building a stable global community. When all world cultural forces are in balance interculturally with each other, the world will remain in a stable racial and ethnic orbit. When cultures are working collectively, they are not one dimensional. This scenario has the potential to be a very beautiful thing.

Cultures are in harmony and sync with each other when no single culture is leading the cultural base. Instead, each culture reacts in unison to the diverse mix of minds, ideas, perspectives, backgrounds, and experiences of all cultures. The interconnectivity of all cultures allows them to reach a balanced cultural sphere and equilibrium that can never be reached solely by a single culture. Earth's species such as birds and fish have flown or swum in unison in murmuration to avoid conflicts with each other. Are human beings ready to completely transform and stop their practice of domination, conquest, division, control, confusion, and destruction among their species? When cultures march in harmony with others and follow various leads, they will be more acceptable to being lead or guided when they experience some shortcomings. Global cultures should create beneficial paths for other cultures to keep them strong in our shared humanity. They will finish their cultural journey at their pace.

The internal makeup of a culture is defined by its members. A culture undergoes gradual changes over time that are transmitted across generations. The members define the culture and the ability to reshape or unshaped the way they think, feel, and act in a certain manner. The culture can be influenced by other cultures, develop technological advancements, and foster economic development, but in the final analysis, it is up to its members to ultimately change their overall cultural behaviors. Humanity's ability to heal and repair itself after centuries of atrocities is greatly affected by our present beliefs, intentions, thoughts, and emotions. They have a profound effect on our continually developing cultural codes. We are the programmers of the social codes which require beneficial activations and upgrades to produce positive outcomes for all culture members. For the sake of our global future, this present global cultural behavior must change and evolve sooner rather than later.

A cultural introspection global behavior check-up and tune-up are badly needed by some members. Over centuries, the cultural fantasy will eventually wear out. Cultures must keep reinventing themselves to stay relevant, but it must be based on humanistic social constructions. Although the mainstream cultural mystique continues, it may be positioned on past fiction, fairytales, mythologies, and conspiracies. It is convenient for cultures to believe that everything is still wonderful. Therefore, members feel good about themselves. However individual culture members are easily replaceable generational cultural unit. New culture members may not have committed the sins of their culture members and ancestors, but they surely have inherited the benefits. As culture members, they benefit directly based solely on their physical profiles, which is an unearned benefit. Even if they never contributed to the wrongdoings of other culture members, it is in their best interest to help find remedies for the betterment of humankind and other Earth's inhabitants.

42

Multiculturalism is here to stay. Its developments are the product of centuries and millenniums. Multiculturalism will not disappear from our global societies. Multiculturalism is nature's way of adapting to life's parameters where the universe keeps its checks and balances. Multicultural representation of all groups is essential. The way some cultures use the images of other cultural groups affects their lives and the way the world perceives and treats them. We must learn to coexist with other global cultures. Diversity is our heritage and our future. Multiculturalism has the potential to be a powerful mantra for the twenty-first century.

Chapter II
The Impact of Multiculturalism on Race Relations

With multiculturalism spreading throughout the world, cultural clashes and conflicts between the mainstream cultures and subordinate cultures have become more pronounced. Throughout the history of humankind, there has always been a proliferation of cultural and racial clashes between groups of people. Oftentimes, it arises, because of a disagreement between groups of different beliefs, values, and practices. Generally, conflict occurs between and within cultures as an inevitable reaction to handling their differences. When different cultures meet and interact with each other, particularly when the distribution of resources is at stake, it is unlikely that all the cultures will maintain the consistency of their cultural history.

However, an appreciation of one's culture should in no way precludes recognizing that other cultures have value, and it should in no way preclude treating members of other racial groups with humanity and respect. World history has shown that disrespect and feelings of superiority by one of the groups have provoked the situations and turned them into racism, discrimination, poverty, exploitation, exclusion, atrocities, and even wars. This global behavior by the dominant cultures has disproportionally impacted the lesser cultures.

The assimilations of different opposing cultures and preventing conflict are very delicate situations. Societies need to be very careful how they manage this cultural transition. It requires acknowledgment, adaptability, understanding, and communication. As a global society, we have not done a very good job in embracing different cultures. Generally, what has occurred is the dominant culture simply fundamentally imposes its political will and culture on the lesser cultures. Unfortunately, this type of mindset has taken us to this point in world history in which the legacy of cultural and racial differences continues today.

Is it Race or Culture?

Is it a racial or culture clash? It may not always be about race. Race is an element of culture, although technically speaking, it is not a scientific term but a social construction. Culture defines what a race is and encompasses many things in society. Society defines what its culture is, which in turn, defines what the races and ethnicities are. Sometimes people confuse race and culture because race is associated with a culture where people have a racial or ethnicity designation within their culture that is shared with other culture members.

There is no clear distinction to determine if a clash or conflict that occurred within a society is caused by race or culture. In a multicultural society, there may be multiple sets of morals or values standards so there may be no standard in determining what is wrong or right if any. However, in some cases, the circumstances may be obvious with little dispute from other cultural members. In other cases, after the situation is analyzed, the initial determination may change after a review of the issue(s). Further, the members of the culture of an independent reviewer make the determination. Because of their perspectives, a final determination may not be unanimously reached or agreed upon. Further negotiation can take place, but all parties still may not be satisfied with the conclusions.

That is why in most cases, very seldomly are their winners in an integrated racial culture game. Hopefully, a compromise between the parties will ultimately merge the disagreements into a satisfactory outcome. Culture members may share their experiences. Once the conversation has evolved, it may become apparent that neither "race" nor "culture" played a larger role. In some cases, it may be a combination of both since both terms are associated with each other.

In some situations, there may be a deeply entrenched dominant culture whose members want to maintain a centuries-long status quo. That type of culture excludes external cultural influences and practice - only the traditions of one culture. The lines between the competing cultures can be crossed, but only one way. The culture rejects any form of multiculturalism and cultural change. Customs and traditions die hard in some cultures. The pushback may continue indefinitely and a compromise - if ever reached - may be so diluted where no one is satisfied with the outcome. This resistance could dissolve into a splintering or stand down by some culture members who will hunker down alongside their stance that may threaten the future of the culture.

There will always be a continued debate as to the reasons for conflicts or clashes within the culture. Generally, the dominant group members will probably say that *culture* is the reason; whereas, members from the subordinate group will side with *race* because of their lived experiences and knowledge. Race, as an element of culture, is insignificant to predicting demeanor, lifestyle choices, accomplishments, and education but culture anticipates them.

Since *race* is just one of the many elements of culture, ideally, in an ideal world, *culture* should probably be the main reason for descensions and conflicts among members most of the time. However, because of the historical realities that *race* has played in our global society, particularly during the past five centuries, its significance and impact loom large. This historical interaction between groups of people in multicultural societies affects cultural experience, and culture affects the experience of one's identity. The idealism of just and fair global societies has not been met for all its societal members. Racism, unfortunately, is the simplest answer and is certainly the one with the robust historical evidentiary documentary trail.

Some members of a culture tend to assume that other culture members think the same way they do. Thus, they become obsessed with their own culture and only see everything that happens through their cultural lenses. They project culture racism into their interactions and behaviors of other group members when none really exists. Some even claim to know and understand the inner workings of the other culture better than the members do. More often, than not their knowledge of the other culture will be immediately dismissed and disputed.

The reason for this cultural difference of opinions may be how cultural members view the degree of racism in their society. Generally, one prevailing thought is that some dominant culture members shaped the existential reality of subordinate members and predetermined their future. On the other hand, some look at racism as a thing in the past, that race relations have gotten better, and we live in a colorblind society. The opinions from some dominant group members are that we live in a more just society and there are no barriers preventing someone from reaching his/her life's potentials.

If forced to choose between biased societal structures and systems, or biased minority communities, many pick the latter. So how some cultural members view this cultural divide, come to starkly different conclusions. These two or more culture group members, with most coincidentally divided by skin tone, live in the same society, but do not live in the same reality.

The attainment of power in a society is the one issue that takes precedent over race or culture. Like most delicate issues, the answer can never be answered and lies somewhere in the middle. There are too many variables. There is an ongoing debate as to whether a universal moral code exists among global societies. Cultural beliefs, values, perspectives, and ideas are constantly changing and evolving. Cultures and subcultures have different social standards and belief systems in what is accepted as moral. Placing blame for this cultural divisiveness will only bring about more divisiveness. Rather than both parties hunkering down in their positions, there should be a spirit of cooperation so the cultural issues can be critically analyzed. Culture members should make a good faith effort to understand and empathize with the other members so that a compromise if needed, can be reached for the benefit of all culture members. It is difficult enough for culture groups to integrate with other culture groups with different life perspectives. But unfortunately, once the concept of *race* is thrown into the cultural equation, it is taken to a whole new level.

Reasons Why Some Global Societies are Undeveloped

The citizens of the world's undeveloped nations are living in extreme poverty when their standards compare to international set living standards. These standards measure human developmental indices. Such indices include but are not limited to Gross Domestic Product (GDP), Gross National Product (GNP), poverty ratio, access to clean and potable water, life expectancy rate, access to economic and social freedom, rate of maternal and infant mortality, access to primary, secondary, and tertiary healthcare, public procurement transparency, public infrastructure, public utility, and many others. These are measurable indices in which statistics have an international standard to help us define if people are poor or living within acceptable living standards. For most undeveloped and impoverished nations, the living standard falls far below the international set ones. Their present plight is not unconnected to the unfair trade, economic, and political policies of the West and East. These unfair trade deals give advanced economies unfettered access to African markets while protecting their own, to the detriment of the African economy, citizens, and its diaspora. There should be a global advocacy for a change in the world's economic and political structure and system. The present system is weighing against undeveloped world's societies versus other cultures and nations in enjoying the global largesse.

The major world events since the fifteenth century such as the Transatlantic Slave Trade and worldwide Colonialism retarded the economic growth of many impoverished nations, particularly cultures of color and those on the continent of Africa, the Middle East, Southeast Asia, Latin America, and in the Caribbean. Haiti, for example, is one of the poorest countries on planet Earth. Historically, the Republic of Haiti was the only slave colony to earn its independence through a slave revolution. [lvii] After these countries won their hard-earned independence, why did some undeveloped countries such as Singapore, Japan, South Korea, and Thailand become more prosperous than countries in Africa or Haiti? After the African countries gained their independence, pressing challenges such as lack of infrastructure, energy dependence lack, national identities, and inexperienced leadership stifled their economics and political stability.

People of color, and particularly those of African descent generally live in most of these poor undeveloped, and impoverished countries around the world. There are numerous reasons why some of the countries remain poverty-stricken despite gaining their independence after World War II and mostly in the early 1960s. For example, many of these former colonized African countries and Haiti still pay a Colonial tax to France. This annual debt to the former colonizers could be almost half of the countries' budget. The exploitation of these former colonies has stunted their economic growth, France, for example, takes in about 500 billion dollars from Africa each year. These countries are obliged by France, through the

48

Colonial pact, to put 85% of their reserves in the central bank of France under the control of the French Ministry of Finance.

As a result, the people in these countries endure extreme poverty and desperation. In some cases, the stubborn African leaders who decline to pay the debt were the subject of a coup or killed. "In fact, during the past fifty years, a total of sixty-eight coups happened in twenty-seven countries in Africa, sixteen of those countries are French ex-colonies, which means sixty-one percent happened in Francophone Africa." Others who submitted to it were provided extravagant lifestyles while their citizens embraced abject poverty and distress. "We often accuse African leaders of corruption and serving Western nations interests instead, but there is a clear explanation for that behavior. They behave so because they are afraid that they may be killed or become victims of a coup. They want a powerful nation to back them in case of aggression or trouble. But, contrary to friendly nation protection, the Western protection is often offered in exchange of these leaders renouncing to serve their people or nations; interest." [lviii]

Even after the countries of Africa gained their independence after WWII, they still rely heavily on the former European powers economically for aid, charity, health, and education matters. The colonizers took few measures to help transition Africa and many of the formerly colonized nations after WWII. This hasty and poorly planned European exit from Africa led to some tenuous country borders and governments, planting the seeds for many of the conflicts we see today. [lix]

The International Monetary Funds (IMF) - (loans for countries in crisis) and the World Bank (loans for developing countries) have a strong influence on the economic policies in many countries. Many African countries have loans with these institutions and other financial institutions. Because the work of these institutions deters economic freedom, most recipient countries have been unable to develop fully after sixty years of independence. The reforming of these institutions is needed to create incentives for countries to increase economic freedom.

Africa should strengthen its position with IMF and the World Bank and push for free markets and trade across the globe. The goal for most of these countries should be to borrow only as needed and make good use of the available funds. These countries must understand the terms and agreements of their loans as they can place a heavy burden on their citizens. The inability of many countries to repay their debt has made them dependent on new loans. [lx]

Thirteen European countries and the United States participated in the Belin Conference from 1884 to 1885. They drew up artificial European borders to slice up the continent of Africa among themselves. Before the creation of the artificial European borders, Africa never had any independent countries. For centuries before the European invasion and conquest, the sovereignty of Africa was based on linguistic, ethnic, and cultural mores. The European countries and the United States only looked at the economic benefits that would enrich their countries when the borders were drawn. Instead, the drawing of the African borders was self-serving to the Europeans. They did not care about the other factors and how they would affect the continent for centuries and millenniums to come.

As a result, after the African countries finally gained their independence after World War II, the negativities from the artificial borders became more pronounced. They are still reverberating today. Now, there is mistrust with the artificial borders that are having an economic fallout that has inhibited economic development and sustainability; good governance; and the free flow movement of trade and people from crossing borders without constraints. The artificial borders have also fostered mistrust between neighboring countries involving chiefdom, land, and religious disputes.

Africa can never achieve the unity it desires until it handles the homogeneous task of critically analyzing the artificial borders created by the Europeans and the United States and their future impact. There is still not one African country that is self-reliant to furnish the needs of its people with food, clothing, shelter, and security. The countries are still relying on the Colonial powers for assistance. [lxi] Before the European invasion and Colonization, Africa was able to sustain its people. The African kingdoms were involved in independent trading and global affairs with other nations in the Middle East, Europe, and Asia for over two millennia.

The European colonizers "partitioned land from European capitals, with limited knowledge of geography, history, and ethnic composition of Africa. In many African countries, a significant portion of their population belongs to groups split by Colonial partitions. During the onset of colonization, European powers preferentially dealt with African local leaders and chieftaincies. Colonial powers employed underhand mechanisms in the territorial acquisition and boundary- making such as deceit, fraud, intimidation, and bribery. Moreover, Colonial powers utilized various techniques to influence African leaders and obtain resource-rich land. [lxii] The Berlin Conference legitimized the partition of Africa; Colonialists designed regional maps without providing any notification to the local African rulers and made treaties among Colonial powers to avoid resource competition. However, many errors were made because of their superficial knowledge of the continent and undeveloped maps in existence.

Lord Salisbury, the British Prime Minister in 1906 demonstrated this arbitrary and under-informed approach at the signing of the Anglo-French Convention on the Nigeria-Niger boundary in 1906, when he said: *"We [the British and the French] have been engaged in drawing lines upon maps were no White man's foot ever trod: we have been giving away mountains and rivers and lakes to each other, only hindered by the small impediments that we never knew exactly where the mountains and rivers and lakes were."* [lxiii] This statement helps us to understand how Colonial powers designed artificial African boundaries without knowledge of the land and local communities.

European powers completed cartographic surveys of territories through boundary commissions from 1900-1930, which allowed total control of colonies. However, these focused solely on land control and disregarded the impacts of partitioning on ethnic groups. Artificial borders split many closely related ethnic groups into different Colonial regions. In the Horn of Africa, for instance, they split Somalis into French Somaliland, British Somalia, Italian Somalia, Ethiopian Somalia, and the Somali region of northern Kenya. Such Colonial borders have massive effects on Somali people who share a common culture, a similar way of life, and the same religion, but live as separate citizens of Ethiopia, Djibouti, and Kenya. Similarly, the Afar people of Ethiopia were split amongst Ethiopia, Eritrea, and Djibouti, and the Anyuaa and Nuer were split between Ethiopia and South Sudan.

Following artificial border designs, African communities could not move freely in their daily activities and nomadic practices, which inflicted economic hardship and social inconvenience. Changing the lifestyle and structural systems of African communities negatively affected their traditional life, administrative structures, and economic well-being. This deprived African borderland communities of economic opportunity by hindering their movements and forcing them to live differently than their traditional life. For example, many Africans are pastoralists and nomadic people that need vast land for grazing and water. However, artificial borders limited borderland people to herding on limited land and forced them into resource competition and confrontation because of limited mobility with other borderland peoples.

Besides improperly designed borders, European Colonial powers employed "divide and rule," "direct rule," and "assimilation" policies, which forced the loss of social norms, identity, and social order for Africans. Moreover, these policies instigated conflicts among local people, dividing them even further, and consequently strengthening Colonial power. Doing so helped gradually develop hostile relations among borderland people, and post-independent African governments and political elites used this division for political means. Some political elites in Africa affiliate more along ethnic lines and play crucial roles in fueling tensions and escalating political disenfranchisement. For instance, the Lou-Nuer of South Sudan and the Jikany-Nuer of Ethiopia are the same ethnic group and live along the Ethiopia-South Sudan border, yet they are considered as two distinct ethnic groups with different nationalities and have developed hostility through resource competition. Despite the effects of colonization and artificial borders on borderland communities, African political leaders have not alleviated these problems but rather used them as political instruments.

> "Improper border design and the partitioning of ethnic groups have contributed to underdevelopment, and instability in African states. In addition, the disconnect between center-periphery relations is demonstrated by the exclusion by some. African states of borderland communities in economic development exacerbate the challenges. The lack of economic, social, and political development and limited upward mobility exposes the borderland communities to several human security problems, including widespread poverty, lack of infrastructure, limited education, and cross-

border intergroup conflicts. The improper design of African borders and use of these designs as political instruments have increased instability and underdevelopment for borderland communities across the continent." [lxiv]

Undoubtedly, the global trade regime has its roots in slavery and Colonialism. The European powers participated heavily in and benefitted from the Transatlantic Slave Trade and Colonialism, while those in Africa, the Middle East, Southeast Asia, the Caribbean, and Latin America suffered the most from these atrocities. They have been left impoverished by the effects of slavery, Colonialism, and neo-colonialism, and are in a weaker position to negotiate with the world's powers. Their weaker position is taken advantage of and leaves them with little in the way or power or recourse for previous wrongdoings. A restructure of trading regimes would require greater parity in the negotiations between trading partners. However, this trade imbalance has thus far been proven to be unlikely because the world's power would have to show restraints in their negotiations with the developing nations. There needs to be more support to the developing nations to access the benefits of a globalized economy more fairly and equitably to enable the redistribution of power in trade between the countries. [lxv] To a significant extent, the European powers leveraged problems of poverty and inequality in the undeveloped countries to achieve their ends.

The centuries-long trade power shift from the fifteenth century has resulted in massive trade imbalances. The power shift can be reversed but only with tougher trade deals, new demands, and a renewed global commitment to fairness. The resulting trade imbalance between developed and undeveloped and impoverished countries has the spawned wholesale destruction of the Earth's natural order.

Unfortunately, Africa and nations of African descent are not being treated very fairly in trade negotiations and are continually being taken advantage of economically by most of the world's powers. "Many countries depend on African resources to sustain their economies and ensure future growth. France has a tremendous stake in its former African colonies, as consecutive French leaders have openly confessed:

53

'Without Africa, France will have no history in the 21st century" ~ Former Prime Minister François Mitterrand, in 1957

"...without Africa, France will slide down into the rank of a third [world] power" ~ Former French President Jacques René Chirac, in 2008

"...a little country [France], with a small amount of strength, we can move a planet because [of our] relations with 15 or 20 African countries..." ~ Former French minister Jacques Godfrain in 2011

"We have to speak the language of Truth: African growth pulls us along its dynamism supports us and its vitality is stimulating for us... We need Africa." ~ Speech by French finance minister Pierre Moscovici, December 2013

"...France, along with Europe, would like to be even more involved in the destiny of your continent..tomorrow's economy will heavily depend on the strength and vibrancy of African businesses... The goal I have set is to double the level of trade between France and Africa in five years. ~ Speech by Current President François Hollande at the Elysée Summit for Peace and Security in Africa, December 2013" [lxvi]

In the past, economists have avoided the sensitive concept of culture as it relates to a culture's economic development. Historically, people of color have been sharply underrepresented in the economic field, which lessens the perspectives of diverse groups, thus the profession has been slow to address racism as a source of economic inequality. They sometimes draw conclusions that are often not reflective of reality. [lxvii] There was a discomfort in defining the multitude of the various elements that define culture in an economic ramp-up. There had been a debate among economists and others in exploring the definition of culture in fixed terms such as beliefs, values, and religion versus elements of cultural change that are shared by members and encompass learning and strategies. The different cultures in the global countries appeared to have played a role in their progression but it does not provide a debate framework as to how the undeveloped and impoverished country could catch up with the developed ones.

This debate impacts why some undeveloped and impoverished countries who at some points were broadly comparable in terms of income per capita, the structure of production, and foreign aid. However, a few decades later, the contrasts of economic development between some of the countries were very pronounced. The culture of the undeveloped and impoverished countries possibly masked other forces at work that are more amenable to change. Is it the results of bad policies or political instability that deters long-term investment? Instead of the cultural behavior traits of the undeveloped and impoverished nations being the culprit, it may instead be behaviors shaped by economic incentives that are amenable to change. So, the absence of cultural patterns of the undeveloped and impoverished countries may not be the true indicator but the natural response to the economic environment. The people's cultural patterns also reflect the environment that they experience. "There are several factors which have fundamentally affected development in various parts of the world and can be detached from conceptions of culture. For instance, the disadvantages of geography, such as access to natural resources, being landlocked, or part of a poor, volatile neighborhood. There is a heavy burden on Africa associated with the historically arbitrary demarcation of international borders. Poverty may have more to do with geography and climate, with natural resource management, and with the toxic interactions between ethnic diversity and artificial borders, than with purely cultural factors."[lxviii]

The development of nations is not only about reducing poverty and expanding opportunities against the background of rising incomes. It is also in a very fundamental way about adopting a set of values that are compatible with humanity's moral development. [lxix] Had Colonialism never been fundamentally imposed on Africa, its development would be significantly different and many of the problems that plague it today would not exist. It is impossible to develop these skills when you spend all your time fighting for survival. In earlier eras, Africa was at the forefront of creativity in developing mathematics, religion/spirituality, philosophy, arts, science, architecture, building pyramids, and other disciplines. "The continent lost millions of people who were in the most productive phase of their lives, particularly from the western coast. Left without a skilled and able workforce, Africa's agricultural and industrial development was greatly undermined."[lxx]

The European powers drew up borders that were theoretic and arbitrary. Border issues have always plagued African nations. Africa is a hugely diverse continent that is stifled with ethnic conflicts.

Virtually the root cause of African conflicts has an ethnicity region dimensions. It is an instrument for political manipulation. Civil wars have always been a prime hindrance to development. When you have a never-ending political conflict, anarchy is rampant then survival becomes the priority over development.

Trying to understand how one group of people or culture succeeds and another culture does not may be misleading. There may be past histories and some internal and external forces that stifle its growth. So, culture may not be solely responsible and the all-encompassing force for the overall success of a society. Some of these cultures have been through toils and strife and still trying to discover a coherent cultural identity. In the past, some of these undeveloped and impoverished cultures were forced to devote their energies to politics and mere survival. Therefore, it will take a little longer for these cultures to find their global niche with the modern global culture.

The answer is very complicated, and the verdict is incomplete. Sustainable political and economic successes rely on leadership that adapts and manages the society's beneficial systems and institutions. The national development that these nations need starts with leadership and accountability. Leaders unite and protect, enabling a group of people to thrive. Determined leaders can often make things happen if they are passionate enough. Divisions keep them from reaching their desired outcomes. External detractors incite individual's rights and freedoms over and above community aspirations and responsibilities. They should not allow those cultural forces to hold them back and determine their future destiny. Somehow, the debilitating internal forces from within those societies and the external forces need to be overcome through determination and tenacity. Political and economic successes for most societies are often top-down. Real leaders lead from the bottom or grassroots level. They rely on leadership that adapts and manages appropriate systems and institutions that also benefit all citizens. Some of these societies have yet to acquire the leaders for national development they deserve. But the capability, energy, and self-determination – as they are undeniable. Fixing the trading system, the scrapping of visas for travels within Africa, working with its diaspora, limiting its foreign dependency, and fundamental changes in the education system are steps toward mending the longtime global systemic inequities.

The West and the East continue to exploit Africa economically and are mostly responsible for Africa's present economic plight. Their reasons for Africa's involvement are usually self-serving. The many present events by the European countries and other world's powers still contribute heavily to the unequal broken world order given to majority countries of color and particularly those of African descent. In recent decades, many African countries have made trade deals with China involving major loans and aid. Likewise, the countries of Africa need to understand the clauses and conditions of those loans because in many cases, they are not revealed to the public. A few African countries are already indebted to China. [lxxi] These countries' poverty and political instability have been formed and shaped by foreign interference. The meddling and interferences have denied the citizens their ability to charter their future and path. Today, one half a millennium later, the African continent, those who live there, its diaspora, and indigenous people worldwide are still vulnerable but not fragile, to other predatory human species on planet Earth.

Science of Risk Perception Research Study

The characteristics that make up the elements and factors of cultures that define their cultural behaviors are certainly an undertaking that is worth being conducted. It may help explain the thought process of a particular culture and add some credence as to why it behaves in a certain manner in its interactions with other cultures and subcultures. The continued polarization in our global society has primarily existed because of the clashes and conflicts of global society's cultures. We know the main reasons why the predatory dominant culture decided to conquer, enslave, and colonize the world in the fifteenth century.

But we do not fully understand the sociopolitical factors that would compel some members of the culture, along with other cultures, to have a majestic era of human-made global developments, but during the same period, also commit incredible heinous, and inhumane acts against lesser cultures that have adversely affected the entire landscape of the planet. The "science of risk perception" may

57

shed some light on understanding the cultural differences between some members of racial groups. Other such sociopolitical factors that this research can address may include racism, the economy, class anxiety, fragile masculinity, political fear, sectarianism, and others.

One such major research study was conducted in 1994. However, it should be noted that there is no such thing as "absolute Truth" in science. The research "found that these race and gender differences in risk perception in the United States were primarily because of 30% of the White male population who judge risks to be extremely low. The specificity of this finding suggests an explanation in terms of sociopolitical factors rather than biological factors. The study reported here presents new data from a recent national survey conducted in the United States. Although White males again stood apart concerning their judgments of risk and their attitudes concerning worldviews, trust, and risk-related stigma, the results showed that the distinction between White males and others is more complex than originally thought." [lxxii]

The research may not have been specifically developed to address the broader historical global racial culture differences between racial groups, but the nature of its subject matter appears to be very relevant. Further investigation of sociopolitical factors in risk judgments was recommended to clarify gender and racial differences. "Cognitive scientists long ago coined a term for the psychological forces that have given rise to the gendered and racialized political divide that we're seeing today through research, and decades of subsequent scholarly work." [lxxiii]

A group of researchers led by Paul Slovic and others published a study that asked about 1,500 Americans across the country how they perceived different kinds of risks, notably environmental health risks. Slovic and his team found that White males differed from White women and non-White men and women in how they perceived risks. For every category of threat, White men saw risk as much smaller and much more acceptable than did other demographic groups. This is what they dubbed "the White male effect." They also found that White women perceived risks, across the board, to be much higher than White men did, but that this was not true of non-White women and men, who perceived risk at pretty much the same levels, suggesting complexities worthy of further exploration.

Eventually, expansions of this study would include a wide range of risks including handguns, abortion, nuclear threat, and capital punishment. [lxxiv]

Over the years, subsequent studies would add layers of nuance to the understanding and interpretation of the 1994 results. By 2007, researchers were explaining the White male effect in the context of cultural cognition, demonstrating that it was only indirectly a product of gender and race—that at a fundamental level, it stemmed from differences in cultural identity, socioeconomic security, and attitudes toward egalitarianism and community. But the through-line was that different groups can perceive the same risk through vastly different lenses. And in the case of White men, it is often a lens that seeks to preserve institutionalized cultural identity and societal status.

They perceive an even greater threat around the horizon: a threat to an elevated social status that they can preserve and restore which is a social status that is inevitably linked to race, gender, and religion. "Individuals selectively credit and dismiss asserted dangers in a manner supportive of their preferred form of social organization," wrote Slovic and collaborators in a 2007 research paper that rings no less true today. [lxxv]

When this perceived need to protect one identity is stoked by people in positions of power, it can turn dangerous and ugly. Identity protective cognition can lead to what Slovic and other researchers call "virtuous violence"— violence that people support or commit because they believe it is morally right. In an August 2020 study, Slovic and a team of researchers found that White conservative men were more likely than all others to support virtuous violence, and "felt socially distant from the enemy, dehumanized them, and believed that the victims were to blame for their fate." [lxxvi]

Every research proposal is just a theory that stands if the evidence supports it based on real facts. "Perhaps, in the end, the name we use to describe social and cultural differences in risk perception matters less than what we do about it. This academic research is valuable but should not obfuscate the real-world violence and harm. Virtuous violence is still violence and there is nothing abstract about identity protective cognition's role in White male supremacy. What the science seems to suggest—and what people like Paul Slovic have observed for decades—is that society's multiple overlapping crises

59

cannot be solved when governing bodies composed primarily of White men, who are outliers in terms of risk perception, are tasked with making decisions about risks for the entire population. The individuals who hold power over decisions about what's risky and what is not should be representative of the community at large, and those individuals should have the agency and authority to be part of the final decision-making." [lxxvii]

Cultures of Denial Research Study

Cultures of Denial is another major body of research work that attempts to explain the global cultural divide that exists among racial groups. There have been some research studies conducted that focus on the crimes of different political systems around the world or of the State, involving human rights violations and crimes. Denial of past global human rights abuses around the globe that have not been addressed, profoundly impact all cultures. There has been a deep historical societal pattern of denial and social fears that make it difficult to understand the true world's history. These studies provide some compelling insights into the forces of cultural denial in the way members see themselves and other cultures. Cultural racial clashes have occurred in all global societies and their various forms of political systems. The cultures of denial research efforts center on human rights abuses committed in most nations in our global society. "Over the past century, national laws, and international treaties have condemned torture and other abusive treatment of detainees as unacceptable governmental practices." [lxxviii] This culture of denial research is also relevant in other sectors of society such as education, environmental issues, racism, the economy, mental health, gender-based violence, class anxiety, judiciary, political fear, sectarianism, and others.

One such research study was conducted in two countries, the United States, and electoral democracy, and Argentina, a dictatorship form of political systems. The study model was based on "Argentina during the last dictatorship (1976-1993) and the United States during the "war on terror" post-September 11, 2001. The study is based on 40 in-depth interviews with members of diverse civic, religious community, and political organizations in both countries." [lxxix]

The Argentina model site was based on a repressive military dictatorship that targeted were a diverse group of people, including armed group members, activists, journalists, students, teachers, religious leaders, labor organizers, guerrilla organizations, and others. These people were subjected to state terrorism by the dictatorship in the forms of torture, disappearances, and arbitrary use of force. The United States model was based on the post terrorist attacks on September 11, 2001, in which a "war on terror" was launched in Afghanistan and Iraq as part of that effort. The Abu Ghraib prison in Iraq and the United States-run Guantanamo prison in Cuba were alleged to have violations of human rights violations alleging humiliation, abuse, torture, due process issues, and others. In both instances, many citizens of Argentina claimed they were unaware of widespread human rights violations, and normal life continued for most citizens in the United States. [lxxx]

There have been different approaches to the study of State crime and what constitutes human rights. Human rights are generally referred to as natural rights e.g. rights by existing, such as the right to life, liberty, and free speech, or civil rights e.g. the right to vote, to privacy, to a fair trial, or education. One such thought was proposed by Criminologists Herman Schwenindinger and Julia Schwenindinger who defined crime as that which violates basic human rights than law-breaking. They equated someone who steals a small sum of money as a criminal yet reward agents of the State who destroy foods to maintain food prices, but a sizeable portion of the populace is suffering from malnutrition and poverty. They viewed any State that practices imperialism, racism, sexism, or inflict economic exploitation are committing a crime. This thought was criticized by noted Sociologist Stanley Cohen who regarded human rights violations such as war crimes and torture as obvious, but other acts like economic exploitation are not illegal just morally wrong. Cohen argues that all type of State governments conceals and legitimate their human rights crimes by using different methods and conceal their human rights crimes. Dictatorships would simply deny that abuses are happening, and democratic states would use more complex ways to justify the abuses.

In Cohen's three-step process called the Spiral of Denial, the State would flat out deny that violations existed despite the media and others having proof that it occurred. If the abuse did occur, the State would justify it by explaining it was self-defense or collateral damage. The third prong was that even if it was justified, it was done to protect national security or the fight against the war on terror. Furthermore, other denial techniques include looking at the victims as terrorists that incite violence; the injury to others because they started it and the State was defending themselves; lack of responsibility because they were obeying orders; condemning the condemners because they are racists, anti-Semitics, or Islamophobia; and an appeal to a higher loyalty of self-righteous justification.[lxxxi]

These Culture of Denial studies, along with several others, are important for understanding the internal mental processes related to denial by individuals and of the State. Both the United States and Argentina, despite having different political systems, have some state violence similarities. First, the ideology of patriotism and national security were used as tools to minimize, normalize, or justify human rights violations. Secondly, the broad range of people who participated exhibited cultural practices that preferred not to ask questions or be told information by avoiding political topics to keep human rights violations out of sight and mind. These studies examine the lenses of individuals through denial practices of highly charged political situations. They also reveal the complicated process of how human rights abuses are circulated in societies. Despite the public circulation of information and the outright censorship and suppression of information to potentially provoke widespread condemnation, many well-meaning individuals looked the other way. It suggests that an individual's consent is crucial to maintaining the status quo that is secured by cultural ideas and practices. The study highlights areas of overlap regarding ordinary citizen's response to human violations under political systems often seen as opposed. It highlights how official denial is culturally reproduced and tacitly condoned.[lxxxii]

The Origin and Concept of Global Racialization

Identifying human species by skin color terminology has been around forever but it was popularized during the European Colonial caste system. Race, as we currently understand it, and as we currently live it, is almost entirely a made-up condition. Race by pigmentation is a European invention that was formed inside the matrix of slavery or Colonial societies founded in the fifteenth century. The word "race" was originally used to refer to any nation or ethnic group. The Europeans coined racial color labels. Much of the existence of race can trace its origins to the Colonization of the Americas. The categories and meanings of race have changed over time and geography. No one was *White* or *Black* until the colonization process needed ways of differentiating various rights, privileges, social, and legal standings between various laborers.

Fifteenth-century European countries were not the modern nation-states of today," so there was no concept of being "Italian," for instance. People identified with regional areas, as Calabrese, Genoan and others. When Europeans did use the term "race" it was employed to talk about tribal groups, such as the "Teutonic races" and while those categories might have been used as indicators of "types" they were by no means seen as limiting or indicative of innate inferiority. Religion and class were the most important divisions, and race as we know it had not been invented." [lxxxiii]

The Europeans declared themselves as White and the rest of the people of color as non-Whites. Later, during the height of the Transatlantic Slave Trade, followed by the labor exploitation of the native Indians and Chinese, they further coined racial labels of Black, White, Red, and Yellow. It included a racial caste system with White people at the top and Blacks, at the bottom of the racial hierarchy. What separates the Atlantic slave trade from any slave trade is the race language established with it later in the Americas and the Caribbean. It discriminates against a whole group of people on basis of their physical profiles and skin tones. Historically, the term Black had different interpretations in European cultures including terms such as Schwarz, svart, Moreno, neg, smith, negro, and others. However, by the mid-fifteen centuries, during the rise of the Transatlantic Slave Trade, the term Black became associated with the oppression and suppression of the African indigenous population and its diaspora. Thus, the terms, Black and Negro were attached to the negativity of skin tones and physical profiles associated with people of African descent.

The concept of humanity began during the Spanish Inquisition (around 1480) when the purity of blood decree was established and those converting to Christianity needed to prove their Christian origins. Racism became even more established during Colonization when two theories were developed to explain why people in other parts of the world looked and behaved differently from Europeans. The actual idea of specific races as they are thought of today developed through a long process that began with Western philosophers, like David Hume, Immanuel Kant, and Johann Blumenbach in the 1700s. [lxxxiv] Skin color, unfortunately, has risen to the front in distinguishing the physical profiles between the human species as the foremost determinant of race.

The European powers launched a world conquest of other global societies initially lead by the Portuguese. From the fifteenth century from 1441, the year of the first mass slave expedition, to 1888, [lxxxv] the year slavery was abolished in Brazil, they assumed a more aggressive stance when they traveled by ships to a lesser aggressive society. The highly aggressive European powers push their belief system and authority on less aggressive societies. Their expertise in sea fearing and the gunpowder technology, invented by the Chinese allowed them to colonize all but ten countries worldwide. They used enslaved Africans to build the Americas and the Caribbean and sadistically eradicated the indigenous people in many of the world's territorials.

The Europeans' false sense of "racial superiority" started in 1492 when they finally defeated the Muslim Moors (Muslim of Northwest-East and Saharan Africa and their Arab allies). Thousands were expelled from Europe and returned to Africa. "They were a noble people of many cultures, nationalities, and backgrounds mostly made up of Africans, Arabs, and North African Berbers (Arab/African Mixed)." [lxxxvi] Some were enslaved and sent to America in bondage. "Dating back to the first millennium AD, Africans existed in Europe, and, from about 711 AD to 1492 most of Spain, Portugal, North Africa, and south France were under Moorish control. Consequently, the Spanish colonizers who ventured forth to "settle" lands outside of Europe did so while harboring color prejudice associated with their subjugation. But racial categories as we now know them had not yet been used to justify the denial of basic rights, which were controlled through the church." [lxxxvii] The Europeans conveniently forgot that the Moors were instrumental in the rebuilding and redevelopment of part of Europe that facilitated learning that led to the Renaissance. A form of historical amnesia set in that led to a chain of events that continues today.

The European powers began to feel they were invincible even though some regions of Europe were still under the rule of the Ottoman Empire rule. Like all new conquerors, the European powers rewrote history and created themselves into a superior or civilizing race. The revised maps and falsified ancient cartography. For example, the Ethiopia Ocean has renamed the South Atlantic Ocean after the 1884-1885 Berlin Conference sealed the Scramble for Africa which colonized all the nations except Ethiopia. They used all the propaganda tools available to justify their world conquest and maintain world dominance. [lxxxviii]

Before the fifteenth century, Europeans considered the continent of Africa as exotic but not necessarily as inferior. With the involvement of more European nations in the Transatlantic Slave Trade, Africans were characterized as stupid, backward, and uncivilized to justify their conquests. These atrocities were easier on the conscience of the enslavers if the perception of the enslaved were viewed as sub-human or non-human. "Europeans knew Africa to be a wealthy, advanced continent in many areas of development and education. They were targeting well-established kingdoms weakened by internal strife, with citizens who had the skills required to develop the Colonial enterprises, including advanced agricultural practices, metallurgy, navigation, and shipbuilding, as well as the resources from the lands. Race did not begin to take on its modern meanings until the mid-16th century, and the terms and meanings that we now give to race in the United States were not concretized until the early 20th century.

There are three seminal moments for British-American colonies that structure race, only the most recent of which was the first United States Census in 1790, establishing race as a set of official categories. That first happened in 1662, when the Virginia Colony passed an act stating that *"Negro women's children to serve according to the condition of the mother,"* thus undoing centuries of European tradition and law regarding paternity, birthrights, and rights of inheritance. Perhaps more relevantly, this act stands as the first real miscegenation law in what would become the United States.

Bacon's Rebellion in 1676 was the second. It was the first rebellion in the American Colonies in which discontented frontiersmen took part. [lxxxix] Feeling unprotected from Native American Nation resistance, workers in Virginia united and violently removed their governor and attacked neighboring indigenous groups. The following Colonial backlash had two important results: Native Americans became the "enemy Other" for the new Americans, and Euro-American workers were awarded privileges over their former comrades of color, thus ensuring divisions between the lower classes, and laying the racist foundations for a class that still divide us. These actions (and a host of other smaller acts) encouraged physical separations between Blacks and

Whites that would become a permanent part of the American tradition and lay the foundation simultaneously for American concepts of race and White supremacy. The post-Jamestown government passed the Virginia Slave Codes at the turn of the 18th century, assigning nearly all remaining Black indentured servants to slavery. [xc] The other colony followed suit in enacting the same kind of laws because of Bacon's Rebellion. The laws persisted in the United States until 1865.[xci]

Intermarriage was discouraged, as White workers were encouraged to believe that they could attain a level of economic and social mobility previously impossible in Europe. Ideologies based on Enlightenment philosophies and the profoundly self-serving ranking of conquered, colonized peoples by the Europeans helped institutionalize European nationalism, anti-indigeneity, racism, wage disparities, and housing discrimination in every country that the Europeans invaded. In short, Europeans brought racism with them wherever they went. In the United States, this practice would lead to the removals of Native Americans, the institution of the reservation system and ghettoization of native peoples, the exclusion of Red and Black peoples from enfranchisement, full legal humanity, and standing, and traditions of separation and oppression that are now entrenched in our culture. " [xcii]

While the Portuguese, English, French, Spanish, Dutch were the primary players in the European colonization of North America, South America, and the Caribbean, Sweden, Courland, Norway, The Danes, Russia, and Scotland, and others also participated. All but ten countries were able to avoid worldwide colonization by the European powers. They were Afghanistan, Nepal, Bhutan, Ethiopia, Japan, Korea, Iran, China, Saudi Arabia, and Thailand.

Global racialization occurred in different terms in the Spanish colonies than it did in the English colonies, but the purpose and effect were the same. For the Spanish, racialization emerged as a structure attaching people of different origins to specific economic strata and modes of labor exploitation. At first, the indigenous as such were enslaved. In the Caribbean region, they were quickly decimated by their separation from former means of physical and cultural survival.

When African labor was brought to the Spanish colonies to replenish the deficit, and some Franciscans (particularly Bartolomeo de Las Casas) convinced the king to ban further enslavement of the indigenous, a multi-stratified labor system emerged that became the organizing principle for defining race. Africans were held as slaves and sold as slaves. While the indigenous could be considered the first "race," that is, relationally racialized concerning the Spanish as racialized, the complex economic system of Colonial settlement produced a more complex hierarchy, organized according to ancestry, that equated radiality with class. If one was a slave, then one was Black and others.

A different mode of racialization occurred in the English colonies. Those colonies were not administered by military conquest, nor by land tenure related to a monarchy. Though at first English bond labor was used on the plantations, the colony shifted to African bond labor after the 1680s for several reasons. As the colonies grew, it became easier for English labor to escape, and blend in elsewhere, which was not the case for the Africans. But this did not yet express racialization. When the English first arrived, they did not see themselves as White, and the terms they used for themselves, for the Africans and the indigenous, referred to geographical origin ("Negro" referred to Africa rather than "race," for instance). The concept of racialization did not take hold until the 1690s.

The English defined a White racialized identity for themselves by racializing the African labor force as slave, other, finally as Black. Racialization occurred through a transformation of color terms from descriptive to racializing, referring to the social category rather than bodily characteristic. In terms of social categorization, race must be understood as essentially relational, a social relationality, and not something inherent in the people so racialized.

The contemporary concept of race derives from the English version. It was in the English colonies that the concept of Whiteness and a notion of "White supremacy" (even a concept of White nation as theorized by Ben Franklin, and other independence luminaries) were developed. Its extension to all European American thinking as a "natural" division of the human species (by a variety of European theorists, such as Buffon, Gobineau, and others.) has been concerning Whiteness, and the Coloniality of White supremacy, as a mode of social identification, and not simply as a link to forms of labor exploitation. [xciii]

As the European settlers' population grew in the Americas, Africa, Asia, and Australia, they simply cleared the indigenous people from tracts of land to make room for themselves and their farms. This disrupted the nomadic life of some of the native tribes and made their survival problematic. The clearance was deliberate and systematic, resulting in the extinction and genocide of the indigenous people. Some natives, particularly those on the East coast of North America, lived in settled cities and villages. The tribal cultures of the indigenous American Indians, the Australian Aborigines. and other natives around the world had little chance to succeed when competing with the European settlers in warfare because of their advanced weaponry at that time. The indigenous tribal cultures had little chance to win in outright competition with the European powers. [xciv]

Because of the Transatlantic Slave Trade and worldwide Colonization, the United States became a European country in a non-European part of the world brought about by European migrants and African slaves. Europeans and England gave birth to America and the origins of American law. The Europeans and America are culturally similar because the United State was a child of English Colonialism. English is the shared national language, and the founding fathers were of the same ethnicity. However, numerous other European immigrants and Asians migrated and settled in the Americas and assimilated into society. They include the Germans, Irish, French, Italians, Polishes, Russians, Spaniards, Portuguese, Croatians, Greeks, Jews, Arabs, Chinese, Japanese, and Koreans, and others.

Likewise, the continent of Australia became a European continent in a non-European part of the world. Portuguese America is modern Brazil. Brazil was settled by Portugal and the official language is Portuguese. The Spanish Colonization in the Americas brought Roman Catholicism and the Spanish language to Latin America. The English Colonization brought the language to North America. France brought the French language to parts of North America (Canada and Louisiana). Protestantism came to the Americas through English Colonization. The English Colonization brought the English language to Australia, New Zealand, most of Canada, and South Africa. [xcv]

English is also one of the official languages in many African countries, namely Nigeria, Kenya, Zimbabwe, and Uganda. The Belgian Colonization has resulted in French being the official language in the Democratic Republic of Congo. Dutch and British presence in South Africa resulted in both Afrikaans and English being official languages. English is also an official language in India and Pakistan. Spanish is spoken in all countries south of the United States, starting with Mexico and continuing into South America, except for Brazil, where the official language is Portuguese. Portuguese is the official language in Angola and Mozambique. Those countries colonized by traditionally Roman Catholic countries (Spain and Portugal) tend to have a large proportion of Roman

Catholics. The British tended to introduce Angelico Catholicism or Protestantism. The English language has spread to more countries and in some places, displaced the French and Spanish languages. There are more English-speaking countries whose primary language is not English but the second language than there are primary language English-speaking counties. [xcvi]

Some former colonized world's cultures were able to maintain their native languages. Most of the Arab nations were colonized by the Europeans but they still speak Arabic as their primary language in the Middle East. Many nations in Southeast Asia were colonized by other world's major cultures, but most maintained their official indigenous languages. Likewise, the British colonized India. While English is the official language in India, the native languages such as Hindi, Tamil, and Bengali are used by a large percentage of the population in their societal major sectors in business, media, and academics.

The indigenous natives of both territories, the Indians in America and the Aborigines in Australia were mostly removed, replaced, and subject to genocide. In America, most natives live on reservations and represent only 1.2 percent of the population. In Australia, Aborigines represent only 2.8 percent of the population.

"List of former European Colonies Global Conquests

The Americas and the Caribbeans

British
- British America (1607– 1783) – New Britain
- Newfoundland (1583-1949)
- Thirteen American Colonies (1607- 1783)
- Rupert's Land (1670-1870) – A private estate stretching from the Atlantic to the Rocky Mountains, and from the prairies to the Artic Circle
- British Columbia (1793-1871)
- British North America (1783 – 1907)
- British West Indies – Bahamas, Barbados, Belize, Jamaica, Leeward Islands (Antigua and Barbuda, Dominica, Saint Christopher (St Kitts)-Nevis), Trinidad and Tobago, Westward Island (Grenada, Saint Lucia & the Grenadies)

- British Guiana (Berbice, Essequibo, Demerara)

Courland (Latvia)
- New Courland (Tobago) (1654–1689)

Danish – (Denmark)
- Danish West Indies (1754–1917)
- Greenland (1814 – today
- Iceland

Dutch
- New Netherland (1609–1667)
- Essequibo (1616–1815)
- Dutch Virgin Islands (1625–1680)
- Berbice (1627–1815)
- New Walcheren (1628–1677)
- Dutch Brazil (1630–1654)
- Pomeroon (1650–1689)
- Cayenne (1658–1664)
- Demerara (1745–1815)
- Suriname (1667–1954)
- Curaçao and Dependencies (1634–1954)
- Sint Eustatius and Dependencies (1636–1954)
- Anegada
- New Walcheren (Tobago)
- Saint Croix
- Tortola
- Virgin Gorda

French
- New France (1604–1763)
- Anguilla
- Antigua and Barbuda
- Dominica
- Grenada
- Montserrat
- Nevis
- Saint Christophe (St Kitts)

- Saint Croix
- Sainte-Lucia (St Lucia)
- Saint Vincent and the Grenadines
- Sint Eustatius
- Acadia (1604–1713)
- Canada (1608–1763)
- Louisiana (1699–1763, 1800–1803)
- Newfoundland (1662–1713)
- Île Royale (1713–1763)
- French Guiana (1763-today)
- French West Indies
- Saint-Domingue (1659–1804, now Haiti)
- Tobago
- Virgin Islands
- France Antarctique (1555–1567)
- Equinoctial France (1612–1615)
- Quebec
- Brazil (Rio de Janeiro briefly, Sao Luis briefly)
- Lles Malouines (Falklands Islands)

Norwegian
- Greenland (986-1814)
- Vinland (Partly in the 1000s)
- Dano-Norwegian West Indies (1754–1814)
- Sverdrup Islands (1898–1930)
- Erik the Red's Land (1931-1933)

Portuguese (Portugal)
- Colonial Brazil (1500–1815) became a Kingdom, United Kingdom of Portugal, Brazil and the Algarves.
- Cisplatina (1808–1822, today Uruguay)
- Barbados (1536–1620)
- French Guiana (1809–1817)
- Misiones Orientales

Russian
- Russian America (Alaska), 1799–1867)

- Fort Ross, California

Scottish
- Nova Scotia (1622–1632)
- Darien Scheme on the Isthmus of Panama (1698–1700)
- Stuarts Town, Carolina (1684–1686)
- Darien, Georgia (from 1735)

Spanish (Spain)
- Cuba (until 1898)
- Belize
- The Bahamas
- Hispaniola
- Puerto Rico
- Trinidad
- Mexico (1521)
- Peru
- New Granada
- Rio de la Plata
- Upper Peru
- New Granada (1717–1819)
- Captaincy General of Venezuela
- New Spain (1535–1821)
- Captaincy General of Guatemala
- Costa Rico
- Banda Oriental
- Real Audiencia de Quito
- El Salvador
- Nueva Extremadura
- Nueva Galicia
- Nuevo Reino de León
- Nuevo Santander
- Settlement at Nootka, near Vancouver Island, Canada
- Nueva Vizcaya
- Las Californias
- Santa Fe de Nuevo México
- Viceroyalty of Peru (1542–1824)

- Captaincy General of Chile
- Puerto Rico (until 1898)
- Rio de la Plata (1776–1814)
- Santo Domingo – Dominican Republic (last Spanish rule 1861-1865" [xcvii]

"Africa"

Belgium
- <u>Belgian Congo</u> (<u>Democratic Republic of the Congo</u>)
- <u>Lado Enclave</u>
- <u>Ruanda-Urundi</u> (<u>Rwanda</u> and <u>Burundi</u>)

Brandenburg
- <u>Arguin</u> (in <u>Mauritania</u>)
- <u>Brandenburger Gold Coast</u> (coastal settlements in <u>Ghana</u>)

Britain
- <u>Anglo-Egyptian Sudan</u> (<u>Sudan</u>)
- <u>Basutoland</u> (<u>Lesotho</u>)
- <u>Balleland</u> (<u>Benin</u>)
- <u>Bechuanaland</u> (<u>Botswana</u>)
- <u>British East Africa</u> (<u>Kenya</u>)
- <u>British Somaliland</u> (<u>Somaliland</u>)
- <u>British Togoland</u> (eastern <u>Ghana</u>)
- <u>British Cameroons</u> (split between <u>Nigeria</u> and <u>Cameroon</u>)
- <u>British Egypt</u>
  - <u>Khedivate of Egypt</u>
  - <u>Sultanate of Egypt</u>
  - <u>Kingdom of Egypt</u>
- <u>Gambia Colony and Protectorate</u>
- <u>Gold Coast</u> (<u>Ghana</u>)
- <u>Colonial Nigeria</u>
  - <u>Niger Coast Protectorate</u>
  - <u>Northern Nigeria Protectorate</u>
  - <u>Southern Nigeria Protectorate</u>
  - <u>Colony and Protectorate of Nigeria</u>
- <u>Northern Rhodesia</u> (<u>Zambia</u>)

- Nyasaland (Malawi)
- Sierra Leone Colony and Protectorate
- Union of South Africa
  - British Cape Colony
  - Natal Colony
  - Orange River Colony
  - Transvaal Colony
- South West Africa (Namibia)
  - Walvis Bay
- Southern Rhodesia (Zimbabwe)
- Swaziland (Eswatini)
- Tanganyika Territory (mainland Tanzania)
- Uganda Protectorate
- Sultanate of Zanzibar (insular Tanzania)

Courland (Latvia)
- St. Andrews Island (in the Gambia)

Denmark-Norway
- Danish Gold Coast (coastal settlements in Ghana)

France
- Albreda (in The Gambia)
- Comoros
- French Dahomey (Benin)
- French Algeria
- French Cameroon (91% of modern Cameroon)
- French Chad
- French Congo (Republic of the Congo)
- French Guinea (Guinea)
- French Upper Volta (Republic of Upper Volta, Burkina Faso)
- French Somaliland (Djibouti)
- French Sudan (Mali)
- French Togoland (Togo)
- French Madagascar
- Gabon
- Ivory Coast (Côte d'Ivoire)
- Colonial Mauritania
- French protectorate in Morocco (89% of Morocco)

- Oubangui-Chari (Central African Republic)
- Senegal
- Senegambia and Niger
  - Upper Senegal and Niger
  - Colony of Niger
- French protectorate of Tunisia

Germany
- German East Africa (Burundi, Rwanda, Tanzania)
- German South-West Africa (Namibia)
- Kamerun (split between Cameroon and Nigeria)
- Togoland (split between Togo and Ghana)
- Wituland (Lamu Island, owned by Kenya)

Italy
- Italian East Africa
  - Italian Eritrea
  - Italian Somaliland (now Somalia)
  - Italian Ethiopia
    - Amhara Governorate
    - Galla-Sidamo Governorate
    - Harar Governorate
    - Scioa Governorate
- Italian Libya

Netherlands
- Arguin Island (in Mauritania)
- Dutch Cape Colony
- Dutch Gold Coast (settlements along coast of Ghana, including El Mina)
- Dutch Loango-Angola (Luanda, Sonyo and Cabinda)
- Gorée (Senegal)
- Moçambique (Delagoa Bay)
- São Tomé
- South Africa

Portugal
- Ajuda (Whydah, in Benin)
- Angola

- Annobón
- Cabinda
- Cape Verde (Cabo Verde)
- Ceuta
- Fort of São João Baptista de Ajudá
- Gorée (in Senegal)
- Malindi
- Mombasa
- Macau, China
- Algarve Ultramar (Morocco)
  - Agadir
  - Alcacer Ceguer
  - Arzila
  - Azamor
  - Mazagan
  - Mogador
  - Safim
- Nigeria (Lagos area)
- Mozambique
- Portuguese Gold Coast (settlements along coast of Ghana)
- Portuguese Guinea (Guinea-Bissau)
- Quíloa
- São Tomé and Príncipe
- Tangier
- Timor-Leste
- Zanzibar
- Ziguinchor

Russia
- Sagallo

Spain
- Bona
- Bougie
- Jerba
- Fernando Po and Annobon (insular Equatorial Guinea)
- Oran
- Port Guinea
- Río Muni (mainland Equatorial Guinea)

- Spanish Protectorate in Morocco
- Spanish West Africa
  - Río de Oro
  - Saguia el-Hamra
  - Tarfaya Strip
  - Ifni

Sweden
- Swedish Gold Coast (coastal settlements in Ghana)

Indian Ocean

Britain
- Mauritius (British Mauritius)
- Seychelles
- Maldives

France
- French Comoros
- Isle de France (now Mauritius)
- French Madagascar
- French Seychelles

Netherlands
- Dutch Mauritius (now Mauritius)

Portugal
- Laccadive Islands (Lakshadweep)
- Maldive Islands
- Socotra

West Asia

Britain
- Aden Protectorate
- Bahrain
- Cyprus
- Mandatory Iraq

- Sheikhdom of Kuwait
- Muscat and Oman
- Mandatory Palestine
- Qatar
- South Arabia
- Emirate of Transjordan
- Trucial States

France
- Syria
- Lebanon

Netherlands
- Jemen, Al Mukha (Mocca)
- Mesopotamia (Iraq, Al Basrah)

Portugal
- Aden
- Bandar Abbas (Iran)
- Hormuz
- Manama (Bahrain)
- Muharraq Island (Bahrain)
- Muscat (Oman)
- Qeshm

Russia
- Russian Armenia
- Russian Azerbaijan
- Russian Georgia

South Asia

Austria
- Banquibazar & Cabelon
- Nicobar Islands

Britain
- Afghanistan

- <u>British India</u> (After independence from Britain, British India became Pakistan (East and West) and India – later East Pakistan got independence from Pakistan and known as Bangladesh)
  - o <u>Bangladesh</u>
  - o <u>India</u>
  - o <u>Pakistan</u>
- <u>Burma</u> (<u>Myanmar</u>)
- <u>Ceylon</u> (<u>Sri Lanka</u>)

Denmark-Norway
- <u>Frederik Oerne Islands</u> (Nicobar Islands)
- <u>Serampore</u>
- <u>Tranquebar</u>

France
- <u>India</u>
  - o <u>Pondicherry</u>, <u>Karikal</u>, <u>Yanaon</u>, <u>Mahé</u>, and <u>Chandernagore</u>

Netherlands
- <u>Bangladesh</u> (<u>Dutch Bengal</u>)
- <u>Ceylon</u>
- <u>India</u> (<u>Dutch Bengal</u>, <u>Suratte</u>, <u>Malabar</u>, <u>Coromandel</u>)

India
- <u>Bombay</u>
- <u>Calicut</u>
- <u>Cambay</u>
- <u>Cannanore</u>
- <u>Ceylon</u> (Ceilão)
- <u>Chaul</u>
- <u>Chittagong</u>
- <u>Cochin</u>
- <u>Dadra and Nagar Haveli</u>
- <u>Daman and Diu</u>
- <u>Goa</u>
- <u>Hughli</u>
- <u>Masulipatnam</u>
- <u>Mangalore</u>

- Surat
- Syriam

Ragusa
- Ragusan India

Sweden
- Parangipettai

Asia-Pacific

Austria
- North Borneo
- Tientsin

Britain
- Australia
  - New South Wales
  - Queensland
  - South Australia
  - Swan River Colony/Western Australia
  - Van Diemen's Land (Tasmania)
  - Victoria
- British Solomon Islands
- British Western Pacific Territories
- Christmas Island
- Cocos Islands
- Colonial Fiji
- Gilbert and Ellice Islands (Kiribati & Tuvalu)
- Hawaii (formerly Sandwich Islands)
- Kingdom of Rarotonga (Cook Islands)
- New Zealand
  - Auckland Islands
  - New Hebrides
- Niue
- Norfolk Island
- Territory of Papua and New Guinea
- Territory of New Guinea

- Western Samoa
- Phoenix Islands (part of Kiribati)
- Solomon Islands
- New Hebrides (Vanuatu, condominium with France)
- Territory of Papua
- Tokelau
- Tonga
- Southeast Asia
  - Malaysia
  - British Malaya
    - Federated Malay States
    - Straits Settlements
    - Unfederated Malay States
  - British Borneo
    - North Borneo
    - Kingdom of Sarawak
- Brunei
- Bonin Islands (Japan)
- Singapore
- China
  - Hong Kong
  - Weihaiwei (leased to the British government)
  - Shanghai International Settlement (merger of the British and American concessions and residency in Shanghai)
  - Tientsin (British concession territory)
  - Canton (British concession territory)

Belgium
- Tientsin (concession territory)

France
- East Asia
  - Kwang-Chou-Wan (廣州灣) leased territory, now the city of Zhanjiang (Guangdong province)
  - French settlements (French Concession of Shanghai, Guangdong, Tianjin, and Hankou)
  - French zone of influence officially recognized by China over the provinces of Yunnan, Guangxi, Hainan, and Guangdong

- Indochina
  - Cambodia
  - Laos
  - Vietnam
    - Annam
    - Cochinchina
    - Tonkin
- New Hebrides (Vanuatu, condominium with Britain)
  - Ay de mi Alhama

Germany
- Bismarck Archipelago
- Caroline Islands (Karolinen)
- German New Guinea
- Gilbert Islands
- German Samoa
- Jiaozhou Bay (Kiautschou)
- Kaiser-Wilhelmsland
- Marshall Islands
- Nauru
- North Solomon Islands
- Northern Marianas Islands (Marianen)
- Palau
- Tientsin

Italy
- Tientsin (concession)

Netherlands
- Burma (Myanmar) (Mrohaung (Arakan), Siriangh, Syriam, Ava, Martaban)
- Dutch East Indies (Indonesia)
- Dutch New Guinea (Western Part of Papua, Indonesia)
- Malacca
- Dutch Formosa
- Dejima

Portugal
- Flores

- Macau
- Malacca
- Moluccas
  - Ambon
  - Ternate
  - Tidore
- Portuguese Timor (Timor-Leste)
- Portuguese Nagasaki
- Solor

Russia
- Kazakhstan
- Kyrgyzstan
- Tajikistan
- Tientsin
- Turkmenistan
- Uzbekistan

Spain
- Spanish East Indies
  - Philippines
  - Marianas Islands (Ladrones)
    - Guam
    - Northern Marianas Islands
  - Caroline Islands
- Marshall Islands

Europe

Britain
British Empire
- Corsica (the Anglo-Corsican Kingdom was a protectorate of Britain, now part of France)
- Cyprus
- Ionian islands (now part of Greece)
- Ireland
- Malta
- Menorca (now part of Spain)

Denmark
Danish overseas colonies
- Iceland

Italy
Colonia (Roman), Venetian Empire, and Genoese Empire
- Albania
- Dodecanese

Russia
- Belarus
- Finland
- Estonia
- Latvia
- Lithuania
- Moldova
- Ukraine
- Poland" [xcviii]

Global Cultural Racial Identities

Because of the Transatlantic Slave Trade and worldwide Colonialism, some countries more than others, have a long, bitter, and ugly history of tension between cultures and racial groups. This history was based on the separation of groups of people in societies from around the world. In Europe, the historical racial narrative of slavery was kept at arm's length in overseas colonies but not on the continent. As a result, the perceptions of race and racial identities in some societies continue to play a role, more so in some than others.

Some societies based their citizen's identities on race, ethnicities, nationalities, or a combination thereof. The political construction of a nation or continent, as well as its history, can play a pivotal role. For example, in comparing the continents of Africa, Europe, and North America, Africa, and Europe have many sovereign nations within their continents; whereas, North America has much fewer ones. As results, Europeans and Africans tend to view cultural identities along nationality, regional, or ethnicity lines than is much more common in the United States which identifies its populace among racial lines. Unfortunately, even today, skin color and race, which have no biological meaning, transcends other cultural elements.

Too, the vast majorities of citizens in Europe, Africa, and Asia tend to be homogenous in terms of race. The possible exceptions are former Colonial power who have more race diversity such as the United Kingdom and France. So, it is logical that such nations and continents would identify themselves with nationality over race, which is a social construction. In multicultural societies where there are multiple races and ethnicities, plus a history of institutionalized racism, race becomes more pronounced.

Some countries in the Americas, and particularly the United States have more obsession with racial and ethnic identities. However generally, countries in Latin America, located in North America, are like Europeans in identifying more with their culture, values, and family traditions. Racial identities are more predominant in European countries in a formerly non-European part of the world where people are more culturally centric than in continental European countries.

The United States is predominately an immigrant country, except for people of African descent by forced servitude, and occupied with a multitude of descendants from around the world. Currently, the dominant values in the United State originated in Western Europe, with people who were imported and sometimes faced some terrible conditions and issues in their native countries. It was then settled by various other cultures including Jews, Eastern Europeans, Africans, Asians, and others to form a mixture of various cultures. The dominant cultures in the United States still share many of the same traditions, cultures, political systems, and religions of Western Europe.

Historically, descendants of European Americans were generally simply referred to as "Americans" and seen as the default for Americans. They presently have the majority population but are projected to lose it around 2045 by most estimates. They designed a racial classification system with Whites on top of the hierarchy with which other cultures are compared. The system reflects their perspectives and paradoxes, so there was no reason to generally define themselves as Europeans.

Europeans and Asians migrated to the United States from their homeland as opposed to Africans who were forced to leave their ancestral homeland in slave ships. The indigenous people were on their native soil. This scenario is repeated by other nations in the Americas and the Caribbean during the Transatlantic Slave Trade as well as the institution of worldwide colonization. In the United States, Great Britain formed the base "mainstream" society culture of the United States against which all the other ethnic and racial groups are defined. Likewise, the other European countries that were involved in the Transatlantic Slave Trade in the Americas and the Caribbean became the base "mainstream" society culture in the nations that they enslaved or colonized. Few exceptions include countries such as Mexico, Belize, Haiti, and Jamaica, and others that finally gained their independence.

These cultural views of "Whites" of exclusivity and superiority carried on in the Americas, Australia, New Zealand, and other colonized places around the world. When the Europeans migrated to the United States from the various countries in Europe, all of them had ambivalent racial statuses. Over time, the strategy of positioning the European nationalities with the White label against the other cultures was successful. They considered themselves as White no matter what country they migrated from, and more importantly, they came to be considered White by their fellow Americans. Before migrating from Europe, they were labeled by their nationalities. [xcix]

Europe was the place where their ancestors escaped from in times of tyranny, religious persecution, and ethnic oppression. When they migrated to the United States and other places around the world, they established a new identity and contrasted with other inhabitants in the country of their residing. "Without the presence of black people in America, European-Americans would not be 'White' - - they would be Irish, Italians, Poles, Welsh, and others engaged in class, ethnic, and gender struggles over resources and identity." [c]

Even some of the old Hispano communities in the Southwest United States largely descended from White European Spanish criollos who settled there long before their conquest and absorption into the United States. They continue the White label, sharing Hispanic cultural traits with mixed-race or non-White Latin Americans. A large portion of Texas, California, Arizona, and New Mexico used to be part of Mexico. Some people of Mexican heritage in this part of the United States did not descend from immigrants; their country immigrated from them.

In the United States, Middle Easterners and Asian Americans, which consist of nations from China, Japan, North and South Korea, countries in Southeast Asia, and India had no history of defining themselves as a monolithic group of people with a shared racial, cultural, or historical history. These cultures reside nearby geographical location, and despite the exchanging of agriculture, architecture, religions, philosophies, vocabulary, music, and other cultural elements, still display a diversity of cultures.

Historically, there has been a long history of conflicts between some of the Asian countries. Yet, they put aside their differences and embrace a common "Asian American" identity in the United States. After they arrived in America, some of their cultural elements such as languages, clothes, food, religions, and others were very different from the dominant European-American culture. As a result, the Chinese Exclusion Act was passed to limit their numbers and Japanese internment camps were created during World War II to keep Japanese Americans from acting on potential sympathy to the enemy state they descended from despite no proof of this fact.

In the United States, the existence of an Asian American identity and a lack of European American identity are the products of the dominant and mainstream European-descended "White" culture. From the mainstream perspective, immigrants from Asia and descendants of enslaved Africans were viewed in terms of their contrast with "Whites" as a collective group that was apparent to the untrained eyes of the dominant culture. On the other hand, there were only subtle differences between the European nationalities. [ci]

Attributing culture or certain behaviors to people based on their skin tone alone is divisive. Such terms make assumptions that people need to act, behave, or think a certain way. Whenever this boundary is crossed, it may be a form of cultural appropriation or race treason. Before the European fifteenth century global invasion, cultures were tied to previously used terms such as nationality or ethnicities instead of one's pigmentation. But those delinquent societies need to change their cultural behaviors. After all, culture arises from the interactions of the human species with their surroundings, environments, or societies. If someone is a member of society but does not share the majority's skin tone, who are other society's members to say that that member cannot be part of the society? The argument that someone does not share the majority culture's skin tone is culture racism.

However, there are no universal identities because over the decades and centuries the intermixing of the different cultures has generated new combinations and variations of cultures. Although race does not have a biological meaning, its usage continues today in some global societies, particularly those involved in the Transatlantic Slave Trade and worldwide Colonialism. Race is separate from culture, but an inevitable outcome of it is ethnicity. Thus, no global society has a single culture that produces a single identity among its members.

Immigration and Multicultural Issues

Multiculturalism is another major issue that many nations of the Western culture are facing, particularly the United States and the continent of Europe. Europe has been grappling with a massive influx of refugees from the Middle East. In Western Europe, the refugee crisis is causing many people holding primarily Islamic ideals to crash with those who have primarily Western ideals. This cultural clash will inevitably lead to conflicts, perhaps violent conflict. Cultural differences compared to political-economic ones often turn violent, as the conflict between Arab nations and Israel, and exacerbate the latter. Destabilization of the Middle East via Western invention has led to the rise of sectarian groups which have led to more war and an influx of refugees. Between 2015 and 2016, more than one million migrants and refugees came to the European Union. In America and Europe, capitalism thrives off the backs of immigrants who must accept menial labor for low wages. Industrialization succeeded because of a steady flow of immigrants who were not often able to collectively fight for better conditions.

Worldwide, subordinate group members continue to practice vagility and migrate to other countries whom they feel are more amendable to their human and civil rights. "Millions are on the move from impoverished rural areas to cities, and from poorer countries to wealthier ones, in search of work. Migrants are especially vulnerable—they are often very far from home, don't speak the local language, have no funds to return home, and have no friends or family to rely on."[cii]

In some instances, many lack the resources to migrate to other countries not only to escape racial issues but also socioeconomic reasons such as poverty and crime that resulted from racism. However, some subordinate groups become so desperate to find a better way of life that they still migrate to other countries at any cause. However, in recent decades, some countries in Europe and America have tightened their immigration laws to discourage them from migrating. Even those who are successful in migrating to countries more amenable to human rights compared to the native countries, still experience racism, discrimination, and biases in their new countries.

The United States' proximity to the United States-Mexico border has resulted in legal and illegal immigrants from Mexico and other nearby Latin American countries. Immigration has been a very controversial issue in the United States for decades. Mexico believed that Texas was part of their territory and the United States believed it part of theirs. As a result, conflict broke out which led to the Mexican-American war from 1846 to 1848. America won the war, and the Treaty of Guadalupe Hidalgo was established. According to the treaty Mexico had to not only give up Texas but also the "Mexican Territory" (now known as California, New Mexico, Arizona) This hotly debated political issue has divided the country for decades to the extent that a comprehensive immigration bill has not been yet passed by the United States Congress.

Trump administration's immigration policies were always going to be central to his presidency. This policy position was announced during his candidacy when he declared that migrants coming into the United States from Mexico were rapists and criminals. One of Trump's first actions as President was initiating a travel ban on Muslims entering the United States. The Trump administration rolled hundreds of executive actions curtailing both legal and illegal immigration to the United States. After many legal battles, including the ban blocked by courts, the Supreme Court upheld an iteration of the ban in 2018. Some of the Trump administration's restrictive immigration efforts have been blocked by courts, including an attempt to include an immigration question in the census and end the Deferred Action for Childhood Arrivals (DECA) program.

Trump administration also separated thousands of families at the United States-Mexico border under the controversial "zero tolerance" policy and built hundreds of new barriers on the border. Refugee admissions to the United States plummeted. In a pair of White House immigration moves during Spring 2020, the administration suspended much of family-based immigration and the number of guest worker visas through the end of the year, with some exceptions, citing high unemployment caused by the coronavirus pandemic. President Biden issued Executive Actions undoing Trump's past immigration orders, reinstating DACA, and repealing the travel ban. But ultimately, the administration overhauled the United States immigration system to largely bar immigrants from the US through successive changes that will be difficult for President Biden to undo. [ciii]

The Biden administration has been burdened with its immigration issues. In 2021, Americans from across the political spectrum welcomed thousands of Afghans amid the hurried withdrawal of United States troops from Afghanistan as the country fell under the control of the Taliban. United States officials launched a nationwide effort to help Afghans resettle in the country with the help of three former United States presidents and more than 250 private businesses. Most Americans are united around resettling Afghan refugees because they are perceived as loyal to the United States, and Americans feel a sense of moral obligation towards them. Many are being housed temporarily at military sites before eventually resettling in cities and towns across the United States. [civ]

The sympathetic feeling and public perceptions do not extend to people in Central America, Haiti, or a few other countries in the world. Hundreds of thousands of migrants and asylum seekers from Central America and the Caribbean, many of whom are fleeing poverty in their home countries, have sought refuge in the United States in recent years. In 2021, nearly 14,000 Haitian migrants and asylum seekers were stranded under a bridge in Del Rio, Texas. Most were quickly deported in a speedily plan, which effectively blocked asylum in the United States. Initially, the migrants were not extended the same humanitarian courtesy, but public perception changed the narrative for a few of them. Many migrants were flown to Haiti on expulsion flights, and additional resources were made available to expel people quickly. Haiti is the poorest nation in the Western Hemisphere. The small Caribbean Island country was struck by a 7.2-magnitude earthquake following the assassination of

President Jovenel Moise in July 2001.[cv] The present immigration policies have tested the measure of our humanity for all human beings from different cultures

Additionally, early America's original sin and centuries of brutal history and long legacy of slavery, segregation, Jim Crow laws, oppression, and injustices against its African American and native citizens have made the multicultural issue problematic. The civil rights movement in the 1950s and 1960s led by Dr. Martin Luther King Jr. helped move the country forward in race relations through legislation, judiciary, and public policy initiatives.

However, there is still a very deep divide among the various racial groups on how far the country has advanced in race relations that still need to be resolved. Along with population estimates that by the year 2045, the nation may no longer have a majority White population. This has led to additional fear and anxiety that many citizens may hamper the past progress made by the country in its quest for a just society for all its citizens. The election of its first President of color, Barack Obama, did not calm the racial tensions and fears in the country. It may have exacerbated race relations given political issues after his Presidential term expired. The country is undergoing continued growing pains, and it will be interesting to see how events involving race relations unfold during the next few decades.

The date of January 6, 2021 will long be remembered in our national history when the United States Capitol, the nation's symbol of democracy was deliberately attacked by internal domestic enemies. The rioting at the United States Capitol has been described as both insurrection and sedition by politicians and media organizations. The chaos has also been described as a failed coup. The protests turned into an insurrection, breaching the home of United States democracy, for the first time since the British army set it on fire in 1814. An argument can be made that the rioting of the United States Capitol was a continuation to support and advance White supremacy? It did not appear to welcome and embraces a multiracial, multicultural inclusive American democracy?

The continent of Europe is also experiencing multicultural issues. Humans have always practiced migration and vagility throughout the history of mankind. During the first world order, particularly in the nineteenth and twentieth centuries, migrants were flowing out of

Europe to the Americas. Now the trend had been reversed and immigrants who have been forced out of their homeland for a variety of reasons are going to nearby Europe from the Middle East, Africa, and Asia after America tightens its immigration laws. Globalization on the world market demands consumers and consumer cultures which help to create a more multicultural world. Many of the people feel compelled and forced to move to more developed countries in the United States and Europe. Some migrants face some dire situations in their own countries that have been ravaged and plundered by multi-national corporations, the International Monetary Funds (IMF), World Bank, and some trade agreements that reduced them to below poverty living conditions.

Unlike the United States, there are very few indigenous people on the continent of Europe. Europe's multicultural issue differs from America in that America looks at racial groups or ethnicity; whereas, Europe views cultural differences among those who have immigrated to various European countries. America, as a melting pot country was founded on a core set of values by its founders but still allowed its immigrants to value their cultural heritage. Europe, on the other hand, does not necessarily have a core set of values that it expects its immigrants to assimilate to. It fundamentally rejects the notion that one value system is better than others and one group must adapt to the other one. This cultural divide, however, has led to conflicts because of historically fundamental dislikes that have existed among racial groups for centuries. Fear about the integrating of the new Muslim populations conflated with the issue of Islamic terrorism has created problems. Some immigrants could become legalized citizens but were not allowed to emerge into the culture, thereby maintaining their cultures, identities, and religions.

Europe also has many countries that deal with immigrants differently based on its history, racial narratives, and relations; whereas, the United States has States, but federal laws have trunked some state and local laws. At this time, the early consensus is that Europe has regarded multiculturalism as endangering their society. It has failed and there seems to be no option other than a conflict between the racial groups. There are not even borders between most European nations anymore. It has become just one seamless continent. There is not even a language barrier anymore. Almost all

Europeans speak at least one or even several languages in addition to their native tongue.

The developed societies around the world must address the long-term migration issues and root causes as to why migrant border crossings are continuing and even surging in recent years. To stem the tide and rising humanitarian crises in Europe and the United States will require long-term strategies for addressing surges at the borders. Developed countries need to work with undeveloped, and impoverished countries, and focus on the root causes which can be mitigated by promoting job creations and long-term public/private investments. These plans will help alleviate the key drivers of migration involving corruption, organized criminal activities, child trafficking, modern slavery, violence, economic devastation, and even the effects of climate change. [cvi]

Humankind has practiced migration and vagility since the beginning of history all over the world. This is an ongoing phenomenon that is always occurring somewhere around the world. People migrate for several reasons, including looking for a better way of life, escape widespread brutal racism, poverty, famine, atrocities, religious persecution, economics, jobs, and educational opportunities. The migration patterns with migrants making these perilous trips and death voyages from undeveloped and impoverished nations to developed nations for a better way of life will continue until these migration issues are addressed. [cvii]

The West, particularly the United States and Europe need to develop more comprehensive reform policies that are just and build societies that are both secure and welcoming, but immigration laws enforced with fairness and respect for human rights. The massive influx of new immigrant groups in the United States and Europe have destabilized specific concepts of race, led to a proliferation of identity position, and challenged present modes of political and cultural norms. [cviii]

Multiculturalism and Global Political Systems

To fully understand the dynamics and interactions of a multicultural society, there is a need to know how different political governments in the world are structured; how the political power is distributed; how they operate; interact with their citizens; and how rules are made and enforced? ^{cix} Depending upon one's experiences, backgrounds, and perspectives, a person may take side with the political system of his country's residing or develop some preconceived notions about other political systems. There are many forms of political systems around the world. The major theories of political systems include Monarchy, Authoritarianism, Totalitarianism, Direct/Representative Democracy, Republic, Communism, Dictatorship, Autocracy, Anarchy, Theocracy, Colonialism, Military Dictatorship, Aristocracy, Socialism, and others. There are overlapping philosophies among them.

Generally, two types of people are attracted to politics. Those who seek power over others and those who seek to extort the powerful. The only people that should be granted power and authority are those that have no desire for either. Under this current system of economic and political rule, social justice and true human equality can only be achieved through our collective political action in opposition to the current racial world order. Although our world consists of different political systems with different concepts, philosophies, racial groups, ideologies, and cultures, they are governed by individuals.

The world's political systems have handled multiculturalism and race within their societies in different ways. Each society has its unique historical background. Societies deal with diverse populations with different histories that provide the backgrounds and frameworks for the political systems to function within them. It takes time, citizen ownership and consensus, and long-term stability to take root and thrive.

There is no political system that is perfect to handle multiculturalism. Multiculturalism has not demonstrated its infallibility in any nation where it has been tried. They all have some advantages and disadvantages. A political system that may be ideal for one country may not be ideal for others whose societal compositions, histories, cultures, and others vary. The best systems are those that can accept criticism and admit their mistakes, offer mass education, able to adapt to a changing society, and make cultural changes and improvements when necessary.

An ideal political system for a multicultural society should be a problem solver. Its structure should not be just ideological but rooted in cultural realities that offer individual rights and freedoms to all citizens. Other features that are conducive to a multicultural society are a political system that has merit-based or elected leaders; enjoys a sustained measure of economic success; a system of checks and balances in place to deal with corruption; a livable standard of living, and a stable political environment.

Some political systems work better when the inequalities of the society hang in balance favoring a certain culture. They allow other cultures to achieve some semblance of parity and equality. A few political systems are leveraged by systems and institutions with noble ideals that are not fully practiced in their cultural realities. These systems remain in a state of deniability about their past inhumanity misdeeds and refuse to even acknowledge them.

Some political systems are better equipped to handle citizen's discontent who engage in social evolutions that are jumpstarted by revolutions while others are governed by celebrated rulers that create hope and unite their citizens. Others may have a better system for public participation while some are set up to respond to critical issues more rapidly than other systems. Also, some political systems just seem to generally do a better job of building coalitions and allowing for different groups to work together.

Some planned economies have historically failed to create prosperity for their entire countries, usually favoring smaller groups or cultures. A purely free-market economy, with no government intervention, has not been tried. Instead, most economically successful nations in the world have mixed thriving entrepreneurs with a combination of government services and regulations. A few political systems ideologically allow the people to rule themselves rather than leaders with personal agendas.

Some political systems, whether they have homogenous or non-homogenous populations have major issues in accepting refugees and immigrants from Mexico, Latin America, Africa, the Middle East, and other nations that may challenge their cultural norms. These refugees and immigrants are often distrusted and viewed negatively with or without good reason except for their cultural and racial differences. Some political systems indirectly encourage segregation by their populace and the resulting society is segregated based on race or ethnicity because its practices are not discouraged or prioritized.

In some cases, a new political system or nation can get off to a good job and treat its citizens with respect and humanity. However, over time, poor and inept leadership can take over and ignore the needs of its diverse citizens and their cultures. All societies, at some point in their history, will reach a point where stagnation or bad leaders take over. In some societies, the country can eventually elect new and better leaders but in others, it may eventually lead to the demise no matter what form of political system exists. On the other hand, it may not be the political system but the political leadership that governs the society that may be the problem.

In most societies, regardless of their political systems, people organizing into different cultures or groups for whatever reasons are unfortunately prevalent. But in an ideal multicultural society, all cultures are equal. A successful multicultural society needs an overriding set of a universal set of laws in the formulation of which all members of the society are involved, and to which all cultures contribute. It does not impose one culture's values but determines them collectively. In those societies, culturalism exclusivity is antithetical to multiculturalism.

Most of the world's nations or societies have either homogenous or non-homogenous political systems. A multicultural or heterogeneous society consists of people with a diverse background with a high diversity of cultures, racial groups, and religions. [cx] The criteria for an ideal multicultural political system are ultimately measured by the services it can deliver to the people, and whether the deliverance is sustainable in the long run. To be sustainable, the system should also be flexible to modify itself to become compatible with a changing diverse multicultural society. Dominant cultures need to re-examine their roles, interventions, and place in our global community. Cultures must learn to respect other nation's sovereignties and reframe from imposing some systems of governance that do not suit them. Societies and cultures need to be respected for their uniqueness and allowed to determine their destiny and charter their paths to develop themselves.

Chapter III
Formation and Development of Major World's Cultures and
Civilizations

Cultures, civilizations, empires, and societies are often used interchangeably. But there are differences. Civilizations or empires may not be the same as modern-day nations and prominent political entities but today they are generally referred to as societies. However, civilization refers to a complex way of life that came about as people began to develop urban settlements. Civilization is a complex entity made of different elements. Civilizations include law, administration, infrastructure, architecture, social arrangements, and others. Culture is a complex whole that includes knowledge, religion, beliefs, customs, dance, literature, morals, philosophy, laws, traditions, art and music, and many others. Culture is the total sum of ways of living built up by a group of human beings that is transmitted from one generation to another. Culture is a part of a civilization.[cxi]

All world's cultures, traditional tribal culture, and modern culture were developed to accommodate people's surroundings. Both were suited to adapt to local environmental conditions. In both cultures, members learned and shared things throughout generations. Both deal with ways of thinking, relating to its people and the universe. Every culture and subculture have different standards and belief systems. This was formed by their history and the development of society.

The beginning of all forms of culture was language. Language may also differentiate one culture from another. "There are three presumed principal forces, like material condition, for the formation of human culture. These are environment, or geographic factor, and function or activity, the economic factor. But there also exists a third element, thought, or the psychological factor, whose presence liberates man from his blind dependence on the environment. This factor is precisely that which makes possible the formation of an ever-growing reserve of social traditions, in such a way that the things accomplished by one generation are transmitted to the next and the discoveries or new ideas of one individual become the common property of the society, and it is that which gives rise to culture." [cxii]

Traditional Culture versus Modern Culture

Traditional culture was held together by the relationship among people who lived close to each other – immediately and extended family, clan, and tribe. Traditional culture was not the sole province of any ethnic group regardless of which continent they occupied or the ethnic group they constituted. There was a clearly defined behavior and relationships among members, but it did not rob them of their individuality. The business and personal lives of its members were the same. There was no separation in economics, trade, spiritual and ceremonial activities. Members did not compartmentalize or separate their business, personal, religious, or political lives. Because of the conservative nature of the traditional culture, it tended to stay relatively the same for some periods.

Ancient traditional culture did change but the conservative nature of it did resist change whenever it could. Technological advances such as ceramics or bow and arrows occurred in the member's way of thinking and doing things. It just happened at a slower pace. Traditional cultures lived in close contact with their environment. This taught that nature must be respected. The societies saw themselves as part of nature, its spiritual beliefs, and values. The traditional culture had a small base of knowledge. They mastered the potential usefulness of plants and animals in their local environment. They possess wisdom in weather, geology, astronomy, medicine, politics, history, languages, and others that laid the foundations for modern culture.

Modern culture developed in areas of the planet as societies grew larger. Mass organization in the form of large workforces and armies and later the development of mechanized means of production led to modern culture. The shift from rural to urban life was at the core of modern development. In modern culture, most people live in conjugal families. It seems to be held by power and things and not by people and relationships although there are contacts outside the immediate household. There is a separation of business and personal life. Members learn to compartment their lives. Modern culture thrives on change. New goods, and services and new technologies, things and ideas are developed at a very rapid rate. Modern culture tries to create its environment. It teaches that nature is meant to be manipulated, the source of jobs and wealth. The culture builds cities, massive structures, and exports to faraway colonies and trading partners. It sees itself as being above nature. Modern culture is built on knowledge. It enhances their power.

Modern culture tends to think of traditional culture as "primitive," "backward," and "childlike,". On the other hand, traditional culture tends to think of modern culture as "hollow," "ignorant," and "childlike,". But modern culture takes over traditional culture because it is more powerful, mechanized, moves a mountain, digs canals, drains swamps, overwhelms, glitters, tastes sweet, goes fast, and advertises. On the other hand, some people in modern culture are very interested in traditional culture. There may be a vacuum in modern culture that truly understands how important spiritual and humane parts of life used to be. [cxiii]

Spirituality and Religion

Religion is one of the many elements of a cultural society. Religion is the epicenter of most cultures. Religious and spiritual factors have always played an important role in man's physical and spiritual dimensions. Throughout the history of humankind and particularly during the past five centuries after a few European powers conquered the world via worldwide Colonialism and the Transatlantic Trade Slave, dominant cultures have fundamentally imposed their Western culture on other cultures. The European's scientific and technical motivations through their expertise in seafaring and gunpowder were the vehicle that contributed to the worldwide invasion that enhanced the Western culture foundation.

Earlier in the seventh century, one of the largest slave trades in human history was the Arabs in Western Africa to Arabian Peninsula. This invasion was the impetus that brought Islam to the continent of Africa. In some cases, African societies adopted foreign religions by their own free will for political and economic reasons. In other instances, the African societies were forced to adopt many of the religious elements of the dominant cultures and were unable to maintain the consistency of their cultural histories. Numerous cultural examples can be used to illustrate how these dynamics were played out over decades and centuries between traditional cultures and modern cultures. The Mali empire was not converted by force but free will while other nations such as Morocco, Algeria, Tunisia, Libya, and others by Arab conquest.

When some people enter a new culture, which may be more mainstream, dominant, and different than their previous one, they leave their comfort zone and start to question their traditions and beliefs and end up asking which religion is right for them. Those that convert to religion usually do it for social or personal reasons. Some may be having challenging times in their lives and need a source of comfort. Some people get it indoctrinated into them as kids before they have a chance to speak for themselves. Or in the case of the African slaves or indigenous people in the Americas, Australia, New Zealand, or through worldwide colonization, Christianity and Islam were either forced on them through propaganda, integrated education, free will, or by force through Colonial conquest.

Subsequent generations of colonized countries converted to the major religions. However, there were exceptions. Although the European powers colonized all but ten countries on planet Earth, a few nations held on to their ancestral religions and were not forcible converted to Christianity. Many of the nations are in the Middle East, India, and Southeast Asia. They held on to their ancestry religions.

The consensus by scientists, anthropologists, historians, and others is that Africa is the cradle of civilization and the origin of humankind. Egypt is considered one of the world's oldest civilizations. The traditional religions of Africa and how they evolved will be examined. Although the religions and spiritualities in Africa will primarily be discussed, the norms and beliefs of other traditional cultures around the world are also included. At that time in world history, nothing happened in Africa that did not happen in other places around the world. Early migration patterns showed that some Africans migrated from Africa to other territories all around the world. Generally, indigenous religions and spirituality were the norms until some dominant cultures invaded other cultures and force their religions and cultures on them.

African religions and practices and other traditional cultures around the world will be understood overwhelmingly as pagan by new world standards and modern culture. There is no specific name for their religion(s) because they were so diverse throughout Africa. Africans and traditional culture were very naturalistic. They were connected to the land and people attached sacred principles to valleys, trees, bodies of water, mountains, and others. They also reverenced the life-sustaining elements related to Africa's Fertile Crescent, including the sun, rain, and wind. Many areas were very astrologically advanced and ascribed a deific essence to the constellations. Many of the world's ancient societies erected massive stones circles aligning them with the sun and stars to mark the seasons. Thousands of these megaliths made of stones were mostly built 6,500 to 4,500 years ago largely around the Atlantic and Mediterranean coasts. The oldest discovered astronomical site is the Nabta Playa around 7,000 years ago in Egypt while the most famous one is the Stonehenge, thought to be around 5,000 years old in England. [cxiv] They paid homage to the moon, stars, satellites, and the occasional comets as symbols of divinity. The teleological appearances in the heavens gave rational to spontaneous divine expressions.

In addition, they also had a mystical connection to their ancestors who preceded them in death. Many rituals and services included necromancy, séances, and hypnotic yielding, to connect with the next world. It was also an African practice to venerate the attributes of certain animals. "Their gods and goddesses were portrayed with animal heads. The ancestor's observations and profound knowledge of nature enabled them to identify certain animals with specific qualities that could symbolize divine functions and principles in a particularly pure and striking fashion. As such, certain animals were chosen as symbols for that particular aspect of divinity." [cxv] They admired the strength, speed, stealth, and savagery of panthers, lions, serpents, rhinoceros, buzzards, eagles, and other earth's inhabitants. Many religious and spiritual forms of worship included paying obeisance to these symbols. [cxvi] These symbols represent an expression of deep spiritual understanding of the external environment within which we live.

Some cultures did not completely understand traditional African and indigenous spiritual connections with nature and denounced the

101

concept as paganism. These animals and celestial bodies were not worshipped by the ancient ancestors but used as symbols of the Divine. This misunderstanding of African spirituality is one of many examples that show a lack the cultural awareness of other cultures. Yet, on the other hand, some cultures adopted some of the same concepts and structures during those periods of African discovery. The architectures of cathedrals, churches, temples, medieval art, and other buildings are prominently displayed by exotic animals in many European countries. Likewise, in modern society, sports teams at all levels use animals, celestial bodies, and even indigenous groups as symbols and nicknames. The mascots represent the team with an identity, bring good luck, and are used for merchandising purposes.

Abrahamic religions which include Christianity, Judaism, and Islam deal with two supernatural powers - God and the Devil; Africa's indigenous spirituality only deals with one. The three major Abrahamic religions are monotheistic because they believe in one, true God. There are differences, particular in their views of Jesus. Africa's indigenous spirituality has no Devil; has several names throughout the continent; may be male or female; and looks at negative evil forces as man-made caused by man's rejection of himself as a deity and the source of evil. It does not place blame on a supernatural rival creation but a greater force of nature in which the human species is just a tiny part of the universal continued transformation process. The human species should in turn use his intelligence to mold and tame nature with beneficial human constructs and ride out the turbulence that is beyond his control.

Africa's indigenous spirituality's Gods looked like them and express their power through their reflections. Their spirituality came from the soul. It was not based on theology or ideology. It served them as a network linking them to their Gods, the universe, and each other. The traditional culture viewed spirituality as a personal relationship with the divine. African systems and spirituality are family and community based. Modern culture's religions are based more on sets of rules, regulations, and rituals to help people grow spiritually.

The fact that women cannot presently be priests in a Catholic church is an example of one of the major differences between the spiritual and religious beliefs of ancient traditional culture and modern culture, involving the Christian ideology. In ancient traditional culture, the deity may be male or female. They were considered as humans and not living in the clouds but manifested through humans on Earth. The idea of all-male deities and priests by modern religious culture is a further manifestation of the omnipotent 'male role' in modern culture.

There have been thousands of religions in Africa. Some of the first recorded deities were formed in Egypt and the Nile Valley but spread all over the continent but there were many others. Because of the numerous tribal languages and dialects, there was no mass communication. There were no shared religions, at least not to the degree that they are in modern cultures. Each tribe had its religious belief systems that used various names for their deities like various names for God associated with modern religions. They were all passed down generally through oral history over generations, although written systems existed, so there is little written record. Now, there remains little information available to the masses of people where the deep philosophical meaning of the traditional African spiritual science can be empowered by individuals other than a few traditional spiritual teachers.

Generally, African religions involved beliefs in multiple Gods and the influence of the power of nature. The "Gods" were aspects of the supreme being living within them and the universe. It varied from tribe to tribe, and they had conflicting beliefs with each other. Because of Western cultural involvements, many of Africa's religions and spirituality have been lost. Too, the colonization of the wide world Colonialism, the Arab-Muslim Trade Slave, and the Transatlantic Trade Slave led to the loss of entire cultures. The only people who would know something about them would be older generations of Africans. However, its remembrance largely based on oral history, although some parts of Africa had writing systems, has been problematic as a large percentage of the population has converted to one of the Abrahamic religions such as Christianity, Judaism, or Islam.

Generally, some mainstream religions and African traditional religions and spiritualities have teachings that are to be understood as they were centuries ago from their origins. Even some modern versions of the traditional indigenous religions followed the same concept of having to be authentic to the original meaning. The learned shared religious and spiritual concepts are transmitted over generations based on the new understanding that is closer to its original concepts and doctrines. Some traditional religions, however, do not seek a pure imitation of its original meaning but build and improve upon their ancient understanding that the ancestors taught.

All the traditional indigenous cultures around the world were not identical. The traditional cultures originated in Africa and migrated to other territories around the world. Many kept some of the ancient beliefs from Africa, but over generations and centuries, they diffuse with other cultures, wherein, the possibility exists that they adopted different beliefs over time. Although these religious or spiritual systems have some ancient African influences, they are products of their cultural mentalities and may not reflect traditional African cultures. They brought with them the African spiritual science and culture. That is why there are similarities between Africa and the earliest ancient civilizations around the world. African spirituality is about tranquility and inner peace that help a person evolves to their best cultural traits. It recognizes the Universe as a force to one's divinity. It is not used as a tool of manipulation that imposed its religious and political will over other cultural members.

Religion in Africa today is multifaceted and has been a major influence on art, culture, and philosophy. Today, the continent's various populations and individuals are mostly adherents of Christianity, Islam, Hinduism, Judaism, and to a lesser extent, several traditional and indigenous African religions. [cxvii]

Roughly three-quarters of Europeans are Christians (75%), almost one-fifth (18%), do not identify with any religion, and about (6%) are Muslims. Hindus, Buddhists, Jews, followers of folk or traditional religions, and adherents of other religions make up 1% of Europe's total population. [cxviii]

In North America, Christianity, the dominant religion, accounts for approximately 75% of the total population of North America. In the United States, approximately 70% practice Christianity, Canada has around 67% while Mexico leads with a percentage of 87%. Judaism accounts for approximately 1.8% in North American. Judaism accounts for about 0.02 in Mexico and 1.2% practice it in Canada. [cxix]

Roman Catholicism is the largest religious denomination in South America and is practiced by over 50% of the population in all South American countries except Uruguay and Suriname. Roman

Catholicism was brought to the continent by the European Colonial powers in the seventeenth and eighteenth centuries which enforced the religion on the indigenous people. The practice of Roman Catholicism among South Americans was made mandatory in most countries during the Colonial period, which would become a factor behind the religion's popularity in the continent. Brazil has the highest number of Roman Catholics in the world practiced by 63% of the country's population. Catholicism was intertwined with government affairs for centuries and at one point had to pay taxes to the Catholic Church. Even after Brazil gained independence, the faith was still established as the official religion until 1891 when the church was separated from the state. [cxx]

The traditional African religious influence also occurred in Asia through the migration from Africa around the world. Religions such as East Asian (Taoism, Shintoism, Sindism, Confucianism) and Indian religions (Hinduism, Buddhism, Sikhism, and Jainism) as well as animistic indigenous religions were also formed that were influenced by their cultures. [cxxi]

Historically, several religions have been practiced by the communities in the Middle East such as Zoroastrianism, Samaritans, and Manichaeism. The largest Abrahamic religions in the world have their roots in the Middle East. In the Modern era, the Middle East is considered a religiously diverse region because of the large number of religions, both major and minor. The Middle East is also home to a significant number of people who are not affiliated with any religious group. [cxxii]

Although Australia does not have an established church or religion, most of the population, or 615 identifies with the branches of Christianity. Today, 25.3% of the population are Roman Catholic, 18.7% are Christians, and 17.1% are Anglican Christians. Atheists and Agnostics make up 22.3% of the population which makes Australia one of the religious countries in the developed world. Taoism, Rastafarianism, Scientology, Unitarian Universalism, and others are practiced by 10.1% of the population. This is followed by Buddhism (2.5), Islam (2.2%), Hinduism (1.3%), and Judaism (.5%). [cxxiii]

Estimates from 2005 classified 54% (3.6 billion people) of the world's population as adherents to an Abrahamic religion, about 32% as adherents to other religions, and 16% as adherents to no organized religion. Christianity claims 33% of the world's population, Islam has 21%, Judaism has 0.2 and the Baha'i'[cxxiv] Faith represents around 0.1%. Christianity is the world's biggest religion, with about 2.1 billion followers based on the teaching of Jesus Christ who lived in the Middle East about 2,000 years ago. Close to two billion people practice Islam that many historians say began in Arabia in the 7th century in a divine revelation given to Prophet Mohammad. Judaism, meanwhile, began more than 3,500 years ago. There are about 15 million Jews worldwide. [cxxv]

Traditional and modern cultural religious and spiritual differences occurred throughout the world. In the United States, some of the first recorded meetings between the European settlers and the local native Indians were on the East Coast in New England in the early fifteen-century. There were several cultural challenges to overcome between the two groups. "Another problem between the settlers and the Indians involved religion. The settlers in New England thought Christianity was the one true faith, and that all people should believe in it. They soon learned that the Indians were satisfied with their own spiritual beliefs and were not interested in changing them. As a result, many settlers came to believe that the Native Americans could not be trusted because they were not Christians. They began to fear the Indians and think of them as evil.

The European settlers failed to understand that the Indians were an extremely spiritual people with a strong belief in unseen powers. The Indians lived very close to nature. They believed that all things in the universe depend on each other. All native tribes had ceremonies that honored a creator of nature. They recognized the creator's work in their everyday lives." [cxxvi] Modern culture has evolved over millennials, molded, and tamed nature, and changed some of the original spiritual and religious concepts of the traditional culture.

There have always been some aspects of contemporary conflicts between modern and traditional culture religious beliefs. There is a conflict between those cultures who want to consider the worldview from modern science-based and post-enlighten-based global humanistic values. On the other hand, some cultures choose pre-modern, scientific worldviews and pre-enlightenment traditional religions based on parochial non-universal ethnicity-based values.

Technological Advancements and Mass Education

No culture can exist without technological advancements and innovations. Science and technology shape cultures and humanity. The Science, Technology, Engineering, and Math (STEM) evolution is rapidly increasing. It has not remained static, particularly during the past two centuries. The more technology advances, the greater it benefits society. Science and technology advance exponentially. Each minor advance spurs many other advancements. [cxxvii] This aggregate effect of new technology brings a cumulative power of ideas in the continued evolving creative process. New inventions, particularly those involving technology, generally increase the rate and development of societies. Historically, technological development and advancement have led to the transformation and modification of cultural values and norms the way humanity operates.

For most of humankind's existence on Earth, knowledge was transmitted from successive generations. This knowledge was transferred through memorization and learning. "The vast majority of the population in the ancient world lived in the countryside and was illiterate; literacy was primarily an urban phenomenon." [cxxviii] This system of knowledge transference severely limits a society's sophistication. The amount of knowledge passed through oral memories is limited when a transmitter dies or may be misinterpreted over the years by other receivers. Without a writing system, most inventions were lost or stolen by another culture. A writing system allows knowledge to be preserved in an accumulated manner instead of being lost in subsequent generations. It allows technological advances and our accumulated discoveries to reach further generations transparently. The realities of technological advancement, spearheaded by the development of writing during the past few centuries, have been facilitated compared to the previous five millenniums.

Likewise, education is an important component in the development of a society that determines the way of life for people. During the past few centuries, the creation of public and private schools and the mass production of books for the masses of people accelerated the rates of technological innovations. For the first time, the masses of people could educate themselves through mass literacy and public education and then apply that knowledge in all facets of their lives. Societal mass literacy and book publishing is a primary reason for the uninterrupted progression of knowledge over the generations. This education advancement has allowed societies the ability to accumulate and preserve knowledge, history, technological advances, and fields of studies from all sectors. This progress has allowed scientists and other inventors to benefit the global society in an official way to prove their hypothesis, prevent biases from others plaguing their results, and a way to build off the work of others and share them.

The global population has exploded during the past two centuries. Before this period, the global population was static with probably a few million people on Earth. Since then, the global population has grown exponentially. Progress in medicine has not only aided population growth and longer lifespans but technological advances. A growing population has allowed more people to stumble onto discoveries, diligently research answers to global issues, and apply new ways to them.

During the early stages of humankind's existence, during the era (until about 12,000 to 11,000 years ago) [cxxix] of hunter-gathers, the Earth's population was low and sparsely populated. A plethora of resources was available and there was not a huge need to compete for food and resources. Their livelihood depended upon their ability to hunt. Accumulating wealth was not a priority in most societies. These skills require to have evolved from the survival mode.

Next came the agricultural revolutions (the first one took place around 10,000 B.C. and the second one between the 18th century and the end of the 19th century). [cxxx] People learned to farm and domesticate animals. Agriculture helped at a time when most groups were still nomads. The population started to increase slowly. Agricultural innovations increased the speed of technology development which produced higher economic productivity and yields. The nature of wealth changed. Now societal power, prestige, and influence were determined by his ability to grow crops and the number of cattle or animals it possessed. A little bit of greed began to germinate in some human beings, but it balanced in the societies. Some people started to increase their wealth to gain respect and have an influence on others. The process of cultivation shifting in global land emerged to increase productivity that exacerbated nature.

Further, people started to store grain to sustain themselves during a bad harvest or agricultural crisis.

Around 1800, ninety percent of the United States labor force was in agriculture. By 1880, approximately fifty percent of the labor force were in agriculture, and the fraction kept dropping until it was twenty-five percent around 1930 and two percent today. Initially, agriculture became more productive because of the widespread availability of better materials, such as iron and steel. This progression allowed for the development of time-saving devices such as plows and reapers. In the 1900s, alternate power sources replaced human and animal effort, increasing productivity even further.

This progression led to the industrial revolution (1760 to 1840). [cxxxi] People began to compete for resources and a better livelihood. The nature of wealth changed. [cxxxii] Societies were able to store wealth in different forms such as bank accounts, stocks, bonds, shares, and others. People could also bequeath their acquired wealth to their descendants. This gain led to the classification of people by class.

The higher quality iron and steel also led to the advent of railroads, making shipping and travel much cheaper. And it also led to the development of machinery for factories and harnessing power from coal and oil, improving productivity even further. Since fewer and fewer people needed to work in agriculture to feed the rest of society, more people were available to work in factories, steel mills, railroads, and universities - all of which continued to be improved and led to further productivity gains. This continued progress allowed for even more population growth because gains in health made survival through childhood much more likely and food was available. And these additional people have jobs that enhance productivity. The world population went from 1 billion people in 1800 to around 7.5 billion people today.

Many modern-day jobs today in the post-industrial revolution (1840 to present), [cxxxiii] focused on increasing productivity. Anyone involved in information technology or software development is trying to help companies and people do things that he was unable to before better, faster, and cheaper. Robots take the place of factory workers. Better vehicles and machinery require less maintenance and upkeep. Engineers are constantly improving upon existing products and developing new ones. Corporations have their research departments, and there is more research going on at universities than ever before. People have higher levels of education than ever before. Corporations (and people) realize that they must continue innovating in modern-day societies. Otherwise, competition will render them obsolete and non-competitive. [cxxxiv]

As people migrated from Africa and started permanent settlements, beneficial technological advancements were created in those territories. The population began to increase substantially. There was a need for people to compete for resources. The nature of wealth changed, and some people developed greed instincts. Bank accounts, bonds, and stocks came into the concept. It gave humans the ability to store wealth in different forms. Also, people can now bequeath their acquired wealth to the progeny, which was not possible before. In this current era, materials wealth brings power, influence, and respect in most societies. It also led to a class and race hierarchy.

Most highly developed countries are now involved in post-industrial. Most of the workforce work is in service-oriented industries such as finance, healthcare, education rather than in industry or agriculture. [cxxxv] Sociopolitical factors contributed to technological and scientific advancement. Wars increased the demand for research and development technologies. Capitalism has played a key role in technological innovations to keep up with the ever-increasing demands of the market mechanisms. The invention of the internet in the 1990s was a major global phenomenon. It catapulted the information age once information was able to be dispersed instantly around the world. It allowed different societies the ability to utilize the intelligence and creativity of people across the globe.

Organized religion is an important aspect of culture in a structured society. In terms of technological advancement and innovations, organized religion has supported it in some instances and not in others. In some societies, religious authorities reigned supreme and played a major role in the development and fundamentally imposed cultural values on their members. In some cases, critical thinking and rationality overruled some technological discoveries because they may have been outside of their teachings, values, and doctrines. In earlier civilizations, it was much easier for a doctrine to be cemented

110

into the fabrics of society since they lacked institutions, systems, and practices to fight it. Organized religion has been through several forms and structures throughout human history. In some societies, religion and politics have been intertwined with each other and part of their fabrics. Religious leaders were also the political leaders who controlled the state. Their religious beliefs framed the education, laws, societal structure, and social stratifications in some societies.

On the other hand, some organized religions like "the protestant ethic and the Spirit of Capitalism influenced people. The Calvinist engaged in work in the secular world, developing their enterprises and engaging in trade and the accumulation of wealth for investment. [cxxxvi]

This scenario does not mean that ancient civilizations did not have innovative technological advances. There were many. Before the technological advancement from a few centuries ago, ancient civilizations invented iron smelting, paper, gunpowder, the magnetic compass, cranks, or windmills that aided long-distance shipping of wooden ships by the wind.

Earlier civilization innovations allowed modern societies that used petrochemical industries and manufacturing to improve raw materials and products such as rubber, steel, aluminum, plastics, computing, steam-turbine with hydraulic gun turrets, and many others. Some products were used in ancient civilizations in some limited forms but progression over centuries allowed for the recreation of these end-products in the modern era. Some inventions were also discovered by accident, which is still the case in modern-day society.

Africa and many other ancient societies have not been at the forefront of science and technology in the last few centuries because of the European colonization in Africa and propaganda that have not highlighted their achievements. However, the list of Africa's inventions is endless. A study of African history and its technological advancements reveal that once the real history of Africa is told to the world, it will stand just as high as any other nations in contributing to the progress of the world.

Different cultures from different parts of the world had different ways of life and activities not practiced by other cultures. At that time of world history, the world was not interconnected, and mass education was not the norm. After the fall of several ancient societies over centuries, such as Egypt and Mesopotamia, it presented a chain of cultural transmission from Greece and Rome to Western Europe and the United States. Since that time, most of the world's culture is only discussed the European conquests. As a result, the histories, and cultures of other countries around the world are rarely discussed except within that culture.

Mass education in global societies should incorporate this segment of world history involving the Transatlantic Slave Trade, the Arab-Muslim Slave Trade, and worldwide Colonialism into their curriculums. The curriculums should also detail an accurate portrayal of the events. Generally, in the past, the few societies taught it did so from Eurocentric lenses that reduce an incomplete picture of world history and the contributions of people from those territories around the world. This effect of omission or inaccurate portrayal of events damages the subordinate members' self-worth and is self-destructive to their sense of self. This mass education acknowledgment will allow future generations the opportunity to deal with these issues more openly and honestly than what happened during past generations. What happened during these archaic institutions that began in the fifteen centuries is a major part of world history? The legacy continues today in all sectors of our global society.

The European colonizers and scholars viewed other indigenous cultures in very unflattering terms such as "primitive", "barbarian", "uncivilized" "savage" and other negative terms in a stone- age society. The associated terms such as the working wheel, social hierarchy, militarization, and industrialization as the true measures of an advanced society. Those cultures who did not identify with those beliefs and values legitimize their unique culture and its core values, dismissing them as uncivilized.

However, this society classification ignores the complexity of culture and the fact that irons technology and military might not be the ultimate measure of an advanced culture. The European settlers entered the countries with the mindset to civilize and save the country since their culture was different because they did not abide by Western values. They had no interest in working with and understanding other world's cultures except using brute force to conquer, divide, control, and destroy.

As the Europeans arrived in Africa to colonize the continent and bring enslaved Africans to the Americas and the Caribbean, they possessed technology and weaponry not known to the African continent. Likewise, weaponry technology did not exist in other territories they colonized around the world. The indigenous tribal people lost in this technology competition. This culture clash between the European powers and the indigenous people around the world highlighted the cultural differences between the groups, which unfortunately led to monstrous atrocities and wars.

Conquering predatory cultures tend to write their history and erase the history and disciplines of study from fallen cultures. They take credit for all the achievements by assuming all ownership in science, technology, healing, medicine, agronomy, arts, science, architecture, astronomy, philosophical traditions, and others. These disciplines were discovered in other past dominant cultures but revoked by the conquering culture.

The European powers were the largest and most far-flung compared to the non-European Empires, is simply because of the technological advantages between the fifteenth and nineteenth centuries. These advantages allowed a relatively small number of people to control a wide area. Also, in an age before mass education and developed concepts of creole nationalism or later indigenous nationalism, there were surprisingly little resistance from the colonized countries to rule from abstract and often exploitative 'mother' countries. However, these empires are impossible today, when a far higher proportion of the world's population is educated and has developed some form of 'national' ideology beyond pure localism.

The European powers saw this as an opportunity to fundamentally impose their political will and culture on the rest of the world. They improved the sophistication of the gunpowder-based weapons that they derived from the Chinese. This tool allowed them to have enormous advantages for fighting wars from a distance. This advantage with their shipbuilding prowess and developmental sea trade routes for commodity markets allowed them to carry out their worldwide mandate. The Europeans saw an opportunity to develop advanced nations constructed upon the principles of political institutions. Everything became mechanized through the introduction of commercial business and industrial sectors. The indigenous

113

people in the conquered, enslaved, and colonized territories during the Transatlantic Slave Trade had a simple lifestyle of hunting, fishing, and socialization that seemed primitive to the Europeans.
cxxxvii

The Western world still has technological advantages over large portions of the world. This contrast now is insufficient to prevent a successful guerrilla campaign by a committed population. Likewise, these empires were impossible before the fifteenth century. This dominance occurred because of the development of ships of a quality that could transmit power from the metropole to peripheries with sufficient strength to create colonies and empires. However, it was not only European powers that took advantage of this period to colonize other parts of the world. Japan colonized parts of China and Korea with similar tools. The drive towards empire building from the dominant cultures has existed throughout human history. Countries such as the United States and China today use their wealth and power to hold influence and access to the economic resources of other parts of the world. This influence is not dissimilar to Colonialism, except without direct rule is no longer possible without vast expenditure.

Global Lands

The utilization of global land was a most major difference between the world's traditional cultures versus modern European Western culture. Generally, global land was determined by whoever was in control at the time. During most of the time in early world history, it was chaotic, varied on a case-by-case basis, and determined by war and conquests.

Ambitious world rulers often expanded as much as they could until they hit barriers or faced strong resistance. Oceans, mountains, deserts, and big lakes often split groups of people. It allowed people on each side of the barriers to evolve differently. In some cases, global land was obtained through purchases. An example is the formation of the United States was the Louisiana purchase in 1803, the Gadsden purchase in 1853, and the purchase of Alaska from Russia. Global land has also been obtained through treaties. Many countries often engage in treaties, usually after a war, that set the border of each nation. Most of Africa was partitioned this way and their haphazard borders are deeply affected among European colonized powers.

Mutual agreements are another way that borders are determined. In 1976, North Vietnam and South Vietnam agreed to unite. In 1947, leaders in India and Colonial Britain agreed to split India into two parts – India and Pakistan. West Germany and East Germany joined in 1989 when the Communism barrier between them no longer made sense.

Globally, there is no unaccounted land. However, borders are constantly changing on the wishes of the people involved. Sometimes the change is non-violent and at times, it is violent. A full third of the world's borders are less than 100 years old. [cxxxviii]

Traditional culture and modern culture had opposite views when it came to the utilization of global lands. Their view of land ownership could not have been more pronounced. Out[cxxxix] of the many cultural difference between groups of people, "perhaps the most serious was the difference in the way that the Indians and Europeans thought about land. This difference created problems that would not be solved during the next several hundred years, and even today, lingering resentment over indigenous lands remains.

Owing land was very important to the European settlers. In England and most other countries, land meant wealth. Owning large amounts of land meant that prisons had great wealth and political power.

Many of the settlers who came to North America could never have owned land back home in Europe. They were poor. And they belonged to religious minorities. When they arrived in the new world, they discovered that no one seemed to own large amounts of land.

Companies in England needed to find people willing to settle in North America. They offered land to anyone who would take the chance of crossing the Atlantic Ocean. For many, it was a dream come true. It was a way to improve their lives. The land gave the European settlers a chance to become wealthy and powerful.

On the other hand, the Indians believed that no one could own land. They believed, however, that anyone could use it. Anyone who wanted to live on a piece of land and grow crops could do so.

The American Indians lived with nature. They understood the land and the environment. They did not try to change it. They might grow crops in an area for a few years. Then they would move on. They would allow the land on which they had farmed to become wild again.

They might hunt on one area of land for some time, but again they would move on. They hunted only what they could eat, so populations of animals would continue to increase. The Indians understood nature and were at peace with it.

The first Europeans to settle in the New England area of the Northeast wanted to land. The Indians did not fear them. There were not many settlers, and there was enough land for everyone to use and plant crops. It was easy to live together. The Indians helped the setters by teaching them how to plant crops and survive the land. But the Indians did not understand that the settlers were going to keep the land. This idea was foreign to the Indians. To them, it was like trying to own the air or the clouds. The Europeans had a materialistic view of the land and its animals and plants. Conflicts eventually arose.

As the years passed, more and more settlers arrived and took more land. They cut down the trees and build fences to keep people and animals out. They demanded that the Indians stay off their lands. [cxl] What consolidated the seizure of land in areas in which indigenous people had no concept of property in land was race.

The Early Seven Original Culture Locations are:

The Nile River Valley

The Indus River Valley

The Wei-Huang Valley

The Ganges River Valley

Mesopotamia

Mesoamerica

West Africa

A culture hearth is a location that saw the origins of a culture from which it later spread. Culture hearths are the center of origin of ancient civilizations which continue to inspire and influence modern societies of the world today. Although many distinct cultures are prevalent around the world, these are the most dominant ones. These culture hearths are the centers of origin of ancient civilizations which continue to inspire and influence modern societies of the world today. All the culture hearths have common criteria such as a habitable climatic zone, the proximity of large river basins, and geographical isolation from other regions of the world by mountains, deserts, or seas. [cxli]

It should not be a surprise that the origins of many of the major world's cultures and subcultures developed during the same time as some of the first recorded ancient civilizations. The world's first recorded civilizations or societies have always been a source of debate among historians, scientists, and anthropologists. These culture heaths include those debated societies. They include present-day societies such as the Indus Valley, Mesopotamian, China, Mayans, Aztecs, Egyptians, India, and West Africa have always been part of that debate.

Though many distinct cultures are prevalent around the world today, the most dominant origins in one of the few areas called "culture are culture hearths" They are the heartlands of various cultures and historically, there are seven main locations from which the most dominant cultural ideas have spread. "These regions are considered culture heaths because such key cultural practices as religion, the use of iron tools and weapons, highly organized social structures, and the development of agriculture started and spread from this area. In terms of religion, for example, the area around Mecca is considered the culture hearth for the Islamic religion and the area from which Muslims initially traveled to convert people to Islam. The spread of tools, social structures, and agriculture spread similarly from each of the culture hearths. [cxlii]

The Nile River Valley
In relative isolation from possible attacks from the sea and the invaders of the sparsely populated desert, the ancient civilization of the Nile River Valley was formed on the banks of the upper Nile River in Africa. In the summer and autumn months, the full-flowing

Nile waters profusely fed the soil giving a rich harvest of millet and rye. Abundantly collected grain crops contributed to the population growth, which in turn led to the emergence of a hierarch and the practice of knowledge accumulation via hieroglyph memos on tablets of wood or clay. Observations of the moon and the sun rotation cycles allowed the ancient Egyptians to form a pattern of time and calculate the number of days in the complete cycle of stars rotation.

The Wei-Huang Valley

The transition from a nomadic lifestyle to soil cultivation, or so-called the Neolithic Revolution, occurred in the Wei-Huang valley in China at about 5000 BC. Although the soil was quite fertile, floods recurred regularly, which gave rise to the need for dams engineering, as well as transportation of large amounts of soil from one area to another. Up to 5000-3000 BC in the Wei-Huang valley territory, no major communities were built, but plenty of small village-like settlements were thriving. Trade relations triggered the appearance of elementary regulation, later grown into centralization. It marked the beginning of the hereditary monarchy's formation: Xia (ca. 2200-1750), Shang (ca. 1750-1100), Xia (about 2200-1750), and the Shang (about 1750-1100). A significant influence on the growth of future empire came from the Indo-Europeans, who introduced bronze and chariots to Yellow River people (as Europeans called them) as well as other objects of the invention already common in Mesopotamia. Formation of the Zhou Dynasty (1122-256) connected with the beginning of Chinese classical civilization.

The Ganges River Valley

The wealth of literature of the Vedic period coincided with Aryans arriving at the Indian subcontinent. The literature also provides an idea of the social organization of Ganges Valley society. During the first centuries of the Ganges civilization, cattle breeding remained a major life provision activity. The large family community started to form during this time often with a confrontation between each other in pursuit of neighbor's cattle. The Sanskrit term gavisti reveals the essence of neighbors' tense relationships and has a common translation as war, but literally, it means "a chase in search of cows." The literature of that period boasts the names of certain clans and their achievements. The names of the most powerful clans of the Ganges civilization have passed the test of time and until now preserved as the names of the geographical regions of India.

The Indus River Valley

Early livestock sites dated to 8500 BC in the Indus Valley, but the cultivation of the soil began with more primitive tools of wood origin, images of which remained imprinted on the archaeological sites of the period. The rich moisture floodplain of the Indus River contributed to the development of a sedentary lifestyle, which required higher social organization. Later developed cotton processing encouraged the development of the earliest textiles. First commodity items inspired trade with other nearest civilizations, located on the same latitude – the Fertile Crescent. Aryan migration with their cultural influence came to India around 1500 BC and coincided with the blossoming of the Ganges River valley civilization.

Mesopotamia

By the degree of ancient, Mesopotamia can be called next, known to some historians as the Fertile Crescent. This was the amalgam of traditions set forth for many centuries to come which has begun with the emergence of agriculture in the fertile soils of Mesopotamia around 8000 BC. One of the major early settlements was Jericho - the city with the longest history of continuous human habitation. Unified Egypt became the next milestone in the formation of a powerful cluster of culture and commerce in the area in the lower reaches of the Nile, north of the Arabian Peninsula and Mesopotamia. Because of the mapping similarity of the region with the crescent, the name of the Fertile Crescent came to use. Interesting enough that in more recent times, this area was settled by Arabs of mainly Islamic religion, the symbol of which is also a Crescent.

Mesoamerica

The movement of tribal groups in search of fertile land hemisphere began in the western hemisphere about 13,000 years BC. However, signs of early agriculture in the region of North America, which includes Mexico and Central America, the developed civilization with common cultural characteristics, began only at 7,000 BCE. Reportedly the cultivation of maize began about 4,000 years BC. However, all the soil work was carried out manually, because of the lack of large domestic animals in Mesoamerica, which in turn explains much later in comparison with other civilizations, the use of a wheel. This fact probably also became an indirect cause of the absence of urban settlements, and the whole area was filled with rather small settlements. The symptoms of typical civilization emerged with the advent of the Olmec rulers at around 1200 BC, giving rise to the construction of expansive ceremonial centers, drainage structures, as well as the creation of colossal artistic objects - famous Olmec heads. The disappearance of the Olmec civilization for reasons still unknown was followed by the era of Maya.

West Africa
As early as 8500 BC the domestication of cattle in Eastern Sudan took place, which at the beginning was a form of nomadic pastoralism. Around 7500 BC permanent settlements began to appear, the sorghum and yams were cultivated, adding each following century a new agro-culture. From around 5000 BC the territory became a host of small Sudanic monarchies such as Ghana, Mali, and Songhai, and their ruling kings were usually regarded as divine beings. Since then, the tradition has set forth to arrange the burial of kings, together with their servants. It was believed that the servants would benefit the kings in the afterlife. At about this cultural era the forces of good in nature and the human mind started to be represented in forms, images, and early texts tending to associate good with rain and fertility, considering it to be universally united divine power." [cxliii]

EARLY GLOBAL CIVILIZATIONS

Civilization is the stage of human social development and organization which is considered most advanced. It always flourished and developed around a river or river basin. People can learn something from every civilization.

    1. Egyptian Civilization: There were masters in Marine and Civil engineering. They knew and developed the

concept of Shipbuilding. We know that they still have ancient Pyramids and Sphinx. From the above point, one can also infer that Egyptians had developed taste in Algebra and Geometry.

2. Mesopotamian Civilization: Known for Hanging Gardens of Babylon. They were good with Medicine, Astronomy, and Mathematics. Astronomy was used to make 12 months calendar using Moon Cycle and dividing the year into two seasons- Summer and Winter. They also supported the fact of the Heliocentric theory.

3. Chinese Civilization: Another civilization famous for its understanding of Mathematics, Architecture, Warfare, and Civil Engineering. Gunpowder, Paper, Compass were developed here. Plus, Seismograph to measure Earthquakes. Umbrellas, Terracotta, Kites, Porcelain, Glassmaking. They also had philosophical lessons in a book called The Analects which was given by Confucius.

4. Mayan Civilization: Mayan Calendar is known for its accurate predictions. They recorded the movements of celestial bodies which were essentially used for Astrological purposes. They were able to predetermine the solar/lunar eclipses which are also used today.

5. Aztec Civilization: They were famous for the smelting of Gold, Silver and combining them with precious stones like Jade, Turquoise. They were first among to use Human waste as fertilizers. They developed efficient means of the irrigation process i.e., Artificial Irrigation and construction of Dams. It is said to be the most populous civilization in Ancient History.

6. Mongol Civilization: The administration was very clever. The same rule applied to minister, high-rank military commander and a commoner. Thus,

Democracy was derived. Mongols were known for technology exchange. As the empire ranged from Asia to Europe- they kept on swapping various interesting Chinese technology with Europeans via Silk Road. The Mongol Empire had an ingenious and efficient mail system for the time, often referred to by scholars as to the Yam, in which a messenger would typically travel 25 miles (40 km) from one station to the next, either receiving a fresh, rested horse, or relaying the mail to the next rider to ensure the speediest possible delivery. The Mongol riders regularly covered 125 miles (200 km) per day. Today it is commonly called Pony Express.

7. Greek Civilization: They developed surveying and mathematics to an advanced state. They are known for great inventions like Water Mill, Aqua duct, Cartography, Alarm Clock, Odometer, Olympics, Concept of Democracy, Calipers, Differential Gears, Archimedes principles.

8. Indus Valley Civilization: The longest surviving civilizations. They were known for inventions like Buttons (ornamental Buttons), Stepwell, Ruler with a precision of 2 mm, Ship Building, Docks, and shipyards. The township was designed with a proper addressing system i.e., Main Street and sub-streets. Every housing was connected to the sewage system. The means of transportation included a bullock cart and chariot. They had uniform weights and measures system. Because of this uniformity, they knew the exact proportions in making metal alloys and push the boundaries of Metallurgy. [cxliv]

Past Western scholars generally saw Egypt as a Mediterranean civilization with little impact on the rest of Africa. Recent studies, however, have started to discredit this notion. Some have argued that various Ancient Egyptians, like the Badarians, probably migrated toward the north from Nubia. [cxlv]

The World's Major Cultures

Below is a comprehensive list of most of the major cultures that make most of the different world cultures. As there is a lot of overlap between cultures, measuring them is particularly difficult. In addition, the media and travel are creating rapid cultural changes. It is almost impossible to know the number of world's cultures that exist. It is not easy to measure cultures directly. Approximately six to eight thousand worldwide is a good estimate. The overall total numbers are based on indigenous and immigrant groups, including diaspora groups minus racial and religious groups. The number of cultures includes ethnic, religious, diaspora, castle, regional, and national groups.

Languages are a useful tool to estimate cultures. There are about five to six thousand languages worldwide, but only about half of them are spoken by children, which means they are disappearing. As many people find out that it is easier to communicate with certain languages, the lesser ones will disappear. Also, as the English language becomes the language of choice for many cultures, the culture associated with it becomes more popular.

Some cultures are beginning to dwindle because of globalization spreading different systems and beliefs. Western culture is found in many areas of the world, and by the same token American culture has become more diverse thanks to immigration. Although it is difficult to measure cultures, there are some clear differences worldwide. For example, Western culture differs significantly from the cultures found in post-Cold War era countries. Further differences are seen in North Africa, Southeast Asia, and other areas. Such differences are apparent in terms of religion, cuisine, and social etiquette. [cxlvi]

African Culture

The continent of Africa is essential to all cultures. "Human life originated on this continent and began to migrate to other areas of the world around 60,000 years ago, according to the Natural History Museum in London. Other researchers, like those from Estonian Biocentre in Tartu, believe that the first migration may have been much earlier, as early as 120,000 years ago. Researchers come to these conclusions by studying human genomes from various cultures to trace their DNA to common ancestors. Fossil records also factor into some of these theories.

Africa is home to several tribes, ethnic and social groups. One of the key features of this culture is the number of ethnic groups throughout the 54 countries on the continent. Nigeria has more than 300 tribes for example. Although essentially similar, these countries in Africa have some subtle differences in their culture.

Currently, Africa is divided into two cultural groups: North Africa and Sub-Saharan Africa. This is because Northwest Africa has strong ties to the Middle East, while Sub-Saharan Africa shares historical, physical, and social profiles that are very different from North Africa, according to the University of Colorado. The harsh environment has been a large factor in the development of Sub-Saharan Africa culture, as there are several languages, cuisines, art and musical styles that have sprung up among the far-flung populations." [cxlvii]

Within the context of the United States, Caribbean Americans, and continental Africans along with their descendants will assimilate into African American culture and the broader Western mainstream culture. Some of these people of African descent and the diaspora will connect closely with the people that look like them. They will adopt some of the subculture identities in American society such as dress, music, speech dialect, food, and others.

Technically, there is no such thing as a unified Black culture since there are people of African descent who represent several nations and ethnicities. However, the integration of these subcultures into the mainstream American culture incorporated many of the different cultural concepts into practice. In the United States, you will typically find three distinct people of African descent.

African Americans
They are descendants of slaves sold to European settlers during the Transatlantic Slave Trade. These people have been far removed from their continental Western and Central African roots and have been in the United States for several generations. These are people of African descent who dealt with the historical human/civil rights obstacles such as American chattel slavery, Reconstruction, the Great Migration from the South,

124

Jim Crow and Black Codes segregation laws, mass incarceration, the 1980's crack epidemic, and others.

Caribbean-Americans
People of African descent migrated from various nations located in the Caribbean Sea, including Jamaica, Haiti, the Bahamas, and others. These people are also descendants of West, and Central enslaved Africans brought to the Western Hemisphere via the Transatlantic Slave Trade. However, the ones currently living in the United States are immigrants who voluntarily migrated there. They are typically new immigrants or first-generation Americans; therefore, they are culturally distinct from African Americans regarding food, music, and dialect.

Continental Africans
They are very similar to Caribbean-Americans in that they voluntarily migrated to the United States and are culturally distinct from African Americans. They are new immigrants from any country on the African Continent such as Nigeria, Ghana, Kenya, South Africa, or recent descendants of continental Africans. The main thing that distinguishes them from the other two groups is that continental Africans are not descendants of slavery via the Transatlantic Slave Trade, but most were part of the European powers Colonialism. Their ancestors have historically remained on the African continent throughout the centuries and millenniums. [cxlviii]

African Tribes
"There are several African tribes in the African continent. The *Afar* tribes are found in Ethiopia, Djibouti, and Somalia. The *Anlo-Ewe* tribes were once inhabitants of Notsie, from where they migrated in 1474 and are currently found in the Southeastern areas of the Republic of Ghana.

The *Amhara* tribes are found in Ethiopia, *Ashanti* tribes in Central Ghana, *Bakongo* tribes along the Atlantic coast, and the *Bambara* tribes are in Mali. The *Bemba* tribes located in Zambia, the *Berber* tribes are in Morocco, Algeria, Tunisia, Libya, and Egypt. The *Bobo* tribes are found in Western Burkina Faso and Mali.

The *Bushmen* tribes are in the Kalahari Desert. The *Chewa* tribes are in Zambia, Malawi, and Zimbabwe. The *Dogon* tribes live in Southeastern Mali and Burkina Faso. Some other tribes found in Africa are the *Fang tribe, Fon, Fulani, Ibos, Kikuyu, Maasai, Mandinka, Pygmies, Samburu, Senufo, Tuareg, Wolof, Yoruba,* and *Zulu.*

African Religions
There are two major religions in Africa and hence most Africans adhere to either Christianity or Islam. Many adherents of both Islam and Christianity also follow African traditional religions.

African Arts
African art has certain themes that are repeated throughout all the art forms, be it painting, pottery or any other handicrafts, and even fabric. Some of the subjects that are commonly portrayed are couples, the depiction of a woman and a child, a male with a wild animal, or the portrayal of an outsider.

According to African culture, the depiction of the couples represents ancestors or even community founders. Often there is also a depiction of twins. However, the representation of the couple is rarely the kind to show sexual intimacy or love, more often it depicts strength and honor.

The portrayal of the woman and her child represents Mother Earth, and the child represents the people living on the Earth. The portrayal of the male with the weapon or with a horse is usually representing the power or status conferred upon man. Finally, the portrayal of the stranger represents a foreigner or an outsider. In ancient African culture, the stranger was not welcome and there always existed a gap between the stranger and the African people in the pictures.

In the African culture, songs are used as a mode of communication. Melodies in African music are organized within a scale of four, five, six, or seven tones. Common musical instruments used in African music are drums, slit gongs, double-bells, rattles, harps, musical hows, xylophone, flutes, and trumpets. Drums are particularly popular which explains the use of several different types of drums like – *Tama* (talking drums), *bougarabou, djembe,* water drums, and the *Ngoma* drums.

African Languages

There are close to 2000 languages spoken throughout Africa. All these languages can be broadly categorized into four major categories, which are *Afro-Asiatic* languages, *Nilo-Saharan* languages, *Niger-Congo* languages, and the *Khoisan* languages. Some of the Nilo-Saharan languages are *Kanuri, Songhay, Nubian*, and the *Nilotic* family languages, which include *Luo, Dinka*, and *Maasai*.

The Niger-Congo languages include the *Bantu* and *Niger-Kordofanian* language families. The *Khoisan* language family includes around thirty languages categorized into five *Khoisan* families. In addition to the languages, there are also certain non-African languages as well as many sign languages.

African Clothing

Vibrant colors have always been a prominent feature of African clothing. A near Eastern influence is evident in countries like Egypt where the *Jellabiya* is worn. The Dashiki is a very colorful men's garment that covers the upper half of the body, while the traditional female attire is called a *Kaftan*, which is a loose-fitting pullover garment, usually with an embroidered V-shaped collar. The *Boubou, Tuareg,* and *Mitumba* are some other traditional costumes found in African countries.

African Cuisine

The African cuisine is a beautiful concoction of tropical fruits and vegetables as well as exotic seafood varieties. There are various regional differences in African cuisine. For instance, Central African cuisine is influenced by the plants grown in the region which chiefly include plantains, cassava, spinach stew, peppers, chilies, onions, okra, ginger, and peanut butter. Meat preparations containing crocodile, monkey, warthog, and antelopes are also found at times.

The East African cuisine rarely features meat forms and includes corn, rice, saffron, cloves, cinnamon, tomatoes, pineapple, orange, lemon, and bananas. The North African cuisine owing to the Turkish influence has inclusion of several popular pastries and other bakery items. Southern Africa, owing to its Malay influence includes spicy chutneys and curries and marinated kebabs and sweets savories in its cuisine. On the other hand, a typical West African meal includes many starchy items and a relatively smaller number of meat products.

African Festivals
In addition to the traditional Muslim festivals like *Ramadan, Eid-ul-Fitr,* and *Eid-ul-Adha,* and other universal festivals like the New Year celebration and Christmas, there are several other festivals in Africa. Many of the African festivals are oriented around the farming and harvesting cycles. Some of these popular festivals include Kwanzaa, *Yam Festival, Adae Kese festival, Festival of Opet, Homowo, Sed festival,* and the *Osirian festival."* [cxlix]

Middle Eastern Culture
The countries of the Middle East have some but not all things in common. This is not a surprise, since the area consists of approximately twenty countries, according to PBS. The Arabic language is one thing that is common throughout the region; however, the wide variety of dialects can sometimes make communication difficult. Religion is another cultural area that the countries of the Middle East have in common. The Middle East is the birthplace of Judaism, Christianity, and Islam. [cl]

Egyptian Culture
The culture of Egypt is beyond just the Pharaohs. It is a complex blend of many cultures of the world which resulted from the complex process of cultural diffusion and cultural assimilation. There is a whole gamut of intricacies that lend the culture of Egypt a mystic touch, which can be cracked only after a detailed study. [cli]

Western Culture
The term "Western culture" has come to define the culture of European countries as well as those that have been heavily influenced by European immigration, such as the United States. Western culture has its roots in the Classical Period of the Greco-Roman era and the rise of Christianity in the 14th century. Other drivers of Western culture include Latin, Germanic, and Hellenic ethnic and linguistic groups. Today, the influences of Western culture can be seen in almost every country in the world. [clii]

American
The land of apple pie and baseball – the United States of America. Of course, we all know there is more to America than apple pie and baseball. Here is more about the culture of the USA.

American People
The American society is a blend of native Americans as well as many immigrants from various countries like Ireland, Germany, Poland, Italy, Latin America, Asia, and Africa. Having gone through a phase of racial discrimination, the United States of America today recognizes four races in the country – *Native American, African American, Asian, and European American.*

Religions in America
The majorities of the United States include Protestant Christians. The percentage of Catholics is slightly less than the Protestants. In addition to this, the United States is a secular state; several people have also adopted other religions like Judaism, Hinduism, Islam, and Buddhism.

American Arts
In the early years, American art and literature took most of its ideas and influences from European artists. During the late eighteenth century and the early nineteenth centuries, American paintings primarily included landscapes and portraits in a realistic style. The industrial revolution was responsible for new influences thereafter.

American literature is also known for the development of popular literary genres such as *hard-boiled crime fiction.* As far as dance is concerned, the USA has its share of dance varieties like the trademark *Lindy Hop* and its derivative Rock and Roll. There are also modern square dance and modern dance. In addition to this, there is a wide influence of several African American dances.

Languages in America
The United States of America does not have an official national language as such. However, the majorities of the American population speak English. Owing to many immigrants from Spain, Spanish is the second-most common language in America. In addition to this, some other languages that exist owing to the

immigrants are Germans, Irish, French, Polishes, Italians, Russians, Spaniards, Portuguese, Croatians, Jews, Arabs, Chinese, Japanese, Koreans, Greeks, and others.

American Clothing
In general terms, American clothing is diverse and predominantly informal. One of the most popular pieces of clothing that originated in America was the *blue jeans*, which were touted as *work clothes* in the 1850s by an immigrant merchant called *Levi Strauss*.

American Cuisine
Like every other cultural element, American cuisine has a strong European influence. The commonly used ingredients in American cooking are subject to change as you move from one region to the other. Some of the popular preparations in American cuisine are the American pie, banana split, brownies, corn dogs, crab cakes, hamburgers, clam chowder, lobster, hotdogs, New-York style cheesecake, and the Italian-influenced pizza.

American Festivals
In addition to the traditional Christmas, Good Friday, and New Year celebrations, Americans also celebrate various other festivals like Hanukkah, Thanksgiving, Easter, Halloween, St. Patrick's Day, Mardi Gras, Rosh Hashanah, and Yom Kipper.

Greek Culture
When we come across the etymological background of words in many comprehensive studies, most often we come across those words which have been introduced into the English dictionary, but their origin is from Greek scriptures. Greek culture is rich and vast. It has got immense information which until deeply studied, remains beyond understanding.

Italian Culture
Italy has been home to many great episodes of the Roman Empire, historical eras like the Renaissance, architectural excellence, art, literature, and the like. To study the depths of the Italian culture, one must perceive the totality of this cultural amalgamation. There are

also very elaborate rituals and customs that adhere to this age-old culture.

Irish Culture
Apart from the celebration of St. Patrick's Day, and the Irish Stout, many other things that amount to the emergence of the Irish culture. Irish cuisine is a noted aspect of the long trails of the struggle that Ireland had to go through in times of economic downturn. Many tales narrate the importance of potatoes and kale in Irish cuisine. However, things have changed immensely with time.

Celtic Culture
Celtic culture has its roots in the European domains. It is one of the oldest cultures that have existed and survived. However, there is a lot more that needs to be addressed about this culture.

Gothic Culture
Inspired by European culture, Gothic culture is now found in many countries. It has a different genre of music, fashion, cinema, and literature. It is a niche culture.

French Canadian Culture
This comparatively small group of people are a result of colonization and settlement. They are not originally from Canada, neither they like to call themselves French. They are a wonderfully divergent formation of two distinct cultures. [cliii]

Eastern Culture
Eastern culture generally refers to the societal norms of countries in Far East Asia (including China, Japan, Vietnam, North Korea, and South Korea) and the Indian subcontinent. Like the West, Eastern culture was heavily influenced by religion during its early development, but it was also heavily influenced by the growth and harvesting of rice, according to the book "Pathways to Asian Civilizations: Tracing the Origin and Spread of Rice and Rice Cultures" by Dorian Q. Fuller. In general, in Eastern culture, there is less of a distinction between secular society and religious philosophy than there is in the West. [cliv]

Chinese Culture

Chinese culture is known to be one of the four most ancient civilizations of the world. Therefore, its culture is very vivid and diverse. It also boasts of a very elaborate written history, which holds some of the oldest facts about the richness of Chinese culture. There are many facets attached to Chinese culture and civilization, such as their medicine, food, martial art forms, and others.

Japanese Culture

Japan's culture is laden with so many elements like Japan's music, costume, dance, attire, food, and many such things that it becomes imperative to know it, inside out. Geisha, Samurai, Kimono, are only some of the elements which have drawn everyone's attention for decades. Some lots need to be explored.

South Asian Culture

South Asian culture is exceptionally rich. The reason is simple. There are in all eight different countries which together form this conglomerate culture, known to the world as South Asian culture. The countries which form the South Asian countries include India, Pakistan, Bangladesh, Sri Lanka, Nepal, Afghanistan, Maldives, and Bhutan. Just like there are variations in their geographical properties, differences also exist in their cultures.

Hong Kong Culture

This is yet another spectacular result of the intermingling of the cultures from the oriental and the occidental worlds. It has got traces of both China and the UK. Despite these overpowering interferences, Hong Kong can boast of ethnic culture.

India

India is known for its spicy curries and healing techniques of Yoga, however, there is much more the Indian culture has to offer. Indian culture has its roots in the *Indus Valley Civilization* from where it witnessed the Vedic Age. India then witnessed the rise and decline of Buddhism, the Muslim invasions, and European colonization.

India Religions
India is a secular country, which includes a diverse population, with various religions. Some of the prominent religions followed in India remain to be Hinduism, Buddhism, Sikhism, Jainism, Islam, and Christianity.

India Art
India art essentially goes hand in hand with cultural history, religion, and fundamental Indian philosophies. The rock carvings, *Chola* fresco paintings, *Madhubani* paintings are some instances of ancient Indian art. Indian Music is also a prominent element of Indian culture which traditionally includes Carnatic and Hindustani music.

India Festivals
India has a wide variety of festivals and celebrations originating from the numerous religions that co-exist in India.

South Korean Culture
South Korea is overall a very tradition-abiding country. They are etched to their roots to such an extent that, it gets reflected in their hospitality when a tourist pays a visit.

Malaysian Culture
When talking about the *Spice Route*, it becomes almost mandatory to refer to the beautiful land of Malaysia. Like many other countries, Malaysia is inhabited by a multitude of ethnic groups, and therefore, has a varied culture. [clv]

Latin Culture
Many of the Spanish-speaking nations are considered part of the Latin culture, while the geographic region is widespread. Latin America is typically defined as those parts of Central America, South America, and Mexico where Spanish, or Portuguese are the dominant languages. Originally, the term "Latin America" was used by French geographers to differentiate between Anglo and Romance (Latin-based) languages, according to the University of Texas. While Spain and Portugal are on the European continent, they are considered the key influencer of what is known as Latin culture, which denotes people using languages derived from Latin, also known as Romance languages. [clvi]

Mayan Culture
Mayan culture has left an indelible mark in its long trails of history about mathematics, architecture, scriptures, and many more such things of interest. They have a long history of agriculture too, and their language is diverse.

Colombian Culture
The culture of Colombia is the result of a mixed pot attribute. It has been in the form of development that was grossly influenced by the European, African, and native Indian cultures. There is such a spectacular facet to the culture of Colombia.

Dominican Republic
There is a host of languages that are spoken here, which implies the variety of cultures prevalent here. However, the official language is Spanish.

Mexican Culture
The land of the Maya, the Aztec, and many other native American tribes, Mexico is known worldwide for the enduring grand culture that has made it up for all to admire. Though the dominant language is Mexican, numerous tribal languages are spoken by the masses. Also, there are some very famous festivals and ceremonies that are world- famous and have been showcased in the world cinema.

Culture of Peru
After procuring freedom from Spanish rule, this nation has stood the test of time, and carved out a culture, unique to them. The culture is an interesting compilation of multiple elements.

Jamaican Culture
Jamaica is a rich culture, which has been influencing other cultures too. There would not be too many people who have not heard about the wonders that Jamaican sports and music render. *Rastafarianism* was a result of the rebellion against colonization, but in present times it is more than just a gang of structured rebels. It would not be an overstatement to consider Rastafarianism as a way of life for many.

Samoan Culture

The land is famous for its picturesque scenic bounty, and it is also known as the land of sailors and ships. There is also a pressing need to know about the emergence of the island country, as it serves as one of the most sought-after tourist destinations. [clvii]

Constant Change

No matter what culture society is in, one thing is for certain. It will change. "Culture appears to have become key in our interconnected world. It includes many ethnically diverse societies, but also riddled by conflicts associated with religion, ethnicity, ethical beliefs, and essentially, the elements which make up culture, De Rossi said, "But culture is no longer fixed, if it ever was, It is essentially fluid and constantly in" This makes it so that it is difficult to define any culture in only one way. While change is inevitable, the past should also be respected and preserved." [clviii]

Concluding Thoughts

These major world's cultures have been heavily influenced socially, economically, politically, and culturally by the present-day Western mainstream culture during the past five centuries. Worldwide Colonialism and the Transatlantic Slave Trade in the fifteenth century led by a few European powers who conquered, enslaved, and colonized the world greatly influenced these major world's cultures and some of their creations. The creation of these major cultures was either appropriated from an existing foreign culture or evolved into what it is today from a mingling of different racial groups and cultures. All the major cultures evolved from the continent of Africa, the origin of humankind, the cradle of civilization, and the home of some of the world's earliest civilizations/empires or societies.

The creation of the Middle East culture, for example, began to evolve before World War II and was confirmed during the war when the Middle East term was given to the British military command in Egypt. The Middle East, which has no clear definition or defined borders encompasses about twenty countries in the region. [clix] The Middle East is bordered by Asia to the East, Europe to the northwest, Africa to the southwest, and the Mediterranean Sea to the West. A few countries in Africa, depending upon one's interpretation of the area, are considered part of the Middle East. Because of its economic, religious, and geographical location, the Middle East has been at the center of many world issues and political affairs. The Middle East is very rich in history and culture.

Africa is the "cradle of civilizations". But to many people who live in the Middle East, it is also known as the "cradle of civilizations". Its two major river systems, the Nile Valley in Egypt, and the Tigris-Euphrates in Iraq (ancient Mesopotamia) were the sites of some of the world's earliest civilizations (Egyptian, Sumerian, Babylonian, Sudan, and Assyrian). This global location is where urban life and centralized forms of political organization arose. The Middle East is one of the highly complex and culturally diversified regions of the world. [clx]

Egypt and a few other countries in North Africa are considered part of the Middle East. Egypt, now considered by the Western culture, is physically located on the continent of Africa. Should Egypt and the other African northern countries be part of the Middle East culture or the Africa Culture? Western culture, presently the world's most dominant culture, made this decision for the north African countries to be considered part of the Middle East. These five major cultures exist today. But over generations, centuries, and millenniums, new cultures will be developed or redefined. However, their influences may lessen or continue to strive to depend upon the abilities of the cultures to handle cultural changes and economic development,

Culture Types and Levels of Measurements

What is the best way to measure the levels of technological advancement of present and future global civilizations? In his paper published in 1964, Transmission of Information by Extraterrestrial Civilizations, Russian astrophysicist and astronomer, Nicolai Kardashev, proposed and devised a three-tier system for the classification of a civilization based on their ability to harness energy. Kardashev's paper was a response to Freeman Dyson's 1959 paper. It discussed the possibility of certain types of very large stars with low surface temperatures equal to room temperature. This was the result of alien intelligence building a sphere around their star (Dyson sphere), developed a scale of technical civilizations based on energy use.

The Kardashev Scale is a purely hypothetical scale for measuring a civilization's technological prowess based on the amount of usable energy it has at its disposal. The Kardashev Scale is a method of measuring a civilization's level of technological advancement based on the amount of energy that a civilization can utilize. Notably, the amount of power available to civilization is linked to how widespread the civilization is (whether it populates a planet, galaxy, or an entire universe). On the Kardashev scale, there are three types of civilizations. It has since been expanded.

The five-page proposal by Nikolai Kardashev postulated that correlating a civilization's technological advancement and population growth with the amount of energy they can harvest and consume. This idea helps us create a theory on how to search for alien civilizations by their technological signatures. It is derived from their potential methods of energy harvesting and usage. [clxi]

Civilization Types

• Type 0: Sub global Culture - This type of civilization extracts its energy and raw materials from crude organic-based sources such as wood, coal, and oil. The O type is about where we are today on planet Earth. The Earth has not made it to Type I yet. We are not presently utilizing the entire planet's energy with the current technology. The Earth may reach Type I in one to two centuries. This civilization extracts its energy and raw materials from crude organic-based sources such as wood, coal, chemical rockets, ionic engines, fission power, rail guns, and oil. Any rockets utilized by such a civilization would necessarily depend on chemical propulsion. Since such travel is so pitifully slow compared to other energy sources, a civilization at this level would be, for the most part, confined to its home planet.

• Type I: Planetary Culture - This civilization would be slightly more advanced than those found on Earth. They would be capable of utilizing all available resources on their home planet, skillfully harnessing the energy output of an entire world. We must fully harness all available energy sources including solar, geothermal, wind, ram-jet fusion engines, photonic drive, and others. This type can control all the energy of their home planet. They may have the ability to control or modify their weather, manipulate planetary phenomena, such as hurricanes, which can release the energy of hundreds of hydrogen bombs. Perhaps volcanos or even earthquakes may be altered by such a civilization.

• Type II: Stellar Culture - This civilization would be able to harness all the energy of a star. The sun's energy is fully harvested, and other planets are drained. It can control all the energy (antimatter drive and von Neumann nanoprobes) of its solar system. This type may be reached in a millennium beyond our stage of evolution. It generates about 10 billion times the energy output of a Type I civilization. This civilization may resemble the Federation of Planets seen on the TV program Star Trek. It may have the power capability of the power solar flares. Type II status may be obtainable in a few thousand years.

• Type III: Galactic Culture - This civilization would be able to harness the energy output of a galaxy (about 10 billion times the energy output of a Type II civilization, and about 100,000 to 1 million years more advanced than we are). A type III civilization can fully harness and control all the energy (Planck energy propulsion) in the Galaxy (mass Dyson Spheres around all galactic stars. It may take 100,000 to a million years to reach this status. [clxii]

Technically speaking, the Kardashev Scale is a three tiers scale with possible expansion to five or even six but that would be pretty much beyond what any of us could even imagine.

*Type IV: A universal civilization, capable of harnessing the energy of the whole universe. This civilization would be *super*galactic, able to travel throughout the entire universe and consume the energy output of several, possibly all galaxies. It would also be capable of projects of gargantuan proportions, such as manipulating space-time and tinkering with entropy, thus reaching immortality on a grand scale. An essentially indestructible and highly utopian civilization.

*Type V: A multiverse culture, capable of harnessing the energy of multiple universes. This type V civilization would outgrow its universe. It would span countless parallel universes, being able to manipulate the very structure of reality.

*Type VI: Even more abstract is the type VI civilization. Type VI exists *outside* of time and space. It can create universes and multiverses and destroying them just as easily. It is similar in concept like to a deity. ^{clxiii}

Concluding Thoughts

This highly debatable way to classify civilizations according to how energy can be controlled in the universe is one opinion that has been generally and widely accepted. If human beings fail to get their global social system to stop their human predation's tribal instinct, escaping to another suitable planet will not be an option. The current technology already developed has been misused in very destructive ways.

A global cultural change would be needed to stop our preconceived notion to resort to violence when certain cultures do not get their way. We need to become the masters of our planet, which we have not before we advance to the next stage. We would need to create a new mentality of global culture cooperation in which undeveloped and impoverished countries are phased out, despite an abundance of natural resources on the planet. Human understanding of social evolutions explains why civilizations rise and fall. It can help us understand why we are in the present cycle. It can more aptly anticipate the next stage of development.

Another debate is that the Kardashev scale ignores the importance of increased efficiency and respect for the natural environment of its planet origin by consuming all available sources of energy. Another theory says the sun may burn off in five billion years. Why use up all the sun's energy and deplete it which will leave to our ultimate demise? Another view is

almost all the energy that hits planet Earth is being used, not necessarily by human beings but radiated back to space. The Earth-atmosphere energy balance is the balance between incoming energy from the Sun and outgoing energy from the Earth. The energy released from the Sun is emitted as shortwave light and ultraviolet energy. When it reaches the Earth, some is reflected space by clouds. Some are absorbed by the atmosphere, and some are absorbed in the Earth's surface.
clxiv

Will technological advances outpace the human's institutional ability to adapt too quickly? When societies, and institutions do not adapt as fast as technology creates change, bad things often result. The ethics of a new technological inventions is another moral argument that must be considered when evaluating possible outcomes of new technology advances. The increased acceleration of technology must be done in a beneficial humanistic manner. Otherwise, the continual implication is not considered and may prove to be disastrous in the long run.

These types of civilizations past types O and I are difficult to predict our technology advances. It also depends on the reality of physics and our limitations within the universe. We know that the realities of Type one is perhaps centuries away and it would take millenniums to reach the other civilizations. Artificial Intelligence (AI) could facilitate the timeline for advanced technology if societies can adapt to the new technology.

Some people assume that this scale would apply to all future advanced civilizations. It may be presumptuous to assume that an advanced civilization would continue to use more and more energy. Perhaps some civilizations could achieve population control and live within their means? Furthermore, there is no way to know if future advanced civilizations would continue to use the Kardashev scale as a computational potential measure of an unwilling civilization.

There are at least two alternative scales: the Sagan scale and the barrow scale. The Sagan scale is based on the amount of unique information a civilization possesses where each letter is an order of

140

magnitude more information than the last one. The barrow scale is based upon the smallest scale in which civilization can manipulate matter. [clxv] There is another view that the amount of data is another way to measure civilizations. You could add data storage to the list of options for scales. Archives are valuable.

The East Versus the West

Western culture is presently the most dominant culture in the world. Most cultures in the world are under the umbrella of the Western culture. It had a vested interest to rule over the world for the past five centuries. However, the Eastern culture, particularly China and India, have made great strides in exerting their cultures on the world during the last few decades. These major cultures set the world's agenda and determine what is discussed and implemented on the world's stage that impacts minor cultures.

However, "there is a stark culture clash between the Asian's collectivist values and the Eurocentric individualist values. These two opposed values systems often collide and create a chasm between members of those societies. The collectivist customs and relational norms of the Asians or East culture contrasts from West culture that prizes individualism. Below is a look at the difference between Eastern collectivist values with those Eurocentric Western values of individualism.

Asian societies are known as collectivist, where one's sense of identity is based on the "we" factor—where your allegiance and sense of purpose are tied to your family, village, and the larger community. Who you are is based on the group you are affiliated with? Compare this to Western notions of individualism where you are taught to value your uniqueness and learn to express yourself and challenge authority. These values are not only very different from traditional Asian ones, but they have the potential to create significant confusion, tension, and strain when these values go against each other in a traditional Asian household." [clxvi]

Western culture is a term that refers to the heritage of ethical values, traditions, customs, belief systems, technologies, and artifacts that define the lifestyles and beliefs of people from the Western part of the world. The roots of the Western culture have their origins in Europe and carry a heritage of Germanic, Celtic,

141

Hellenic, Slavic, Jewish, Latin, and other ethnic and linguistic groups. Mainly based on Christianity, one sees oneself as an element of the divine and life in service of God. Beginning in ancient Greece and ancient Rome, Western culture continued to develop with Christianity during the Middle Ages, nourished by the experiments of Enlightenment and discoveries of science and spread itself throughout the world between the fifteenth and twentieth centuries because of globalization and human migration.

Eastern culture is the ensemble of beliefs, customs, and traditions that distinguishes the people of the Eastern part of the world made up of the Far East, West Asia, Central Asia, North Asia, and South Asia. Based mostly on Buddhism, Hinduism, Confucianism, Islam, Taoism, and Zen, the Eastern culture explores the spiritual aspect of exploring the inner world of a human being believing that the universe and its existence is a never-ending cyclic journey with no limits. Eastern culture encourages its people to gain control over their emotions and state of mind through meditation and practices the principle of virtue in all aspects of life. It is also a culture that is built upon community and collectivism. Eastern culture believes that a human being is a social creature and is an integral part of society.
clxvii

- Eastern culture is based on the main schools of Buddhism, Hinduism, Confucianism, Islam, Taoism, and Zen; whereas, Western culture is based mostly on Christianity, scientific, logical, and rational schools.
- Eastern culture has a circular view of the universe based upon the perception of eternal recurrence; whereas, Western culture has a linear view of the universe based on the Christian philosophy that everything has a beginning and an end.
- Eastern culture uses the spiritual and missionary approach of searching inside oneself for answers through meditation; whereas, Western culture takes on a pragmatic and emotional approach in searching outside oneself through research and analysis.
- Eastern culture believes that the key to success is through spiritual means. Western culture believes that the key to success is through material means.

• Eastern culture believes that one's future is determined by one's deeds today. The Western culture believes that one's future is unknown. It is determined by God.
• Eastern culture believes that a human being is an integral part of society as well as the universe and practices collectivism. In Western culture, individualism is stronger, believing that a human being has individualistic and an independent part of society and the universe. ^{clxviii}

Concluding Thoughts

There is no clear definition of the East or West except in general terms. The West mainly consists of the United States, Canada, Western and Central Europe, and the Anglosphere of New Zealand, Australia, and parts of South Africa. The East, in geography, is much larger than the West. The West includes smaller, but powerful groups of nations. Dividing the world into two broad civilizations is vague, to begin with. Particularly when the societies' history, culture, languages, philosophy, religions, legal, political systems, and other factors must be considered.

In mainstream society, the term "Western Civilization and Eastern Civilization" is generally used to describe the world's dominant cultures. But it is not quite that simple when analyzed from a truly global perspective. The terms are generally used to differentiate between the Greco-Roman European and Anglosphere culture and the traditional East Asian, India, and Southeast Asian cultures. Neither culture has any kind of homogenous culture, and none of the countries are monoliths. ^{clxix}

In some cases, the difference between the East and West was a geopolitical phenomenon. Neither the East nor the West was a homogenous concept. For example, the French were allied with the Ottomans against the Germans. The Europeans and Middle Easterners were always in close contact with the Mediterranean a sort of unifying sea. On the other hand, the East, for example, had a conflict between the Mongols and Turco-Persians, and even today, the Syrians and other refugees chose the West in disputes. Other Eastern examples include the Sunni versus Shia, Moslems versus the Hindus and Chinese, Hindus versus the Chinese, and Vietnamese versus the Chinese and Japanese. In a way, globalization is a way that humanity will reach the balance between the two desiderates – individual freedom and accomplishment which is predominant in the West, and social cohesion and harmonious society, which is a feature in the East. [clxx]

Consider too, Africa, the second largest continent on Earth, the cradle of civilization and the origin of humankind, is not a part of the East or West. Neither has particularly strong cultural, or geopolitical ties to African nations except perhaps North Africa and South Africa. Africa is also not a homogenous continent. North Africa has a different culture from the Sub-Saharan and even places like Ethiopia which has its unique culture. North Africa is also strongly associated with the Middle East.

Chapter IV
Counterculture, Subculture, and Cancel Culture

Counterculture and Subculture

All societies have their own cultures which might be different from each other. However, there could be subcultures and countercultures within mainstream culture. Subcultures share the primary values of the mainstream culture, but they have characteristics that differentiate the subculture group from the rest. On the other hand, counterculture does not share the common culture, and they go against it. Counterculture is more like a deviant group in a particular community. Counterculture captured a new generation's willingness to move past cultural and sociopolitical boundaries.

Counterculture is a situation where a group of people goes against the mainstream culture of a particular community. Usually, the members of a certain community are supposed to adhere to socially accepted cultural and social behavioral patterns. However, there can be some members of the group who do not like to follow the accepted social ethics and values. Then, they form their own rules and behaviors. These group members can be identified as counter cultural. The main characteristic of counterculture is its own rules and ethics, which are different from the primary culture. Also, a counterculture in one community may not be a counterculture in another community. This difference is due to the culture and norms of different communities. Importantly, countercultures show a total opposition to the mainstream of the dominant culture and detested authority.

Members of the Counterculture group are not only at odds with the social mainstream values and norms. They also detest the authority structure of the group. These differences have the potential to create a cultural and political revolution. As criticism of the established social order became more widespread among the newly emergent youth class, new theories about culture and personal identity began to spread, and old, non-Western ideas-particularly regarding and embracing religion, social organization, and spiritual enlightenment.

New cultural forms perceived as opposed to the old emerged, including the pop music of the Beatles, which rapidly evolved to shape and reflect the youth culture's emphasis on change and experimentation. Underground newspapers sprang up in most cities and college towns, serving to define and communicate the range of phenomena that defined the counterculture: radical political opposition to "the establishment," colorful experimental (and often explicitly drug-influenced) approaches to art, music, and cinema, and uninhibited indulgence in sex and drugs as a symbol of freedom.

The most visible radical element of this counterculture was the hippies. Some formed communes to live outside of the established system. This aspect of the movement rejected active political engagement with the mainstream and following the dictate of Timothy Leary, an American psychologist, and writer who was a leading advocate for the use of LSD and other psychoactive drugs. He coined the phrase "tune in, turn on and drop out" as a popular counterculture slogan to change society by dropping out of it. [clxxi]

A subculture is also a group of people who share the values of mainstream culture, but at the same time, they have their own set of identities. Subcultures do not go against the dominant culture, but they have their way of distinguishing themselves from the primary culture. For example, there can be youth subculture, university subculture, music subculture, and others. These sub-cultural groups may have their style of dressing, vocabulary, and set of rules. These things may reflect the dominant culture as well. Thus, they do not oppose the mainstream culture. However, subcultures are not a threat to a community, and they define a group identity only.

• When considering counterculture and subculture, the main difference we see is that the counterculture goes against the mainstream culture, whereas, subculture shares the values of the main culture while adapting their own identities.

• Also, counterculture is looked down on in societies, but subcultures are mostly accepted.

• Counterculture in one community may not be identified as a counterculture in another community, but sub-cultural groups may be identified as the same everywhere.

• Moreover, we can say that counterculture is a type of subculture because the group identifies itself as different from the mainstream culture.

• Similarly, they have their own set of rules and identities which differentiate them from the dominant culture. [clxxii]

*"Their difference is that subculture refers to the small group present in a large cultural group; whereas, a counterculture is a group of people against the main culture." [clxxiii]

When the Vietnam War ended, the counterculture as a widespread movement fizzled out. The vast majority's groups of people found jobs and started families. They became enmeshed in every sector of mainstream society. [clxxiv] "The fashion dominance of the war era counterculture effectively ended with the rise of the disco and punk rock eras of the later 1970s. As members of the hippie movement grew older and moderated their views, the 1960s counterculture was absorbed by mainstream society. This left a lasting impact on morality, lifestyle, fashion, and a legacy that is still actively contested. The changes have great influence and are sometimes framed in the United States as "culture wars".

Some global cultures may preclude their classification as part of the counterculture. Because of their socioeconomics roots, history of oppression, suppression, racism, and discrimination the indigenous populations and African descent cultures have been deprived of the economic and political opportunities that other cultures have long been accustomed to. Perhaps, the evolvement of the unequal and broken world order to a more equal one will change this scenario in the future.

The Counterculture appeared in the early1960s in both America and the United Kingdom. It became influential throughout the Western world in Japan, Australia, New Zealand, and Eastern Europe until the early 1970s. In Europe, it mainly consisted of young people but there were also influences from others who became adults after World War II and after it. Jeff Nuttall in his book, Bomb Culture (1968) thinks that the alternate attitudes of counterculture in Europe grew out of the shadow and fear of the Hydrogen bomb. As the Cold War developed, there was a constant reminder of the

147

proliferation of nuclear weapons. These events lead to massive demonstrations attended by thousands of people who felt that the government had no attention to disarming or stopping the arms race. These activities further led to disillusionment and feeling of alienation. "New cultural forms emerged, including the pop music of the British band, the Beatles, and the concurrent rise of the hippie culture, which led to the rapid evolution of a youth subculture that emphasized change and experimentation. [clxxv]

The roots of the American Counterculture are slightly different. Although Americans had the same fear of nuclear annihilation, another factor was the working of the Civil Rights Movement to end racial segregation in the United States and the increasing involvement and escalation in the Vietnam War. Other issues include "sexual mores, women's rights, traditional modes of authority, experimentation with psychoactive drugs, and differing interpretations of the American dream." [clxxvi] "The modern Civil Rights Movement spawned the student movement, the gay liberation movement, new feminists, and others during the 1960s and 1970s." Later movements by other advocacy groups have grown out of the protest traditions and ambivalence of subordinate cultures' suffering, discontent, and optimism for change. [clxxvii] It had a profound effect on the rest of the world. The European and American countercultures influenced each other. [clxxviii]

The roots of the counterculture movement go back to the Transcendentalism of the 1840s. While the counterculture of the 1960s grew out of multiple sources and dynamics, other aspects had roots in the nineteenth century. Notably within the intellectual landscape of New England transcendentalism. The 1960s counterculture bears a striking similarity to the 1840s with a utopianism elitism. It is "associated with Henry David Thoreau, a leading philosopher, and poet who was a leading transcendentalist who asserted the existence of an ideal spiritual reality that transcends the empirical and individuality are associated with the term." He explored nature, the belief of imagination, and loved to be alone that went against society's norms at that time. [clxxix]

148

Cancel Culture

Cancel Culture is a very controversial and hotly contested form of "culture war" debate that exists among cultures. There are very strong opinions on both sides of the debate. It has caused a shift in the thinking of cultural behaviors by all cultural members. Cancel culture is an extreme form of peer pressure or social group shunning. A group comes down hard on individuals, "public figures, companies, and others when they feel that elements in their group norm have been violated, or something said or done was considered objectionable." [clxxx]

Cancel culture is "a modern internet phenomenon wherein a person is ejected from influence or fame by questionable actions. It is caused by a critical mass of people who are quick to judge and slow to question. It is commonly caused by an accusation, whether that accusation has merit or not. It is a direct result of the ignorance of people-caused communication technologies outpacing the growth in available knowledge of a person." [clxxxi] It is a modern form of ostracism that can be online, on social media, or in person[clxxxii] that attempts to combat racism, sexism, or other types of social abuses.

In the wake and aftermath of Mr. George Floyd's violent death in 2020 and within the framework of culture and race, there is a renewed global racial awakening is on the horizon. There has also been a shift in culture thinking among cultures concerning the contents in books, music, television shows, movies, and others.

There is an ongoing debate that cancels culture holds people accountable for their actions that were not possible in the past by using social media. For example, the inability to rely on the criminal justice system to punish people who committed a crime or expressed racial or sexist behaviors. There has been a perceived and growing understanding that levels of violence, inequities, and injustices have not been the same for all cultures. Those individuals have turned to cancel culture for retribution.

Dr. Anthony of Macquarie University asserts that by stopping, muting, canceling, or erasing someone or something, "we can somehow alleviate some of the pain, and redress some of the inequities, around certain things that have happened. It is becoming an important tool of redress for people who have been historically treated terribly. Now there is a wave of how we deal with this and start to think responsibly around racial inequities and imbalances of power historically, and how they impact the way we think and behave today. We get rid of is a complex question that should be dealt with in terms of its specifics. No one should be able to do whatever they want when it involves representing other people's cultures and treating others badly. What is happening in the average person is being called upon to become a media and cultural critic, to become literate in racial and sexual politics." Cancel cultures allows a subordinate member in a society a certain amount of power from a dominant or mainstream culture that they would not ordinarily be inclined to get. [clxxxiii]

As claimed by Dr. Julia Moore at the UNC Charlotte, this form of cancel culture is happening because Americans and the world are starting to have a long-overdue conversation about race and culture that have been centuries in the making. It has been very hopeful and encouraging to see allies from all cultures involved in this debate. There has been a cultural consciousness awakening among many members of society. Other cultures are now realizing how people of color have been suffering. It is important to understand that the 1960's Civil Rights movement advanced race relations only so far. That is because morality and ideology cannot be legislated. The country and even the world are divided in terms of racial, ethnic, cultural, and economic experiences. There has never been a real discussion of why racism existed, and the atrocities were done to people of color worldwide. Now decades later, the same issues have resurfaced because the root causes have never been addressed. A band-aid approach was generally taken by the world's societies, but the slaying of Mr. George Floyd ripped the band-aid off. [clxxxiv]

Then there is an opposite belief that cancels culture has become toxic and run amuck in recent years because of "canceling" things that are considered offensive or inappropriate. This notion of instantly "canceling" someone when a disagreement exists with a group consensus is a disproportionate reaction. Rather than changing anyone's mind, the other party is likely to withdraw completely from the issue, become more entrenched in their views, and be less willing to listen to the other views. It also impacts the person(s) that canceled this situation because they may cease to be challenged in another cultural setting and allowed to grow culturally. It can ruin people's careers, mental and emotional well-being that may be a careless mistake and prevent them from growing culturally and learning from their mistakes.

When someone cancels a company, the possibility exists that that reduces its mission and vision statement, innovations, products, services, employees, stockbrokers, and other components of the business, simply because of a sociopolitical stance of disagreement. Likewise, the canceling of public figures and celebrities may reduce their careers, reputation, popularity, and humanity by simply talking points of disagreement. [clxxxv]

In some cases, cancel culture tactics can cause a restriction on free speech and the first amendment right. Because of the culture and political climate, a self-censor may exist where some people are disinclined to tell their political views, personal opinions because of being worried about repercussions in their workplace or future career opportunities. [clxxxvi]

Although the term "cancel culture" is a relatively new phenomenon used in modern societies, its concepts in our culture have been used for millennia. All cultures have had half-Truths, blatant falsehoods, biased and ignorant opinions, misinformation, fallacious reasoning, and arguments throughout the history of humankind. Its past standards were determined by the cultures and societies during that time. The cultural dynamics changed or improved over time when their descendants understood certain aspects better than in earlier times. Societal ideologies changed during subsequent generations after being challenged internally or by other cultures. Likewise, the way we look at cultural conflicts or clashes today may be accepted or rejected in the future.

Perhaps the invention of the internet has had an impact on cancel culture. It has allowed people the ability to communicate at the speed of light which may have outpaced the ability of some people to thoroughly analyze an issue to slow their judgment. Some people are too quick to conclude from the limited, biased, and inaccurate information that they receive. Additionally, people make snap judgments which may notoriously be inaccurate at times.

Today we have the temerity of web surfers who utilize popular social media websites such as Facebook, Messenger, TikTok, WeChat, Instagram, QZone, Weibo, Twitter, Tumblr, Baidu Tieba, and LinkedIn. Other social media services by internet users include

YouTube, QQ, Quora, Telegram, WhatsApp, LINE, Snapchat, Pinterest, Viber, Reddit, Discord, VK, Microsoft Teams, and more. clxxxvii

This increase and diversity of social media sites may unconsciously cause some people to initiate a cancel culture message with their fingertips before fully engaging in the thinking process. On the other hand, many internet users send objective, rational, reasoning, and educated information too. The important thing to understand is that social media is a fundamental instrument in the lives of people, companies, and businesses around the world. While some believe that engaging in components of the cancel culture is a responsibility of free speech and can hold people accountable for their actions; individuals, groups, and businesses can be "canceled" and censored because of malicious and false information that was generated on media platforms.

In our political system of government, everyone has first amendment rights but there have always been consequences. Everyone has the right to protest, agree or disagree on issues and urge others to join their cause. But by whose standards and cultures are such protests justified, at what cost to our freedom, and at what cost are we as a culture willing to sacrifice? Perhaps as a society, our views of cancel culture have taken on a broad spectrum of culture wars that are broadly defined in nature as a catch-all phase for a variety of scenarios. But based on the present use of social and news media outlets under their parameters, clearly defined terms may be challenging.

It is only by understanding how far we have come as a society and what cultural force brought us here that we can truly address our shared historical ongoing issues involving race and culture clashes. It will require us to place ourselves in the continuum of the unaddressed and unresolved issues that came before us and their impacts on what will come after us. This enlightenment may involve untying the cultural contents of the past. As a society, the members must decide what cultural elements endure and what do not. This debate is complicated because we must deal with the fortitude of our present existence while reckoning with a diverse society that demands some semblance of parity and equity existence among all cultures.

Chapter V
Achieving A Multicultural Global Society

To achieve a multicultural global society and a better way of life for all the world's citizens will require an understanding and adjustments to the world's cultural values and lifestyles, a sharing of power and increased inclusiveness among all the world's cultures, and a major restructuring of all the world's social institutions and systems.

What is being seen globally is that the contributions of subordinate cultural groups have been stifled by the dominant cultures regardless of the level of development, political systems, region, or type of economy. The world cannot afford to lose out on the diverse mix of minds, backgrounds, experiences, skills, ideas, and perspectives of all the cultural and racial groups. Many of the greatest discoveries and inventions have come from members of all the world's cultures. As an interconnected global society, everyone should have an input in determining the planet's fate.

Multiculturalism is often misunderstood and often deliberately misinterpreted. It can be considered a compromise in a pluralistic society between segregation and assimilation. An essential feature of a multicultural society is cross-fertilization. The different cultures swap customs, practices, and concepts. Segregated societies create racism. Segregation, whether imposed or voluntary, is antithetical to multiculturalism. On the other hand, assimilation, when forced to adopt the host culture can lead to racism. [clxxxviii]

Cultural Competition of Global Natural Resources

There is no need for racial-cultural clashes between cultures. The complicated concept of cultural identity grows from the shared cultural experiences, histories, and internal cultural elements of each society is certainly a factor but may be not the underlying reason for culture clashes. Another fundamental reason for these culture clashes may be the actual or perceived lack of resources and the resultant competition of them, rather it is renewable or nonrenewable natural resources such as global land, food, stone, soil, water, oil and gas, energy, precious metals, as well as economic goods and services, monetary powers, and others.

There is a compelling argument that this cultural competition for "scarce" resources and superiority ideology stems from a basic human trait shared by some members of all cultures. On the other hand, it is debatable whether presently we are facing a "scarce" resource issue on planet Earth. That trait is usually greed. The dominant European/American culture is the latest perennial power showcasing it on a global level. Unfortunately, it added a deranged ideology of racial superiority and inferiority to the mix that has caused major problems to people of color during the past five centuries. These barbaric behaviors are the result of hostile environments. When some cultures come from global areas where the resources are scarce, they cannot perceive the abundance in the world. This choice to invade other cultures has left an indelible legacy and mark on the global society that will reverberate into the unforeseen future.

Since the beginning of humankind, a review of great societies and their cultures finds a common organizing principle in their political systems. There are a few people at the top of the hierarchy, a mass beneath them, and a smaller minority at the bottom. The people at the top exploit the people below them, primarily those in the majority, and divert their attention by telling them that all their problems stem from the group at the bottom. The people in the middle are given a false propaganda narrative that they are superior but held back and weakened by those at the bottom who are inferior to them.

In this carefully crafted established scenario, those at the top of the hierarchy control all the societal daily over-arching economic power, systems, institutions, social and cultural activities for their selfish benefit. The only caveat to this framework that differs from others in the past is that the folks at the bottom of the hierarchy are people of color. They have been relegated to the fringes, corners, or margins of the global society during the past five centuries because of their skin tones and physical profiles. Race has been corruptly used as a tool to further inflame passions, thus justifying their action.

The diluted misunderstanding of this propaganda narrative is now wrapped in mainstream culture mentalities.

This pattern holds regardless of the society, nation, or political system. Throughout the history of humankind, since the human species organized as tribes and now cultures, conflicts, clashes, and dissension have stemmed from a small group of greedy individuals trying to destroy or overcome another small group of greedy individuals. They controlled their own by opposing other tribes and taking from them whatever they wanted. They avoided accountability because the tribe(s) the conquered tribe members brought into their leadership wholeheartedly. In essence, the oppressed and distressed majority brought into their dilemma through willful ignorance or tactical stupidity as the enforcers of the status quo. The greedy individuals diverted the attention of others in society. They were being distressed too. It keeps the elites in power. Their attention is confused from doing something about their grip on power.

A change of perspective makes it clear that the enemy of peace and prosperity among the various world cultures is not an inevitable clash of racial cultures, but rather the inability or unwillingness of each culture to look at how and why it organizes itself as a society and nation. There are enough natural resources and global wealth in the world. There is no justification or clashes and conflicts among racial cultures. To survive and keep the few folks at the top of the hierarchy living wealthy lifestyles, they were determined that the group at the bottom, primarily people of color were neutralized.

All culture members and global leaders must hold themselves accountable for their tribal culture greed. It will take away from the needless energy from all kinds of political, economic, racial, and religious clashes. They must change the basic human character and structure of the various global cultural tribes. So perhaps cultures may not change fundamentally until the global society address one of the underlying reasons. It is greed. The fall of great empires such as Egypt, Rome, China, British, Spanish, Persian, Mongol, Caliphate, and Russian did not change at their demise so the common denominator may be greed. [clxxxix]

Perhaps Mahatma Gandhi was right when he said that "the world has enough for everyone's need, but not enough for everyone's greed". [cxc] The consumption of natural resources should be divided

155

more evenly among all global societies. We have too much consumption among the developed societies and too little among the undeveloped and impoverished societies. Ironically, in many instances, the utilized natural resources in developed societies come from the global lands of the undeveloped and impoverished societies. The natural resources are taken to the developed societies at the expense of members from the subordinate cultures. Undeveloped countries supply raw materials to developed countries. The refined goods that are produced in developed countries are then sold for real profit, further enriching the already rich. The mining industries in third-world countries exist only because of inventions and discoveries made mostly in the West. They have fueled a need for third-world resources from developed countries. Cultures need to take their share of the world's resources and allow other cultures to have theirs.

We presently have technological advancements on Earth to redistribute access to resources to the undeveloped and impoverished societies, but do we have the political will and the moral courage to do so? Global reformers need to usher in a renewed commitment by reining in the unfettered greed and make the system work for all the world's citizens rather than the select few. We need to address the "greed" issue and truly help undeveloped and impoverished societies develop. It will work toward balancing the unequal broken world order and reset the uncontrolled cultural trajectory of our global society.

Embrace Cultural and Racial Differences

Culture creates a person and plays an integral part in the development of a global society. Culture shapes us, but many events molded culture, and we must shape these just as much.

In most global societies, there is an inevitable bias that occurs when evaluating a different culture from our own because it is viewed from the context of one's culture. It is possible to minimize the effects of such biases but there is no such thing as pure objectivity. Understanding the nuisances and intricacies of a culture different than one's involves an effort to dismiss all preconceived assumptions. This awareness can prove to be tough. The erroneous perception about cultures is a major problem. We must work through the healing process by seeing the past accurately with the mindset that the current landscape can change. The current racial and cultural divide needs to be acknowledged so the painful realities and shed light on the repairs.

Multiculturalism allows people of different cultures to gain more exposure to other cultures. In turn, it can give them a greater appreciation and tolerance for those cultures and potentially to other cultures they have not been exposed to yet. As they begin to get exposed to facets of cultures other than their own, it broadens the worldview in general.

Multiculturalism also allows for a better exchange of ideas, information, and ways of doing things. By gaining input from people with other cultural viewpoints and perspectives, other cultures can gain benefits that would not have occurred within a more insular society, simply because their way of looking at things is different than their culture. [cxci]

As members of humanity, we need to make a concerted effort to see each other for who we are and not just a member of a particular racial group. This understanding of factors shapes our identities. They include cultural and religious beliefs, race, gender, age, physical and mental abilities, and socioeconomics circumstances. We must recognize the way our cultures have trained us, unconsciously to think about people of a different background, beliefs, or physical profiles.

We need to get to know one another better as individuals. We should decide on others based on what their experience with you personally is. Each person has a unique story. We should listen to one another with the intent to understand their viewpoints. We should listen carefully, with the humility to know we can learn from anyone without thinking ahead to see how we will respond. We should ask questions so we can dig deeper collectively, to learn more about one another. Also, we must speak to one another as people of equal value. Have your words flow from your heart, which is influenced by how we see and hear things. Our languages have the power to tear other people down or build them up. Our words can inspire fear or hope to pull people apart or bring them together. We should use our words carefully to reflect our humanity. More importantly, our actions must match our words.

A solution to achieving a multicultural society is to recognize the differences in our cultures by embracing them even with all the issues. We do not have to have the same cultures and think the same way about things. There is nothing wrong with coming from different backgrounds and having different perspectives. Our respect for cultural differences can summon them as a source of strength and make the society or nation a more vibrant place for all its people. There is a moral responsivity and obligation to come together as one member of humanity because there should be something higher than one's self-interest or a commitment to one's distinct culture.

It is vitally important that our newfound empathy for other cultures be put into action. This compassion is a powerful responsibility. It may be some cultural members uncomfortable. When we face adversity, we may be tempted by our humanity to each other. But we must be sure of our shared humanity as our shared commitment to the mutual good-will of all people.

It is also important to value one another as individuals and as a group. We must be civil to each other and show our humanity even and especially in disagreements. As distinct cultures, we have much more in common than we do in differences. We should look at each other as people of equal worth, value, and dignity. We need to be good citizens and good neighbors is everyone in the community. It is the hope that the next generation is successful in contributing to the common good of the world. We must model humanity now more than ever. If we see one another, hear one another, and speak with one another with humanity, we can make this a better multicultural global society. ^{cxcii}

Enlightened members of the dominant culture can play a role in the effort of building cultural bridges by ensuring everyone is an essential part of society. They must be aware that their privileges come with a responsibility to be cognizant of experiences of other cultures that differ from theirs without questioning their legitimacy. They should understand that legitimate frustration and even anger exist from real injustices of other cultural members being treated differently than privileged members. Realizing that sometimes discrimination may be real, and tangible that may require the rights of subordinate members to defend themselves. This awareness will call for a certain amount of patience, compassion, and understanding, irrespective of their individual experiences and identities. Below are ways for the privileged and non-privileged culture members to become allies in bridging cultural clashes:

- They should work towards becoming more conscious of their privileges and try to recognize areas that would prohibit their enlightenment. Efforts should be made to be supportive by decentering themselves to learn, listen, and witness. Speak up with compassion whenever appropriate by seeking engagement rather than escalation so that it can be a learning moment.

- As dominant group members, they should be conscious of their status in society that allows their voices to be given priority over the lived experiences and knowledge of subordinate members.

- They must recognize that resources and power are not equally distributed in society. They should pay careful attention to the power imbalance and be willing to share power with other cultural groups. We must see how inequality affects all of us and acknowledge how society privileges some members and oppresses other members, to varying degrees.

- They should offer constructive criticism to non-enlightened members when they encounter members with intentional, implicit, and subconscious biases. They should reframe from personal attacks because some members may be conditioned into this behavior from their culture and environment and not consciously or actively trying to be racists.

- Generally, dominant group members decide whose concerns are valid in society. The more privileged an individual is, the more conscious they should be to not delegitimize the valid concerns of other cultural members.

- Make a good faith effort to build dialogue with people who think differently than you by looking at the perspectives from their cultural lenses as a learning experience. This awareness should not be viewed as a betrayal of their group's cultural identity. There are no cultural winners in society. An emerging strong, mature, stable multicultural society is the goal. The dialogue requires the consent of all participants, be engaging, and should not be communicated from the perspective of one side.

- There is a natural inclination to get defensive when confronted by a racial or cultural divide. Although being transparent is difficult, we must all be willing to move beyond the status quo by making a sincere effort to work through issues.

- Leave some room for self-reflection and growth without fear of failure or blunder. See blunders as an opportunity to learn and grow and not a flaw of character.

Some global societies will have some group members with interracial identities who diffused into their culture that will have additional internal and social identification cultural clashes. They will encounter an identity culture crisis. It will clash not only with other cultural group members but also among themselves. Below are ways to navigate around these types of cultural clashes:
- Embrace the cultures of other groups and their traditions. Avoid thinking that their culture is a threat to your own by ignoring theirs and pretending that they do not matter. You can have both. If you explore their culture, you will likely find there are traditions, celebrations, and practices in other cultures that you want to incorporate into your life.

- Take the time and effort to learn about other cultures. It can be your circle of friends, co-workers in the workplace, and others from all walks of life. Learn about their cultural backgrounds, beliefs, attitudes, habits, and practices. You may be surprised by some similarities between yours and theirs.

- Understand that other groups have culturally informed beliefs, behaviors, and traditions that are essential to how they define themselves. Do not make other culture members choose between your culture or theirs. They should not have to compromise who they are, and neither do you.

- Try to look for common ground between your culture and the cultures of others. Try to understand that their cultural background has shaped their expectations, beliefs, and behaviors. Also, be oblivious that some aspects of their cultures may not be open to compromise.
- Do not think that your culture is the objective right way to do things or diminish the cultures of others. It is unfair to expect others to disown the beliefs. They have held since birth or immediately pick up elements of your culture. Be patient and open to doing things differently.

- Seek to create new, blended traditions and cultures that celebrate and respect both cultures. The key is continuous, open communication and negotiation.

We must expand our idea of culture beyond ethnicity and race that has been the preferred method for the past few centuries. Even within one's own culture, a cultural divide exists even among those with similar backgrounds. Because of technological advancements, we have gone from an endless stream of choices with different perspectives and assumptions. This information forms our reality. Cultures are increasingly living in alternative realities even within the same culture and society.

Historically, cultures have generally placed their group's interests ahead of other cultures. Ethnicity, an element of culture and a learned behavior; whereas, a fictional race is unalterable because a person is born that way. Ethnocentrism, however, is based on culture and impacts the way we view other cultures. The alternative is to lose all cultural diversity and become cultural clones worldwide. It is not healthy to see problems and issues with the same cultural perspectives and lenses. It limits and stifles our creativity and imagination in solving our collective issues and place the entire planet in peril. One of the world's greatest strengths has been a diverse multi-ethnic global population. This reality provides a toolbox of ideas from all cultures needed to solve our global problems and issues.

161

Ideally, if world's culture members start seeing themselves as part of the larger society involving all the cultures. The impact of the world social constrict is deep and far-reaching. It needs to be acknowledged, and its implications confronted heads on to heal the wounds. It has gone on much too long in this global society. There are a demographic group of cultural members who are shielded and blind to their privileges and unearned benefits. As the racial and cultural differences continue, the enlightened, open-minded culture members must also use their privileges to reach out to those blind to it and enlighten them. Together, it will take a team effort.

There is a difference between ignorance and evilness of culture and race. The impacts on others can be just as damaging. Ignorance can be educated, but evil is a much more difficult problem as its scope is far-reaching. Fortunately, in our global society, ignorance is more prevalent than blatant evilness. There is reason to be encouraged by the process of education and understanding that could alleviate some of the more dangerous and complex aspects of race and culture. They have unfortunately embodied in the very fibers of our global society.

As a global society, we must embrace our shared cultural history. There should be a renewed commitment to other cultures. There have always been a dynamic interaction and interdependence between cultures. We must find the strength to explore these more complicated aspects of our shared existence to become the key to harnessing our lack of inclusiveness. In turn, this may help us better cope with the fear of the unknown, greed, paranoia, willful ignorance or tactical stupidity, suspiciousness, and the lingering cognitive science of identity, status, and risk that unites the discussion of our current crisis.

Our past and existing global cultural relationships have not fulfilled the needs of all cultures. Different cultures have been too caught up in their own cultures and do not fully understand what is missing from a shared cultural relationship. We can find our way out of this cultural wilderness by accepting the unique perspectives and ideas of what other cultures bring to our global society.

Cultures need to engage in their unbridled self-discovery to find their way out of this cultural wilderness. This disclosure can be done by intentionally searching for the yet unexplored side of their culture. The cultures' urgency of self-discovery will become less intense after their members see the merits in other cultures. The knowledge of cultures will broaden their horizons and propel them to respect certain cultural features lessening their overconsumption with cultures. This awareness may heighten the response to their creative energy flow to start them on the path to a new multicultural identity.

Cultures need to acknowledge their past cultural behaviors and lack of inclusiveness. They must embrace multiculturalism in the future by being fiercely committed to new qualities of positive cultural traits. The culture's urgency of self-discovery will become less intense after the culture members see the merits of other cultures. This knowledge of other cultures will broaden their horizons and propel them to respect certain cultural features and lessen their consumption with their own culture. There is a renewed hope that the cultural sharing of experiences will usher in a new era of a multicultural future. We are at an incredible moment of cultural connection and transformational. Sharing it with other cultures will remind us that this culture expansion is a gift to each other.

Colonial Borders in Africa

The continent of Africa does not belong to other world cultures except the African people who live there and its diaspora. Africa has experienced some of the worst atrocities in humankind's history. If Africa is going to be successful in the long run, a total reorganization of the continent needs to be considered. During the past couple of millenniums, Africa has been the subject of the Arab-Muslim slave trade from the sixth to twentieth centuries, the Transatlantic Slave Trade from the fourteenth to nineteenth centuries, continent-wide Colonialism in the nineteenth and twentieth centuries, King Leopold Congo genocide in the nineteenth and twentieth centuries, and Apartheid in the twentieth century among thousands of other inexcusably heinous atrocities.

Africa may need to carefully analyze the 1884-85 Berlin Conference European's scrabble of Africa map to see if it fits the need of its citizens moving forward. The continent needs an organizational structure that will serve the best interest of Africa and its diaspora. When the European powers colonized Africa, they drew up political boundaries to control the global lands. They were not interested in how the boundary lines impacted the African people. Groups of people who did not get along with each other was placed in the same political boundaries. These artificial caused conflict and tribal wars. The Europeans drew up these boundaries based on what would help them and not on what was best for the people of Africa.

The European model that developed the continent of Africa is highly questionable decades after the countries received their symbolic independence. There appears to be a definite principle in the progress of any distinct group of people who want to start a journey of progression. It was exemplified by the Roman, British, and American empires. Those past and present great societies changed the ancient Egyptian model for development. Many generations later, many descendants of the original people do not know who led and controlled their global land before other dominant predatory cultures took over. The people of Africa must make their case.

The African leaders and their people alone need to be responsible for the reorganization of their continent without foreign interference. Should the Africans remove the artificial borders created by the West and return to Africa's natural borderlines? Or should Africa reorganize the existing borderlines, working on developing and create a new Africa? The author does not propose any specific reorganization model. The people of Africa must make that decision. If Africa ever comes up with a new political system, it should promote a unified Africa model. Before the European invasion and conquest, the sovereignty of Africa was based on its languages, cultures, and ethnicities. A new model should promote African unity void of any known conflicts or dissension among its populace.

There are numerous global societies in world history whereby societies' demographics changed, and multi-cultures caused changes in their organizational structures. "In the last two decades, the Sunni Arabs were suddenly ruled by Shiites rather than ruling over them, and of the Soviet Union, where a Russian-Slavic majority feared becoming a minority in the 1970s." [cxciii]

Historically, when any African nation won its independence after World War II and tried to free itself from Neocolonialism, it is met with civil unrest, or a coup d'état sponsored by the former Colonial master to put their puppet in power. This history is notoriously evident in former French colonies. African unity comes into play.

Any decision about the reorganization of Africa must be done collectively. That means the African Union or whoever initiated it must be done in unison that reflects all fifty-four countries reorganizing from the original model of the thirteen European countries and the United States. The backing of the United Nations, a major global governance institution, can also strengthen their case.

Cultural Identities and Labeling

Global societies and cultures need to eliminate the color code designation (Black, White, Red, Yellow) or terms to identify its citizens by race, which has created a racial caste system. Race has no biological justification as a classification of the human species. Before the advent of the Transatlantic Slave Trade and worldwide Colonialism, people identified by their nationalities or ethnicities. Some groups of people and a few countries have already moved away from the color designation.

The removal of these labels and identifications can go a long way toward removing the reductive representation of these groups and help restore their humanity, dignity, and respect. A few nations that identify its citizen by terms that denote their identification by skin tones and physical profile need to evaluate this requirement in their systems and institutions.

This practice of identifying citizens based on skin tone is divisive and continues the historical legacy of racism that occurred in those societies. Some countries also provide some latitude with the citizens selecting their preferred identification because some have interracial backgrounds. Some countries in the Americas and particularly the United States have more obsessions with racial and ethnic identities. Racial identities are more predominant in European countries in non-European parts of the world where people are more culturally centric than in continental European, African, and Asian countries. "At this cultural moment in the United States, we still live in a socialized social and cultural hierarchy, and our language continues to reflect our ongoing attempts to grapple with that realty."[cxciv]

To contrast using race and color code designations, biologists and anthropologists used "populations and sampling", This method is biologically meaningful in identifying people and maps out specific traits. Some do not correlate with any ideas of race.

Many more multicultural nations used the same identifiers such as nationality and ethnicities that existed before the Transatlantic Slave Trade. Ideally, in multicultural societies, the identification of groups was tied to something other than the pigmentation of their skins. After all, societal cultures arise from the interaction of people in their surroundings. It may prove valuable in building cultural bridges by ensuring everyone is an essential part of society.

Unfortunately, on the other hand, the problem may not be the way people are identified but their perception by some cultures in a society that harbors perceptions and assumptions. It may take a complete societal overhaul for race relations to improve. But it may be a good start in the long journey toward racial conciliation.

Cultural Linguistic Reawakening

The actual number of languages in the world is unknown. But based on the known reliable sources, there appear to be around seven thousand. It is estimated that "over forty percent are at risk of fading away from regular use. Pressures for certain people to stop using their native tongues have persisted for centuries. And in some cases, they threaten to reduce the number of native speakers down to zero.

As the number of active speakers of a given tongue dwindles, so can understanding about what that language's words and phrases refer to. The potential loss of these languages, and all they represent, has motivated many to step up their preservation efforts.

Though people often talk about "revitalizing" a language, forms of speech are not animate objects: They cannot slide away on their own. People stop speaking and using languages for a reason, and in some cases, the influence is a blunt force when colonizers or oppressors actively work to stifle a language.

Genocide, for example, eliminates or reduces the number of speakers of a language tied to the targeted people. During forced assimilation, as well, oppressors often make people stop speaking their native languages. In North America, Europeans explicitly carried out both these kinds of campaigns. White settlers attacked and killed millions of Indigenous peoples while forcing them off their lands, and during the 19th and 20th centuries, they made Native Americans attend boarding schools where students could only speak English.

Some of those United States schools operated that way until about 50 years ago. Today, the ongoing mistreatment of Indigenous communities in the United States takes a toll on Native American languages. With higher rates of chronic health conditions and largely insufficient access to health care, Native communities have been hit particularly hard by the pandemic. The Cherokee Nation, one of many tribes working on boosting their language use. It has lost over 30 first-language speakers to COVID-19.

Global communities have felt pressures like these for centuries, which is why so many languages are going dormant — and why there are hundreds of active efforts to revive them. A few years ago, a survey of 245 language revitalization programs around the globe to learn about how each one operated.

Of all the activities these programs offered, about a third were focused on teaching the language in environments like immersion schools or designated classes. Other initiatives supported different kinds of language development or continuity, like putting a language on TV or online to increase the odds that someone interacts with it more regularly. And programs that collect and store audio or grammatical rules can provide new ways to learn outside conversations with a fluent speaker.

Even short-term efforts can inspire more language use with the help sponsor free workshops for kids in a community in southern Mexico that speaks Isthmus Zapotec, a language native to that region. The team knew that the monthly programs would not produce fluent speakers, but the lessons still encouraged kids to ask family members about what they learned, building up their vocabulary as they did so.

Though boosting the number of speakers might be one revitalization goal, there are other metrics for success. In the survey sent out, the team asked participants who, if anyone, speaks the language that the program's revival effort focused on. Just over 30 percent of respondents said adults and children participated to some degree. Some intervention efforts were strictly preventative and meant to keep most of the community speaking the language in the future.

Though communities can help reverse a language's decline, the original pressures that made the language less common in the first place may still exist. Healthcare settings, for example, often make it difficult for people to use their language — which can then negatively impact their treatment. In Australia, poor communications between medical staff and Aboriginal patients have led to procedures without informed consent and delayed care.

Schools often dismiss or discourage the use of non-dominant languages, too. Up through the 1980s, Brazil banned classes taught in anything besides Portuguese. In the United States, Arizona requires that students learning English use the new language, despite research showing that United States students in bilingual education programs do better on tests examining their English proficiencies than students in English-only classes.

But that does not mean that all is lost: Efforts to welcome linguistic diversity and help speakers grow or maintain their community does work. The Maori language indigenous to New Zealand, for example, has seen the number of speakers skyrocket in recent decades. [cxcv]

As a result of the European Colonization of the Continent of Africa, the official languages of the former European powers remain the official languages in major societal sectors such as business, media, and academics. Although numerous native African languages are used in many nations, such as Hausa, Swahili, Manding, and others, some linguists predict that many will become extinct in future decades.

Societal Cultural Symbols

Historically, very few issues illicit strong emotions and controversy than the display of Confederate and Colonial-era monuments, statues, and other artifacts in public places in most global societies. The world societies are deeply divided between ideological camps with increasingly elusive common ground. Some people in societies place monuments or statues to reflect and honor their values. It is a symbolic expression of shared cultural values. They do not teach history but are a statement of the values for a community. If a culture can impose the meaning and interpretation of the symbols on other cultures, it becomes a form of political power when they can control the debate.

It became evident that some of these symbols were not teaching history but became political statements. In many cases, they were statements reflecting the present political environment, not the past, and a testament to the future. For example, most of the Confederate statues in the United States were erected between the 1890s and the 1950s. They started about thirty years after the Civil War and match up exactly with the era of Jim Crow segregation. [cxcvi] Understanding the values and the reasons why they were constructed reflect what the community that maintains them. As the demographics of the societies change over time, the symbols may no longer reflect the values of the population. [cxcvii] These symbols mean different things to different people at different times in history. Individuals cannot change the meaning of symbols that have been defined by history.

There are thousands of ancient statues. The Egyptians but also in Sudan, Greece, Rome, and the Persian empires. Many suffered damages with broken noses throughout Europe, Africa, and Asia. There are many theories for the defacement[cxcviii] of statues. They include disabling them as an opposing force to dilute or deactivate their life force. The precise motives for the vandals remain unknown. [cxcix] "Thus, ruining the nose, the statue would lose its ability to 'breath.' Effectively killing the statue's power was a way for grave robbers to ensure the spirits did not come for them." There is an opposite theory that the defacement was done to implant falsehoods that the events of Egypt were not of native Nubian African royalty but a Mediterranean culture of Greek origin. But in most cases, the mutilation was driven by political and religious motivations. [cc]

Many societies had fractions within them that disagreed with the public display of these symbols. Several countries in the Americas, Africa, Europe, and other societies had a cultural reckoning in many communities with Confederate and the worldwide Colonial-era statues and monuments. After the United States won its independence, the statue of George III was pulled down. The country freed itself from tyrannical rule by pulling down the statue of the King as a symbolic gesture to make the historic change from the rule of the monarchy to the rule of democracy. [cci]

In May 2020, in the wake of the slaying of Mr. George Floyd initiated major protests, rallies, and marches worldwide against systemic racism and racial injustices. Great Britain, for example, took down or is planning to take down statues of notable White supremacies and slave owners such as Edward Colston, Robert Milligan, Robert Baden-Powell, Cecil Rhodes, Robert Clive, John

Mitchel, Oliver Cromwell, Henry Dundas, Sir Thomas Picton, and Georg Granville.

Other examples include the Italian fascists under Mussolini ridden their society of offensive statutes of former oppressive regimes. Likewise, Germany took down Nazi statues after World War II, so did the Soviet Union with Joseph Stalin's statues and the Chinese under Mao. Afghanistan and the United States took down statues of Saddam Hussein and the Taliban. Iraq, Syrian, and Turkey had similar problems with ISIS in their societies. ISIS destroyed many of its historical and religious monuments, statues, and artifacts in the Middle East.

Societies that insist on keeping their statues and monuments that may offend a segment of their population also tell the public about those communities and reflect their shared values. A segment of the societal population believes that the symbols should not be maintained on public land at public expense and should be moved to privately owned venues such as museums, private property, and graveyard sites.

Others believe the symbols should not be removed because they are part of history. They do not change what happened in the past. This debate asserts that the removal of the symbols equates to erasing history. They believe a plaque be attached to the symbol explaining its historical nature. Yet others believe the symbols should be removed because of moral and psychological reasons of what they represent and promote and the conscious and subconscious intimidation who endured past suffering.

Many other global societies have addressed the statues and monuments issue in different ways. For example, in Germany, its government worked to systematically rid of Nazi-era memorials and architectures. Germany tried to ban and eliminate all the Nazi symbols. The Nazi's seat of power was converted into educational spaces; the SS and Reich Security Service into a museum; the High Command of the Armed Forces into the German Resistance Center; and Berlin's Olympic Stadium reopened as a celebration of Jewish athletes.

In Spain, the streets of former Dictator, Francisco Franco, have been renamed. In Japan, the nation still uses the Rising Sun flag, a controversial symbol of the country's imperial history, and offerings are to the Yasukuni Shrine that honors Japan's war dead, which China and South Korea see as glorying Japan's wartime crimes. [ccii]

In Taiwan, many statues of Chiang Kai-shek were erected all over the country. The former president of the Republic of China who fled to Taiwan in 1949 after losing to the Communist army. But after Taiwan transitioned to democracy, many citizens wanted the statues taken down. About two hundred were taken to a park in the north part of the island, however, thousands more remain elsewhere on the island met resistance.

In Ukraine, every one of the 1,320 statues of Lenin has been destroyed. Another 1,069 Soviet-era monuments have been destroyed as part of the ban in May 2015 signed into law by President Poroshenko. In South Africa, the statue of British Colonialist Cecil Rhodes, who slaughtered Africans by the thousands was taken down in 2015 after a student protest at the University of Cape Town. [cciii] In Bucharest, Romania, at least six statues of Marshal Ion Antonescu, who conspired with Hitler, helping him to kill at least 250,000 Jews during World War II, have been removed. [cciv]

On the other hand, the United States made a different choice with the Confederacy. In some communities, symbols are slowly being destroyed, replaced, or removed from public places around the country. But a large segment of the population wants the cultural symbols to remain in place. The issue continues to be a hotly contested issue throughout society.

Moreover, cultural symbols preserving historical sites and retaining the memories of aggrieved cultures from the Confederate and Colonial-eras have met preservation challenges. Historically, preservations centered around the experiences and perspectives of dominant culture members. Entries of people of color in the register of Historic places represent a small percentage. Increasing the historical societies and demographics of people involved in the planning and preservations of sites and structures is another challenge to overcome. In addition, resources and reinvestment in the communities will be a further challenge to preserve and renovate those sites and landmarks to their former glory. [ccv]

Societal should rethink cultural symbols as permanent artifacts. Perhaps, they should be living objects with historical and symbolic meaning, upheld by powerful forces and structures that need to be challenged by future generations. The symbols were created for symbolic and political reasons. If removed, they would be for the same reasons. As global communities become more diverse and open, their symbols need to reflect that reality. It is a step by communities in showing who they are and what we value. This debate further points out the need for greater clarity in the history teaching curriculums in societies.

Concluding Thoughts

During the past five centuries, the dominant American/European cultures have decided the world's mainstream cultures through conquests, colonization, and enslavement of people of color and their indigenous lands. It has led to the inevitability of an unharnessed collision course between the world's cultures and subcultures in which race has, unfortunately, became a central element in our global society. These events allowed the dominant cultures, through their present control of most of the world's systems and institutions and the clever use of propaganda to help prop its culture to be valued as the best and worth more than other cultures. One problem is everything is filtered through the cultural pattern's lens of the dominant societies that nullify other cultures as sidebars. Journalists representing different perspectives and backgrounds in mainstream media as regular participants of societies are needed.

Reality is the state of things as they exist. This phenomenon is opposed to an idealistic or notional idea of them. Unfortunately, the reality is determined by what most people believe. What most people feel is determined but what mainstream media promote. It is vitally important that the media portrayal of subordinate cultural members in society improves. Presently, a very negative portrayal of subordinate cultures involves excessive coverage on account of criminal activities and sociocultural conditions that create very negative images in marginalized and disenfranchised communities. It also influences the negative treatment of subordinate cultures in the criminal justice system and society at large. With limited amounts of subordinate members portrayed in the media, it might be the only exposure other culture members see for an entire cultural group. [ccvi] In recent decades, the media has become nationalized along racial and cultural stratifications in many societies. These various sources of information coupled with a multitude of different media outlets and venues delivering partisan identity news. The new sources of news have contributed to the premise that cultures do not have anything in common. Venues need to be created where cultural members can hear each other's side of the story.

Mainstream media create stereotypical lenses with which to view each other from media coverage, television programs, and public service announcement that spotlight the achievement of all cultural members will have a positive effect on the communities. Likewise, the regional, national, and international media need to improve their coverages concerning culture and race. It seems easy to pull on the heartstrings of viewers involving members of the mainstream culture. But faces of subordinate culture members are often associated with negative headlines. We have conditioned the viewers and news to a practiced apathy. Subordinate cultures should be encouraged to promote a positive image of their members by documenting and disseminating information on its success and contributions into the development of the overall society. Media plays into cultural and race relations and can affect the perception of a subordinate culture group. This diverse cultural spectrum is a website, and all cultural members are connected.

Complacency has led to the stagnation and demise of many past great societies. All cultures must keep reinventing themselves each generation with a cultural diffusion of new energy, technological advances, values, ideas, and realizations based on strategic plans. People's beliefs, values, and ideas are constantly changing. The culture and subcultures within a society must continue to heed the services and values of its populace. History has shown that when these cultural elements become coercive and repressive and do not uplift and elevate the members, the extinction of that society is a real possibility. Society must continue to strive to complete its essential mission as an instrument in the service of all cultural members.

There are now other major cultures from the East that are also impacting world societies. China and India are growing at an incredible pace but still have low income per capita. China is globalization's present success story with the world's biggest emerging market. These countries giving attention to education, particularly in highly tech fields make it conductive to expand automation and artificial intelligence. Too, China has a mostly homogeneous population and culture and lacks any viable leadership for the Chinese Communist Party that reinforces its stability. [ccvii]

Cultural racism will probably never completely disappear in the world. It has been so intensely a part of our global culture, particularly since the fifteen-century. However, we can make it disappear in a large portion of our global population. Those outliers will be label as outcasts who operate on the fringes of societies where they belong. The masses of people will shun them. We must teach our children and adults the concepts of culture and race are, how they developed over the past five hundred years, and what they mean. Cultures must proactively engage and collaborate with other global cultures to identify ways to tackle this issue collectively in curbing unacceptable culture clashes and committed to keeping cultures safe from abuse.

It will require the dominant mainstream cultures to develop a more profound understanding of the basic cultural and philosophical assumptions intrinsic to other societies. They need to develop an awareness of how people in those societies see their interests. It will require an effort to identify elements of commonality between all global cultures. For the relevant future, there will be no universal culture, but instead a world of different cultures, each of which will have to learn to coexist with the others. We need to have the political and social will to change our global society. We must accept our history without distortions and its contradictions. Then, precisely as we imagined our way into this modern society, we need to reimagine our way out of it. It will allow us to rebuild and redevelop a better global society, and reality for all world's cultures.

Summation

As a global society, we need to continue building on enlightening cultural bases for counteracting and stabilizing the mainstream cultures. This framework can transform our existing mainstream cultures and lead to the centering of the world's cultures with informed opinions, multiple perspectives, and experiences that will be in balance and harmony with each other. We must decide if we will continue with the constant tension and clashes that exist between the dominant culture and other subordinate racial cultures. Will the pendulum finally swing to a balanced sphere and a hint of a return to equilibrium so that the world cultures will stabilize in the long run? The ideas promised by many global political systems must be realized with the realities for all their cultural members. We do not have to accept the existing cultural clashes between racial groups as inherent to our human nature. So far, the world's cultural realities have been a disappointment and fallen short of their noble ideals.

The destruction, diminishment, and devaluation of subordinate cultures have been the primary mission of some dominant cultures since the beginning of humankind. It is evidence in wealth accumulation, health outcomes, life expectancy, quality of life, judicial experiences, educational opportunities, political power, and every measurable index or matrix. In general, all subordinate cultures presently have is the false hope for a better tomorrow by denying them the right to self-rule, universal rights, safety, security, self-determination, peace, and equality under the rule of law. This cultural and racial arrogance was inspired by false teaching and put forth in a global social construction designed to keep them weak, dependent, divided, and confused.

The intentional process by the elitists and dominant culture of trying to erase the historical memories of the ancient traditional African culture links and the subsequent miseducation of their descendants have been problematic for all cultures. Propaganda and mass education have misled many people and prompted them to not look at historical issues critically and analytically. Some people have been radicalized and indoctrinated from birth through biased cultural lenses which control the false narrative that their culture prefers. Some societies feel compel to create and promote that false narrative that worships a dominant culture concept that promotes superiority to other cultures. These cultures base their Truths on their power and control. Their goal is to devise strategies to prevent information that conflicts with the information of their command. The easiest way to control culture is to manipulate their perspective on reality with a view of history that benefits the dominant culture. Therefore, their perception of the past and the present is molded by forces designed to eliminate opposing viewpoints.

The only thing that will bring back a sense of harmony, balance and, reciprocity between cultural groups is to uncover the hidden undisputed Truth that will transform the world and ignite the consciousness to make all of us aware of our shared historical pasts and roots. It will allow all culture members to have a feeling of connection with other cultures besides the one they are presently affiliated with. The new self-discovery of historical global cultural facts that were previously incorrectly taught to some cultures will allow the centering of culture members and cultivate relationships with other culture members who are doing the same in their pursuit and manifestation of restored historical memories. Cultures need to be challenged on their version of the Truth produced by their beliefs, values, behaviors, perspectives, viewpoints, talking points, paradoxes, customs, norms, practices, habits, and views. Cultures should at least debate to learn from other cultures. There will always be room to agree to disagree if the framework of the debate is rooted in facts or reality by a shared universal cultural perception in different global societies. Through the rediscovered Truth, cultures can rekindle the consciousness of their members and control the collective cultural perception that creates reality. Cultures who are resistant, to tell the Truth about themselves will circle their delusions until there is nothing left to harness them to reality.

The unvarnished Truth about history must be told, and its reality must not be cherry-picked and parceled by cultures to achieve a certain objective. We must disseminate the knowledge and rationalize it through erudition. One culture's Truth may be another culture's falsehoods or distortions. There are levels of bias informed by different cultures who have different agendas of the Truth. Studying a more complete history with multiple perspectives and discussions of lasting implications has practical value for all cultures that make up the fabric of our global society. The distortion and restriction of how history is taught have real and tangible effects that may be dependent upon culture's opinions, paradoxes, and perspectives. This recovered consciousness of internal conflict and turmoil can produce much anxiety for cultures. Although some past historical cultural events may be painful for their descendants to acknowledge, people should not hide from past legacies and try to block the memories. These delayed Truths help cultures to fully reckon with the past or to comprehensively account for the impacts and traumas to other cultures.

Despite different cultural perspectives and paradoxes, the Truth can only become a reality when it is fully known by all cultures and shared as real history. It will be a colossal failure of epic proportions for cultures to continue to not learn true world history. Learning promotes change so that the descendants of cultures do not repeat the mistakes of their ancestors no matter how unpleasant history may be. The cherry-picking of history only allows one culture's point of view. Likewise, you cannot combine some aspects of lies and the Truth in the same historical context and present it as credible history. Each facet of history stands on its own and should be sorted out and based on its merit and not the totality of the verifiable event. Future generations deserve to be taught authentic, connective histories so cultures can deal with cultural and racial issues better than past generations. All culture members should be aware of its historical issues, otherwise, it will not be a functional cohesive societal unit. It is our collective history. When the multiple perspectives of all cultures are included, the wholeness of the reality is closer to reaching the Truth. When the Truth is debated and analyzed from all cultural perspectives, only then we can finally reach a stage of enlightenment.

This new level of self-discovery by cultures will allow them to be conscious of who they are and what they can become. It will increase their awareness and understanding of other cultures around the world. Cultures will have the ability to unlearn what they have been conditioned to learn and uproot their seeds of suspiciousness, greed, fear of the unknown, and paranoia that were planted in their cultural mentalities over generations. It will allow cultures the ability to perceive other cultures from the perception of their best cultural traits as valued members of humanity. This self-discovery will give cultures the moral courage and the political will to question what they have been taught and to question their overall cultural behavior. It will equip cultures with the humility to admit what they do not know about other cultures and seek more knowledge about them. It will furnish cultures with patience when they do not understand other culture's outlook on life because there are many ways to do things. It will supply all cultures with the ability to find their purpose and even at times to mind their business because accepting cultural differences and adapting to change apply to all. It will foster a culture change to enable a multicultural future. Transitioning to a multicultural future requires cultures that embrace and complement beneficial humanistic social constructions in a reimagined global societal reality.

It is important to understand how the Truth has survived despite the efforts of the dominant culture to deny global cultural links to dominant and subordinate culture members. Despite centuries of slavery, worldwide Colonialism, and numerous inexcusably heinous atrocities, the absolute Truth of our past is eternal and has survived because it is something that cannot be destroyed. The Truth can only be destroyed if the descendants abandon it or neglect it. There is undeniable and compelling evidence by historians, anthropologists, and archeologists who are periodically discovering cultural artifacts and sacred objects, ancient texts, historical documents, ancient civilizations, astronomical sites, walls, tombs, monuments, gravesites and burial grounds, food sources, and other excavations at archaeological sites in ancient times, slavery era, colonialism, and the present imperialism era. [ccviii] These scientific proofs unmasked timeless misconceptions about our ancestral culture past. These discoveries of historical facts should allow intellectual honesty among all culture members to acknowledge the positive and negative character traits of their cultural behavior. As a result of these global discoveries, everything is now out in the open. There is nothing left to hide.

It is very difficult to hide an open secret because the Truth is constant and does not change. The Truth can be hidden, buried, suppressed, distorted, concealed, covered up, and ignored, but never silenced and erased. The Truth only lasts if we protect, reveal, and spread it. All cultures must seek and adopt the Truth and become creators of our individual and collective cultural destiny. An understanding of the absolute Truth of our past can transform our present cultural behavior and create or broaden our shared culture vision and future. It will allow cultures to distance themselves from the hidden Truth to achieve a greater degree of analytical profundity, accuracy, and dispassionate understanding of other cultures. Cultures can revise their cultural beliefs to reduce discordance when their attitudes, behavior, or actions clash with one another. Only cultures who do not wish to seek the hidden Truth can be deceived and easily exposed. The Truth is difficult for some cultures to acknowledge but it is necessary to promote the healing process.

In a self-discovery effort, cultures must continue to look inward at themselves through periodic introspections. They must carefully do a critical analytical assessment of their cultural elements, and memes in the ongoing search for the Truth. This appraisal will allow them to own their past and present mistakes, celebrate their achievements, learn from them, and transform their cultural behavior. In universal time, the Truth will be revealed, and the displaced and culturally deprived descendants will fully reclaim their cultural links and rightful place in our global society. Time is the natural universal revelation of the hidden Truth, which caters to cultures of all epochs. The world's perception of reality is sometimes dictated by its delusion. If some cultures are trying to avoid reality, how can they face it? Some problems cannot have a solvable solution because their resolution depends upon the mere acceptance of the absolute Truth. In the final analysis, the Truth can only be destroyed and dismantled by culture members who do not revive it and fail to pass it to their descendants as an inheritance.

Cultures need to adapt to the ever-changing environment in terms of cultural variants or memes, and technologies. How cultures deal with these constant changes will determine their future performance outcomes and sustainability. For cultures to survive, thrive in the long run, and adjust to a changing environment, they must find out how they fit into the larger society. If cultures have a difficult time finding their place or role in society, they must make additional adjustments, migrate to a new environment before it is too late, or the real possibility of their demises may exist. Culture members must always maintain their awareness and be vigilant in coping with ongoing cultural environmental and technological changes that they will experience. Societal culture change is inevitable. How cultures deal with it is a choice.

Unfortunately, some cultural members will never embrace the Truth, regardless of how presented to them. Some of them feel justified by their actions and cultural ideology. They are stubbornly unable to see the Truth when it was, repeatedly shown in their face. They think that their beliefs are an honest presentation of the facts. When cultures believe in things about other cultures that they do not understand without hearing their sides of the story, they were already looking for ways to be against them. They are attracted to their continuous idiocy and cowardice and have no interest in intellectual curiosity. This distortion of facts and reality is particularly problematic when you have global cultures with histories of bigotry. The Truth is therefore is harder to gain traction.

Some culture members refuse to embrace a basic honest assessment of their history. They want to maintain the status quo, fiction, and mythologies and conspiracies of their culture. This omission comes at the expense of learning their cultural history in a critical analysis that details the very unpleasant parts of its history. Their inability to grasp the concept of different perspective and face the Truth have made them defensive, reacting quickly to any threat to their social status. Instead, they drum up and amplify creative anxieties, manufacture controversies, and create a moral panic among their cultural members by redefining their interests to manipulate emotions and spread fear. They will fabricate rationalizations to justify their reactions but fail hopelessly to question their motives. The cultures prefer to maintain their misguided convictions by creating additional problems as the solution to previous unaddressed issues. They make endless excuses, usually by trying to shift the blame. They do not like anyone to challenge their positions. The hubris of these cultures have historically exhibited behaviors that are outside the cultural norms.

Understanding the dynamics of how culture and the role that race, ethnicity, ethnocentrism, xenocentrism, and nationality play in our global society is essential. It is needed to overcome many of the multicultural and racial issues that we face in our global society. It will increase our understanding of the role, dynamics, and interactions that these factors play in our societies. We must learn to somehow embrace our cultural and racial differences. Any society or nation's ideology that fails to recognize the dignity, rights, and worth of its citizens will eventually collapse and suffer an ending date. If we are going to be successful at finally eradicating systemic racism and injustices, and the cultural divide in our global society as humanly as possible, we learn to fully embrace the numerous cultures and racial groups that exist on planet Earth.

The two world events that started in the fifteen-century, the Transatlantic Slave Trade and worldwide Colonialism, made our global society more diverse than ever before. It resulted in a more pluralistic world. It has led to the opportunity for more people from so many different cultures to interact with each other. As a result, culture clashes and culture shocks were inevitable. However, these interactions with each other do not have to be negative. When we finally learn as a global society to suspend our assumptions and judgments against each other cultures and instead embrace our different backgrounds and perspective as a positive, can we finally reach our potential as a global society, and ward off that same inevitability.

The major transformational atrocities such as the Arab-Muslim Slave Trade, the Transatlantic Slave Trade, worldwide Colonialism, Jim Crow, Apartheid, the Holocaust, King Leopold Congo genocide, Modern slavery, and thousands of other foreign invasions around the world during the past few centuries and millenniums have been instrumental in awakening our global society of the dangerous precedent of not addressing our racial and cultural issues. But as a global society, we still have a long way to go. Unfortunately, not all cultures will make it, and some will not rise because nature never meant for it to be that way. As some segments of the global society engage in racial and cultural reconciliation, it will still take some time. During the interim, there will be some hurt, pain, and suffering by all cultures before we finally heal as a global society.

The continued failure of the dominant culture(s) and the world's leadership to even acknowledge the roles that race, and culture play in perpetuating most of the past and present injustices and inequalities around the world is still very problematic. It seems that the world has stopped looking for a vaccine to cure our global-wide cultural and racial pandemic. The five-hundred-year history of global oppression and suppression since 1441, when the Portuguese's first public sale of kidnapped and enslaved Africans was made, needs to be acknowledged to heal the wounds to bring lasting change. [ccix] Unfortunately, it seems most societies and cultures are in denial of global human suffering and abuses. Generally, they are aware of the suffering and oppression but choose to ignore it rather than discuss uneasy subjects. Even people who witness these global acts and atrocities will still deny their existence. In essence, the uncomfortable topic of racial cultural oppression makes cultures act blindly to reality, but it needs to change.

May be there is a silver lining in our global cultural future. For the first time, the unfortunate slaying of Mr. George Floyd by the Minneapolis police department led to worldwide protests, rallies, and marches for police reforms and an end to global systemic racism and racial injustices. These protest activities have been ongoing in many countries for centuries but not on a global scale. This movement occurred for several weeks during a global pandemic. This monumental push for global racial awakening, however, needs to continue beyond the global COVID-19 pandemic. The political sustainability fate of these worldwide protests remains uncertain. Constant periodic cultural maintenance must be taken, or else we will not get the permanent change that is needed. In the interim, the deeply embedded and entrenched institutions, systems, and networks that have been complicit in these global injustices and inequalities need to have their past and present roles, critically analyzed, and corrective remedies and actions are taken for the betterment of the human species.

As a global society, we should be taking the best that all cultures offer, including the ancestral traditional culture, and learn from them. All cultures bring something to the table. No culture is better and above another culture. No culture is superior to other cultures. Millennia later, the ancient builders of the Egyptian pyramids show mathematic, and physics formulas still yet unknown by modern cultures. Human species have evolved as any species should, and their tolerance for differences have emerged. Modern culture continues to mold and manipulate nature in more areas and learn more about the environment and surroundings because of our continued evolvement as a species. But it still does not mean we do not especially give homage to the ancestry cultures, who were more tuned with nature and spiritual science than we are. They laid the foundation for our present existence.

If global culture members researched and dove deeper into a study of world history, ancient history, theology, Kemetic Science, spirituality, ancient languages, law, philosophy, and other disciplines in good faith, they may at some point in their lives, deprogram their existing cultural thinking and possibly open their minds and hearts in the search for the Truth. Some profundity of these disciplines may prevent cultures from becoming too rigid in their perspectives and help culture members to be pluralistic, and open to other cultures, religions, and mythologies. This understanding will allow cultures to emerge from their present fixed state to constantly evolving ideals, remade by successive generations to move forward in our collective power to reshape a new global society. Often our cultural leaders possess modern intelligence and environmental ethics that clouds their ability to act with compassion, decency, and a basic moral compass.

While there are reasons to be troubled by our present global cultural plight, there are also better reasons for optimism and hope for our future shared cultural history. As we reflect on the history of the past, we must not lose knowledge that our current actions and decisions regarding our kindred human beings are the history upon which future generations will critique our era. We must never lose sight of their impacts and future implications on our global society. All cultures should accept the time they lived in and the opportunities offered to them. The object of cultures is to make the best of their situation and the generations that follow them. As a global society, we can agree to a cultural pact by coming together to work on our common human interest but respect our cultural differences. We must believe that our best times still lie ahead and along the way, cultures will be comforted by one another. When our cultural forces are in balance with each other and moving in harmony, our destination is the brightest star. We cannot and will not realize our full potential as a global society unless we have all cultures working to forge a new sense of shared associations and vision that can enable a much more diverse world to journey together into the twenty-first century and beyond.

The changing racially diverse global demographics and a shift in attitudes may be the impetus that finally shepherds this racial and cultural divide. There is a rising tide of demographic changes that represent the most racially diverse generations in many of our global societies. Modern societies' younger generations have taken a more developing, evolving, and civilizing stance on racial and political issues than previous generations. They are taking lessons from past generational mistakes and changing their approach. They are learning our true shared history and embracing cultural commonalities while respecting differences. The internet is the great equalizer. The flow of knowledge has put these mainstream cultures in the spotlight because of their history. The plight of the younger generation while still perilous is beginning to see the world for what it is. Cultural cooperation and unity amongst like minds are essential for success. It will not be easy but must be done before a few cultures destroy the planet. This generational cultural shift will soon require modern corporations and businesses to also reflect the consensus views of their majority employees and consumers. This new brand of consumerism will be viewed by their needs and perceptions. The political systems around the world need to ensure that the interests of financial markets and businesses do not prevent societies from taking care of basic human needs. We must prioritize humanistic values and principles above market forces and hedonistic cultural selfishness that provide a real mechanism of growth for all cultures. Despite the recent triumphs of technological advancements, it will never offset the devastating effect it left on the subordinate cultures and particularly people of color who occupied those territories.

The modern culture can never outpace the legacy of the traditional culture. Both cultures had motives and flaws entangled in ways too obscure to grasp. Although their cultural interplay has been inseparable, it has become the defining cultural relationship in our global society. The accomplishments of the modern culture during the past few centuries developed and built off previous eras and earlier cultures. Unfortunately, some modern dominant cultures believe that it was their achievements alone. During recent centuries, the modern culture has been irrepressible, pushing global boundaries while calculating the next move. They both enabled each other, but some cultures in the modern era have been wielding unearned power to the detriment of cultures. The dynamics between the traditional and modern cultures have always been fraught with insecurities. However, the self-serving path that some of our modern cultures have chosen has had a detrimental effect on the humanity of some cultures and other planet's inhabitants.

It took thousands of cultures and thousands of years to construct and develop our global society. The ancient traditional civilizations were instrumental in their developments. There is no single cultural consensus on interpreting historical facts, ancient cultures, and the role they play in modern culture. Although cultures in the Modern era made tremendous progress in technological advancements, the traditional cultures laid the foundation. Since the origins of humankind and societies in Africa are only a few thousand years, how can the developments in the Modern era be accurate discovery mechanisms? Ancient traditional cultures accomplished baseline technological realities and competency that modern cultures cannot comprehend or replicate in some disciplines. Modern cultures think in terms of the discoveries of their lifetimes as the answer to the Universe. We don't have the capability and capacity to understand how ongoing technological advancements will change the global and universal landscape in the unforeseeable future.

The great problem of the Modern era is to restore the humanity the dominant culture lost the moment it decided to conquer, colonize, and enslave most of the world's cultures of color in pursuit of the world's riches, and material gains, and enhance their power and influence over world affairs. As humankind drifted into materialism and greed, their societies became more divorced from the spiritual consciousness of nature and basic concepts developed by our traditional culture. The centuries-long debate between the concepts of dualism versus materialism as the key to the Universe remains largely unresolved. "These alternative views of reality may also be related. Reality can be a mental experience in which both concepts are complementary, and the optimal global culture balances both." [ccx] The ultimate measure of cultures may be how well they relate to their environment and other cultures.

It is important to recognize the Truth of our cultural impacts, to take stock of the enormous destruction that we have reaped on some of the world's cultures. This present global behavior is unacceptable in a civilized global society and must be restructured as we maneuver through these cultural and racial minefields. The developed countries, many of which have some degree of responsibility for the present plight of undeveloped and impoverished countries, need to display some accountability by helping remedy situations where scarcity of resources leads to human suffering. We must restore our traditional cultural and natural balance that the present unequal and broken world order created through numerous misdirected, misguided, ill-conceived, obscured, disguised, and unguided social constructions.

As the world navigates unprecedented challenges to reduce cultural clashes, cultures have a golden opportunity to hold global space for building unity, promoting dialogue, increasing understanding, and social healing for different communities. The central question for the world, whose economies and cultures are rapidly fusing with a more diverse global society – is whether it is possible to rediscover our humanistic identity and mutual responsibility without culture clashes? The world needs to muster

185

the moral courage to push for change. It must find a centering balance to regain the equilibrium of its traditional culture and the modern scientific and technological culture that will bring back the very heart and essence of our ancestry cultural traits that respect the essential attributes of humanity, creativity, respect, decency, and inclusiveness. We can emerge with a renewed hope and focus of shared vision, admiration, and respect for all cultures. The global brand of multiculturalism is continuing its societal accessibility mantra while having varying degrees of success and understanding of the world's cultures. If we change the narrative, the culture will also change. This narrative reawakening will not unfold until all world's cultures are involved in the world's strategic plan and have input in the shaping of the globe's destiny. Only then will the natural order of the universe be restored, in cultural relationships born of necessity.

Work Cited

[i] Samuel P. Huntington, The Clash of

[ii] Antonia Cirjak, How Is Race Different From Ethnicity And Culture?, June 2, 2020, Society

[iii] Harry Belafonte and Michael Schnayerson, My Song: A Memoir, October 11, 2011

[iv] Ibid

[v] Sterlin Williams, Understanding the Far-Reaching Global Impact of the World Racial Order, p. 49-53, February 11, 2019

[vi] John Spacey, 20 Characteristics of the Modern Era, Simplicable, August 22, 2019

[vii] Ahmet Gencturk, Transatlantic slave trade: Legacy of entangled affair between imperialism, racism, slavery, Monthly Review, August 10, 2021

[viii] Christa-Gaye L. Kerr, The United Nations and Reparations for the Trans-Atlantic Slave Trade and Colonialism

[ix] Barbara Ransby, Henry Louis Gates' Dangerously Wrong Slave History, MAY 3, 2010

[x] Dr. Molefi Kete Asante, YouTube, Responds to Henry Louis Gates, 2015

[xi] Sebastiane Ebatamhi, This is How the West Destroyed African Civilization through Colonalism, The African Exponent, August 16, 2020

[xii] Jacob Zikusooka, Stanford Graduate School of Business, Facebook

[xiii] What is the Doctrine of Discovery?, Unitarian Universalist Association, uua.org,

[xiv] Jordi Savall, The Routes of Slavery, Millennium of Music, June 4, 2018

[xv] Christopher Rodriquez, Portugal and African Slave Trade before Columbus, STMU History Media, October 7, 2016

[xvi] https://www.facebook.com/BlackHistoryMiniDocs/posts/3024510017575534, Black History Mini Docs, September 29, 2019

[xvii] Frank Drouzas, Courageous conversations surrounding mental health in the Black community, The Weekly Challenger, August 20, 2021

[xviii] Derrick Clifton, 9 clueless things white people say when confronted with racism, July 11, 2014 and updated May 30, 2021

[xix] Bremmer Ian, Us vs. Them – The Failure of Globalism, p. 91-94

[xx] Mark, Pagel, Does globalization mean we will become one culture?, November 18, 2014

[xxi] O I A. Michael, The Changing Meaning of Race (National Research Council), 2001, Volume 1, p. 24

[xxii] Ibid

[xxiii] African Proverbs in African Literature, A Critical Resource, Cameroon,

proverbsafricanliterature.wordpress.com

[xxiv] Bobby Hemmitt, Master Teacher of Kemetic Science, YouTube video

[xxv] Scott L. CHAUNDA, A Discussion of Individual, Institutions, and Cultural Racism with Implication, Oakland University

[xxvi] Scott L. CHAUNDA, A Discussion of Individual, Institutions, and Cultural Racism with Implication, Oakland University

[xxvii] Seven Major Characteristics of Culture That are Essential for Life, Historyplex

[xxviii] What are the Cultural Elements and Which are the Most Important?, www.lifepersona.com

[xxixxxix] Administration, Difference Between Subculture and Counterculture, November 14, 2014

[xxx] Culture Clash as a Great Conflict Research Paper, May 7, 2019

[xxxi] Albert Gomez, Afro-Latinx Revolution: A documentary about identity and racism in the heart of Loíza, January 22, 2021

[xxxii] How To Handle Culture Clash In An Interracial Or Intercultural Relationship - What It Means To Be In An Interracial Or Intercultural Relationship

[xxxiii] ACW, The Development of Civilizations - Analysis of Vultures and Civilizations, June 2, 2017

[xxxiv] How Important Is Culture in Shaping Our Behavior? October 01, 2012

[xxxv] Scott L. CHAUNDA, A Discussion of Individual, Institutions, and Cultural Racism with Implication, Oakland University

[xxxvi] Ibid

[xxxvii] Jessie Graham, RACISM: A Society of Misunderstood Cultural Clashes, June 29, 2016

[xxxviii] Eliza Shankar-Gorton, The Surprising Science of Race and Racism, December 06, 2017

[xxxix] Jeff Thomas, The Oakland Post, January 13, 2021

[xl] Scott L. CHAUNDA, A Discussion of Individual, Institutions, and Cultural Racism with Implication, Oakland University

[xli] Nadar Kareem Nittle, Understanding the Difference Between Race and Ethnicity, Nadia Kareem Nittle, January 30, 2020

[xlii] Jennifer Betts, Examples of Race and Ethnicity, Your Dictionary

[xliii] Cole, Nicki Lisa, PhD. "The Difference Between Hispanic and Latino." ThoughtCo, February 21, 2021, thoughtco.com/Hispanic-vs-latino-4149966

[xliv] Jennifer Betts, Examples of Race and Ethnicity, Your Dictionary

[xlv] Ethnocentrism. Cultural Anthropology, Lumen

[xlvi] What is Ethnocentrism?

[xlvii] Benjamin Elisha Sawe, August 9 2017 in Society Home Society

[xlviii] Ashley Crossman, Sociological Xenocentrism, December 04, 2020, Quora

[xlix] Aishani Menon, Xenocentrism: Concept in and Examples, Quora

[l] Surbhi S., Difference Between Ethnicity and Nationality, January 20, 2018

[li] Alan Gomez, United States birthright citizenship explained: What is it, how many people benefit, October 30, 2018

[lii] Elaine Gould, M.ED, Strategies for Teaching Social Skills in the School Environment, Williams & Mary School of Education, November/December 2010 Link Lines

[liii] Dennis Wagner, 1829 Andrew Jackson – To The Victor Belong the Spoils, www.stateoftheunionhistory.com/2018/09/1829-andrew-jackson, September 20, 2018

[liv] Portugal confronts its role in the Transatlantic Slave Trade, Africa

[lv] Catherine Buni and Soraya Chemaly, The Science That Explains Trump's Grip on White Males, January 14, 2021

[lvi] Michelle Jackson & Ruth Terry, Preserving Black Historical Resorts Is a Radical Act, Yes! Solution Journalism, June 24, 2021

[lvii] Rebecca Bodenheimer, The Haitian Revolution: Successful Revolt by an Enslaved People, August 12, 2019

[lviii] Mawuna Remarque KOUTONIN, 14 African Countries Forced by France to Pay Colonial Tax For the Benefits of Slavery and Colonization

[lix] MINTER William, Invisible Hierarchies: Africa, Race, and Continuities in the World Order, (Constituencies in a Polarizing World - Part III), (Science and Society), 2005, vol. 69, p.449

[lx] MINTER William, Invisible Hierarchies: Africa, Race, and Continuities in the World Order, (Constituencies in a Polarizing World - Part III), (Science and Society), 2005, vol. 69, p.449

[lxi] https://youtu.be/auQU1RZhFU0, The Berlín Conference, 1884, 13 European countries and the USA, 2019

[lxii] Jeffrey Herbst, "The Creation and Maintenance of National Boundaries in Africa," (International Organization, 43, no. 4, 1989), 673-92

[lxiii] Lord Salisbury quoted in Anene, J.C, The International Boundaries of Nigeria, 1885-1960 (London, The Framework of an Emergent African Nation, Longman Press, 1970), 3

[lxiv] Tessew Gashaw, Colonial Borders in Africa: Improper Design and its Impact on African Borderland Communities, November 17, 2017

[lxv] Christa-Gaye L. Kerr, The United Nations and Reparations for the Trans-Atlantic Slave Trade and ColonialismP

lxvi Ilisha, Bleeding Africa: A Half Century of the Françafrique, March 25, 2014

lxvii Brian Good, Economics Is 'Too White' and 'To Male' According to Top Federal Reserve Policymakers

lxviii Augusto Lopez-Claros, What role does culture play in development? December 10, 2014, World Economic Forum

lxix Augusto López-Claros, what role does culture play in development?, December 10, 2014, Global Indicator and Analysis at the World

lxx Ahmet Gencturk, Transatlantic slave trade: Legacy of entangled affair between imperialism, racism, slavery, Monthly Review, August 10, 2021

lxxi Mbamalu Socrates, Africans deserve to know details of deals their leaders sign with China, 2018

lxxii Melissa L. Finucane, Paul Slavic, C.K. Metz, James Flynn and Theresa A. Satterfield, Gender, race, and perceived risk: The 'White male' effect, July 14, 2010

lxxiii Catherine Buni and Soraya Chemaly, The Science That Explains Trump's Grip on White Males, January 14,2021

lxxiv Ibid

lxxv Ibid

lxxvi Ibid

lxxvii Ibid

lxxviii Barbara Sutton and Kari Marie Norgaard, Cultures of Denial: Avoiding Knowledge of State Violations of Human Rights in Argentina and the United States, Sociological Forum, Vol. 28, No. 3, September 2013

lxxix Barbara Sutton and Kari Marie Norgaard, Cultures of Denial: Avoiding Knowledge of State Violations of Human Rights in Argentina and the United States, Sociological Forum, Vol. 28, No. 3, September 2013

lxxx Ibid

lxxxi Hectic Teacher's A-Level Sociology Site, Human Rights, March 25, 2017

lxxxii Barbara Sutton and Kari Marie Norgaard, Cultures of Denial: Avoiding Knowledge of State Violations of Human Rights in Argentina and the United States, Sociological Forum, Vol. 28, No. 3, September 2013

lxxxiii Anjana Cruz, Europeans invented the concept of races as we know it, July 21, 2017

lxxxiv Eliza Shankar-Gorton, The Surprising Science of Race and Racism, December 06, 2017

lxxxv Jordi Savall, The Routes of Slavery, Millennium of Music, June 4, 2018

lxxxvi Marie Francoise, Syracuse University, Quora, November 01, 2019

lxxxvii Anjana Cruz, Europeans invented the concept of races as we know it, July 21, 2017

lxxxviii Ibid

lxxxix https://en.wikipedia.org/wiki/Bacons_rebellion

xc Donald Earl Collins, Nothing Sacred: From Jefferson to Jan. 6,

America's Toxic Mythologies are Destroying U.S., September 6, 2021
[xci]

https://www.nps.gov/ethnography/aah/asheritage/chesapeake_pop2.htm
[xcii] Anjana Cruz, Europeans invented the concept of races as we know it, July 21, 2017
[xciii] Steve Martinot, The Colonially of Power: Notes Toward De-Colonization
[xciv] Yahoo Answers
[xcv] Yahoo Answers
[xcvi] Yahoo Answers
[xcvii] The History Junkie, European Colonization

[xcviii] List of former European colonies

- Wikipedia -

en.wikipedia.org/wiki/List_of_former_European_colonies

[xcix] Sarah Kendzior, How do you become White in America? The Correspondent (The Reader), 2018
[c] Cornel West, Race Matters (p. 107 – 108)
[ci] Tim Braden, Why are Whites in the USA generally not referred to as 'European Americans'?, March 28, 2018
[cii] Suggested Citation:"8. The Changing Meaning of Race." National Research Council. 2001. America Becoming: Racial Trends and Their Consequences, Volume I. Washington, DC: The National Academies Press. DOI: 10.17226/9599

[ciii] John Blake, The Capitol insurrection could be a bigger racial reckoning than the George Floyd protests, CNN, January 17, 2021
[civ] Taylor Daemon, 'Unfathomable Contrast': Biden Under Fire for Expelling Haitians, Globe World News Echo, September 25, 2021
[cv] Shaun, Biden faces harsh criticism for expelling Haitian asylum seekers, Web Press Global, September 23, 2021
[cvi] Sterlin Williams, Understanding the Far-Reaching Global Impact of the World Racial Order, February 11, 2019
[cvii] ibid
[cviii] ibid
[cix] Political Science Exam #1 Flashcards, Quizlet.com
[cx] Staff writer, What Is a Homogeneous Culture?, April 8, 2020
[cxi] Yahoo Answers
[cxii] ACW, The Development of Civilizations - Analysis of Vultures and Civilizations, June 2, 2017
[cxiii] Stanley Knick, Director, Native American, Resource Center, University of North Carolina at Pembroke, Traditional Culture and Modern Culture: Man's Fall from Grace, May 25, 2011
[cxiv] Eric Betz, Nabta Playa: The World's First Astronomical Site Was Built In Africa And Is Older Than Stonehenge, June 20, 2020
[cxv] Mr. Imhotep, Education website, https://linktr.ee/Mr.imhotep &

https//www.instagram.com/mister imhotep/
cxxvi Yahoo answers
cxxvii

https://www.reference.com/world-view/main-religions-africa-cab77768ae35ed94
cxxviii

http://www.globalreligiousfutures.org/regions/europ
cxxix World Atlas, The Major Religions In North America
cxx World Atlas, The Major Religions In North America
cxxxi

https://en.wikipedia.org/wiki/Eastern_religions
cxxii World Atlas, The Major Religions In North America
cxxiii World Atlas, The Major Religions In North America
cxxiv The Spiritual Life, We are here to help, Abrahamic Religions
cxxv Ibid.
cxxvi American History: A New World Clash of Cultures, October 03, 2013
cxxvii Mik McAllister, Quora, March 4, 2016
cxxviii Ancient world literacy rate, Why was there no literacy in ancient Egypt?
cxxix Hunter-Gatherer Culture, Anthropology, Social Studies, World History, Resource library I Encyclopedic Entry
cxxx The Agricultural Revolution: Timeline, Causes, Inventions and Effects, History 102: Western Civilization II/ History Courses, Chapter 7/Lesson 1

cxxxi The Editors of Encyclopedia Britannica, Industrial Revolution, February 21, 2021
cxxxii Social Science, LibreTexts, December 15, 2020
cxxxiii Ashley Crossman, Post-Industrial Society in Sociology, May 30, 2019
cxxxiv Brian Feldman, Quora, August 6, 201
cxxxv Social Science, LibreTexts, December 15, 2020
cxxxvi

http://en.Wikipedia.org/wiki/Religious_views_on_capitalism
cxxxvii Yahoo Answers
cxxxviii Maps: All the World's Borders by Age
cxxxix Balaji Viswanathan CEO at Invento, Quora
cxl American History: A New World Clash of Cultures, October 03, 2013
cxli Sergei Shcheglov, What Is A Culture Hearth?, April 25, 2017
cxlii Ibid
cxliii Yahoo answers
cxliv Karen Shah, Quora, July 26, 2017
cxlv Was ancient Egypt a Mediterranean civilization?, People also Ask
cxlvi Staff Writer, How Many Cultures Are There in the World? , March 26, 2020
cxlvii Anthony Washington, Quora, Jul 09, 2019
cxlviii

cxlix Historyplex, The Different Yet Surprisingly Similar Cultures of the World cl Kim.Ann Zimmerman, What Is Culture?, July 13, 2017

cli Historyplex, The Different Yet Surprisingly Similar Cultures of the World

clii Kim.Ann Zimmerman, What Is Culture?, July 13, 2017

cliii Historyplex, The Different Yet Surprisingly Similar Cultures of the World

cliv Kim.Ann Zimmerman, What Is Culture?, July 13, 2017

clv Historyplex, The Different Yet Surprisingly Similar Cultures of the World

clvi Kim.Ann Zimmerman, What Is Culture?, July 13, 2017

clvii Historyplex, The Different Yet Surprisingly Similar Cultures of the World

clviii Kim.Ann Zimmerman, What Is Culture?, July 13, 2017

clix

https:www.britannica.com/place/Middle-East

clx

https://www.everyculture.com/Africa-Middle-East/Introduction-to-the-Middle-East.html#ixzz6jXnHWoDg

clxi www.Gaia.com/article/type-one-kardashev-scale

clxii Whitestar, Physics Forum, September 7, 2003

clxiii Fernando Lorenzo, Quora, September 3, 2019

clxiv National Weather Service, National Oceanic and Atmospheric Administration, United States Department of Commerce, USA.GOV

clxv

https://en.m.wikipedia.org/wiki/Kardashev_scale

clxvi Culture Clash, Reconciling Asian collectivist values and Western individualist values, May 02, 2019

clxvii Administration, Difference Between Eastern and Western Culture, April 20, 2014

clxviii Ibid

clxix Linus Slovak , Quora

clxx Dan Vasii, Consultant, Quora

clxxi The Editor of Encyclopedia Britannica ,
https://www.britannica.com/biography/Tiothy-Leary, May 27, 2021

clxxii Administration, Difference Between Subculture and Counterculture, November 14, 2014

clxxiii Aimie Carlson, Difference Between Subculture and Counterculture, May 4, 2020

clxxiv Carol Peracchio, Whatever Happened to the Counterculture?, September 24, 2010

clxxv Aimie Carlson, Difference Between Subculture and Counterculture, May 4, 2020

clxxvi

http://en.Wikipedia.org/wiki/Counterculture

clxxvii Patrick G. Graham, Ph.D, Derek Chauvin's Fate is a Test for our Democracy, April 7, 2021

clxxviii Kenny Wilson, The Decline of the 1960s Counterculture and the Rise of Thatcherism, December 31, 2012

clxxix Henry David Thoreau and the Counterculture
clxxx

https://www.dictionary.com/e/pop-culture/cancel-culture/
clxxxi

https://www.urbandictionary.com/define.php?term=Cancel%20Culture
clxxxii   126.
https://en.wikipedia.org/wiki/Cancel_culture
clxxxiii Sarah Maguire, Has Cancel Culture Gone Too Far, July 2, 2010
clxxxiv Lana Harris, Something went wrong, June 10, 2020
clxxxv Prottay M. Adhikari, Quora, November, 2, 2020
clxxxvi

https://www.cato.org/publications/survey-reports/p...
clxxxvii

https://en.wikipedia.org/wiki/Social_media
clxxxviii Edward Barrow, Quora
clxxxix Clyde Lindsay, Quora, February 20, 2019
cxc Vivien Cumming, How many people can our planet really support?, March 14, 2016
cxci Vivien Cumming, How many people can our planet really support?, March 14, 2016
cxcii Ron Harris, The Memphis Commercial Appeal, Who do we get back to civility? December 27, 2020
cxciii Monica Duffy, The United States' Demographic Revolution Doesn't Need to Be Destabilizing, February 3, 2021
cxciv Yolando Moses, Is the Term "People of Color" Acceptable in This Day and Age", Sapiens, December 7, 2016
cxcv Leslie Nemo, More Than 40% of Languages Are at Risk of Fading Away Completely, February 10, 2021
cxcvi Becky Little, How the US Got So Many Confederate Monuments, History Stories, HISTORY
cxcvii Brian Rayca, Museum Registrar, United State Military Academy, July 19, 2019
cxcviii Cheyenne MacDonald, Why statues from ancient Egypt are often missing their nose: Expert says tomb-robbers deliberately destroyed vital parts to prevent vengeful spirits from coming after them, Dailymail.com, March 14, 2019
cxcix Laura Geggel, Why Are the Noses on So Many Ancient Egyptian Statues?, March 26, 2019
cc Cheyenne MacDonald, Why statues from ancient Egypt are often missing their nose: Expert says tomb-robbers deliberately destroyed vital parts to prevent vengeful spirits from coming after them, Dailymail.com, March 14, 2019
cci Teach History.org, Pulling Down the Statue of George III
ccii Amanda Erickson, How other countries dealt with monuments to dictators, fascists and racists, The Washington Post, August 15,

2017 and updated March 19, 2019

[cciii] Laurel Wamsley, In Reckoning With Confederate Monuments, Other Countries Could Provide Examples, August 22, 2017

[cciv] Erica Hellerstein, Oh, Wonderful, Another Long Debate on Removing Confederate Monuments from the State Capitol. We Went So You Didn't Have To., March 22, 2018

[ccv] Michelle Jackson & Ruth Terry, Preserving Black Historical Resorts Is a Radical Act, Yes! Solution Journalism, June 24, 2021

[ccvi] Sterlin Williams, Understanding The Far-Reaching Global Impact Of The World Racial Order, February 9, 2019

[ccvii] Bremerton Ian, Us vs. Them - The Failure of Globalism, p. 91-94

[ccviii] Sasha Matthews, A look at Africa's Stolen Artifacts, June 22, 2017

[ccix] Slavery in Portugal, Wikipedia, https://en.wikipedia.org/wiki/Slavery_in_Portugal

[ccix] John Uebersax, Director, Californians for Higher Education Reform, May 3, 2018, Quora

A

B

C

Calabrese 63
California 72, 86, 89
Caliphate 155
Calvinist 111
Camus 16
Canada 68, 71–72, 104, 131, 143
Cancel-Culture xviii, 145, 149–52, 196
Capitalism 88, 110–11
Caribbean-Americans 125
Caste vi, 11, 36, 62–63, 165
Catholicism 68–69, 104–5
Chattel Slavery xxvi-xxviii, 124
Cherokee Nation 167
Chiang, Kai-shek 171
Chinese 132, 170, 174
Chinese Communist Party 174
Chinese Culture 132
Chinese Exclusion Act 87
Chirac, Jacques René 54
Christians xxx, 104–6, 129
Chronocentrism 23
Clive, Robert 169
Cold War xvii, 123, 147
Colston, Edward 169
Commensalism xx
Communal xxxii
Communism 94, 115
Confederate 168–69, 171

Confucianism 105, 142
Constitution xvi
Continental 165
Continental Africans 124–25
Corporations 92, 110, 183
Consumer Ethnocentrism 23
Counterculture xviii, 145–48
Courland 66, 70, 74
COVID-19 167, 182
CPR 35
Croatians 68, 130
Cromwell, Oliver 170
Cultural Appropriation 24, 87
Cultural Diffusion 11, 25, 128, 173
Culture Hearth 117
Culture War 147, 149, 152

D

Danes 66
Deferred Action for Childhood Arrivals (DECA) 89
Del Rio, Texas 90
Denmark xxv, 70, 84
Diaspora xxxiv, 10, 12, 48, 56–57, 63, 123–24, 163
Dictatorship 60–61, 94
Direct/Representative Democracy 94
Democracy 60, 91, 94, 122, 169, 171
Djibouti 51, 74, 125

Greeks 68, 130

H

Haiti 48, 71, 86, 90, 125
Hellenic 128, 142
High Command of the Armed 170
Hinduism 104–5, 129, 133, 142
Hindus 104, 143
Hispano 86
Hollande, Francois 54
Holocaust xxvii, 181
Homogenous xx, 85, 95–96, 143–44
Hong Kong Culture 132
Humanistic xix, xxii, xxxii, xxxiv, 42, 106, 140, 177, 184–85
Hume, David 64
Hunter-Gathers 108
Hussein 170

I

Indentured Servitude xxvi
Indians 63, 68–69, 106, 115–16
Indigenous People xxv, 21, 36, 57, 64, 67, 86, 92, 100, 105, 113, 116, 166
Indus River Valley 116, 119

Instagram 151
Interfaith 39
International Monetary Funds 49, 92
Internet 11, 32, 110, 149, 151–52
Iran 66, 78
Iraq 61, 77–78, 136, 170
Irish Culture 131
Islam 99–100, 102–6, 117, 126, 128–29, 133, 142
Islamic 88, 92, 117, 119
Israel 88
Isthmus Zapotec 167
Italian Culture 130
Italian Somaliland 51, 75

J

Jainism 105, 133
Jamaican Culture 134
Japan xxiv, 48, 66, 81, 87, 114, 131-132, 143, 147, 170-171
Japanese Americans 87
Japanese Culture 132
Jewish 142, 170
Jews 68, 85, 104, 106, 130, 171
Jikany-Nuer 52
Jim Crow Laws 91
Johnson And Johnson 24
Judaism 102–6, 128–29

K

Kant Immanuel 64
Kardashev Nicolai 133
Kardashev Scale 137–40, 195
Kenya 51, 68, 73, 75, 125
Kermit 9
King Martin Luther Jr. 91
King Leopold Congo 163, 181

L

Latin American 20, 89
Latin Culture 133
Leary Timothy 146
Lenin 171
Linguistic xxii, 20, 50, 128, 142, 166, 168
LinkedIn 151
Louisiana v, 68, 71, 114
Lou-Nuer 52
Lyrical and Critical Essays 16

M

Macquarie University 149
Madagascar xxi, 74, 77
Malaysian Culture 133
Manichaeism 105
Manifest Destiny 22–23, 35
Maori 168
Mayan Culture 134
Mayans 117

Mediterranean 20, 101, 122, 135, 143, 169
Mesoamerica 116, 119–20
Mesopotamia 112, 116, 118–19, 136
Messenger 122, 151
Mexican 86, 89, 134
Mexican Culture 134
Mexico 20, 68, 72, 86, 89, 95, 104, 119, 133-134, 167
Microsoft Teams 152
Middle East Culture 135–36
Military Dictatorship 61, 94
Milligan, Robert 169
Minneapolis, Minnesota 2, 181
Misogyny xvi
Mitchel, John 170
Mitterrand, Francois 54
Modern Culture xvii, 16, 97–99, 101–3, 106, 115, 182, 184
Monarchy 67, 94, 118, 169
Mongols 122, 143
Moore, Julia 150
Moors 64
Moscovici, Pierre 54
Moslems 143
Multiculturalism 6, 43–45, 88, 92–94, 96, 153, 157, 163, 186
Multiethnic 39
Multigenerational 39
Multiracial 39

Roman Catholicism 68, 104-
105
Romania 171
Rome 112, 142, 155, 169
Russia xxiv-xxv, 66, 76, 78,
83–84
Russian 71, 78, 136, 155

S

Sagan Scale 140
Saharan Africa 64
Salisbury, Lord 51, 191
Samaritans 105
Samoan Culture 135
Saint Augustine, Florida xxx
Saudi Arabia 66
Science of Risk Perception 37,
57
Scientology 105
Scotland xxv, 66
Shia 143
Shintoism 105
Sindism 105
Singapore 48
Sinocentrism 23
Slavic 142
Slovic, Paul 58–59
Smithsonian 12
Snapchat 152
Socialism 94
Somali 51, 73-75, 125
Somalia 51, 75, 125

Somaliland 51, 73–75
South Africa xxix, 68, 74–75,
125, 143–44, 171
South America 24–25, 66, 68,
104, 133
Southeast Asia 4–5, 35, 48,
53, 69, 81, 87, 100, 123
South France 64
South Sudan 51–52
Southwest 86, 135
Southwest United States 86
Spaniards 68, 130
Spanish Inquisition 63
Spirituality xvi-xvii, xxii, 5,
32, 55, 99–100, 102–4, 182
Stalin, Joseph 170
Subculture xviii, xx, xxiii, 3,
6, 10–11, 13, 34, 47, 57,
97, 117, 124, 145–48, 172–
73
Sunni 143, 164
Sweden xxv, 66, 77, 80
Symbiosis xix
Syrian 143, 170

T

Taiwan 171
Taliban 90, 170
Taoism 105, 142
Telegram 152
Teutonic Races 63
Thailand 48, 66

Worldwide Colonization xxv,
66, 68, 86, 100

X

Y

Z

www.ingramcontent.com/pod-product-compliance
Lightning Source LLC
Chambersburg PA
CBHW030241030426
42336CB00009B/207